WATERWAYS GUIDE 3

Birmingham & the Heart of England

Collins

Also available:

C Collins NICHOLSON

Waterways guides and map

1 **Grand Union, Oxford & the South East**

2 **Severn, Avon & Birmingham**

4 **Four Counties & the Welsh Canals**

5 **North West & the Pennines**

6 **Nottingham, York & the North East**

7 **River Thames & the Southern Waterways**

Inland Waterways Map of Great Britain

Published by Nicholson
An imprint of HarperCollins*Publishers*
Westerhill Road, Bishopbriggs,
Glasgow G64 2QT

www.harpercollins.co.uk
www.bartholomewmaps.com

River Thames Guide first published by Nicholson 1969
Waterways guides 1 South, 2 Midlands and 3 North first published by Nicholson 1971
This edition first published by Nicholson and Ordnance Survey 1997
New edition published by Nicholson 2000, 2003, 2006, 2009
Reprinted 2006, 2007, 2009, 2011

Wildlife text from *Collins Complete Guide to British Wildlife* and *Collins Wild Guide*.

This product uses map data licensed from Ordnance Survey® with the permission of
the Controller of Her Majesty's Stationery Office.
© Crown copyright 1999. All rights reserved. Licence number 399302.

Ordnance Survey is a registered trade mark of Ordnance Survey, the national mapping agency of Great Britain.

The representation in this publication of a road, track or path is no evidence of the existence of a right of way.

Researched and written by Jonathan Mosse, Judith Pile and David Lobban.
Designed by Bob Vickers.
Editorial and project management Cicely Frew

The publishers gratefully acknowledge the assistance given by British Waterways and
their staff in the preparation of this guide.

Grateful thanks is also due to the Environment Agency
and members of the Inland Waterways Association.

All photographs reproduced by kind permission of Derek Pratt Photography, apart from:
Shutterstock/ p52 Alan Scheer, p154 Christian Musat (speckled wood), p154 Steve McWilliam (large skipper),
p154 Robert Hardholt (holly blue), p154 Jens Stolt (orange tip), p155 Andrey Novik (devil's-bit scabious); Paul Huggins
p154 (banded demoiselle, mute swan, moorhen); p155 HarperCollins Publishers (great crested grebe); p155 Frank Lane
Picture Agency/Ted Benton (marsh fritillary).

Every care has been taken in the preparation of this guide. However, the Publisher accepts no responsibility whatsoever
for any loss, damage, injury or inconvenience sustained or caused as a result of using this guide.

The Publisher makes no representations or warranties of any kind as to the operation of the websites
and disclaims all responsibility for the content of the websites and for any expense or loss incurred by
use of the websites.

Printed in China.

ISBN 978-0-00-728162-6

Wending their quiet way through town and country, the inland navigations of Britain offer boaters, walkers and cyclists a unique insight into a fascinating, but once almost lost, world. When built this was the province of the boatmen and their families, who lived a mainly itinerant lifestyle: often colourful, to our eyes picturesque but, for them, remarkably harsh. Transporting the nation's goods during the late 1700s and early 1800s, negotiating locks, traversing aqueducts and passing through long narrow tunnels, canals were the arteries of trade during the initial part of the industrial revolution.

Then the railways came: the waterways were eclipsed in a remarkably short time by a faster and more flexible transport system, and a steady decline began. In a desperate fight for survival canal tolls were cut, crews toiled for longer hours and worked the boats with their whole family living aboard. Canal companies merged, totally uneconomic waterways were abandoned, some were modernised but it was all to no avail. Large scale commercial carrying on inland waterways had reached the finale of its short life.

At the end of World War II a few enthusiasts roamed this hidden world and harboured a vision of what it could become: a living transport museum which stretched the length and breadth of the country; a place where people could spend their leisure time and, on just a few of the wider waterways, a still modestly viable transport system.

The restoration struggle began and, from modest beginnings, Britain's inland waterways are now seen as an irreplaceable part of the fabric of the nation. Long abandoned waterways, once seen as an eyesore and a danger, are recognised for the valuable contribution they make to our quality of life, and restoration schemes are integrating them back into the network. Let us hope that the country's network of inland waterways continues to be cherished and well-used, maintained and developed as we move through the 21st century.

If you would like to comment on any aspect of the guides, please write to Nicholson Waterways Guides, Collins Geo, Westerhill Road, Bishopbriggs, Glasgow G64 2QT or email nicholson@harpercollins.co.uk.

▌CONTENTS

Map showing the waterways of Britain	4
Key to map pages	6
General information for waterways users	8
Ashby Canal	15
Birmingham Canal Navigations – Main Line	28
Birmingham & Fazeley Canal	39
Coventry Canal	48
Erewash Canal	62
Grand Union Canal – Leicester Section and the River Soar	71
Grand Union Canal – Main Line	101
Oxford Canal	123
Staffordshire & Worcestershire Canal: North	133
Stratford-on-Avon Canal	143
Worcester & Birmingham Canal	149
Trent & Mersey Canal	157
Index	174

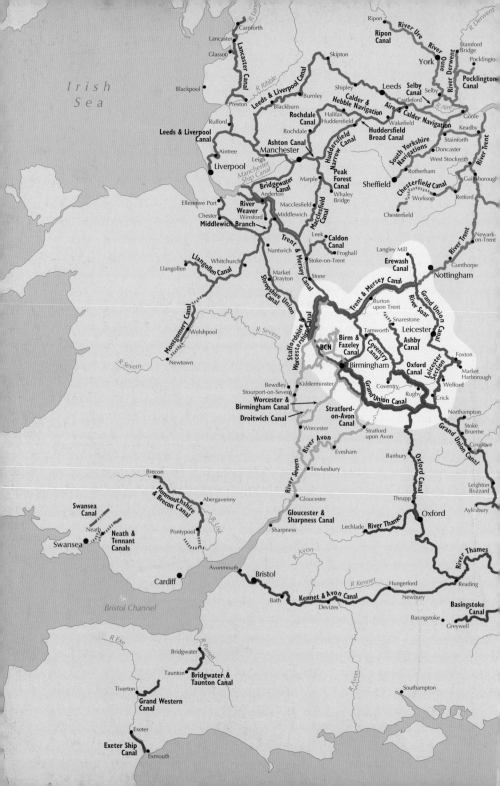

The Waterways of Britain

Kingston upon Hull

R Humber

Lincoln

Fossdyke & Witham Navigations

Kyme Eau

South Kyme · Boston

King's Lynn

Wisbech

R Great Ouse

R Bure

R Yare

R Nene

Peterborough

R Waveney

R Great Ouse

Cambridge · R Cam

Bishop's Stortford

River Stort

Hertford

Chelmer & Blackwater Navigation

Hemel Hempstead

Chelmsford · Maldon

Watford

River Lee

Slough

London

R Thames

Chatham

River Wey

River Medway

Maidstone

Guildford

Tonbridge

Godalming

Dover

Brighton

KEY

Waterways featured in this guide

Unnavigable section

Waterways featured in:

Guide 1

Guide 2

Guide 4

Guide 5

Guide 6

Guide 7

The Inland Waterways Map of Great Britain covers the canal and river navigations of England, Scotland and Wales.

English Channel

Crewe
Alsager
Kidsgrove
Nantwich
Newcastle-under-Lyme

STOKE-ON-TRENT

Leek
Cheddleton
Carsington Water
Ashbourne

Barlaston
Stone
Uttoxeter

Market Drayton
Eccleshall

162-163
Trent & Mersey Canal
Burton upon Trent
140-141
173
Hoo Mill
Great Haywood Junction
164-165
Dallow La
Stafford
Tixall
Gnosall
Deptmore
170-171
168-169
Barton
Newport
Staffordshire & Worcestershire Canal
138
Rugeley
166-167
Moir
Penkridge
Alrewas
Fradley Junction
137
Cannock
Coventry Canal
Brewood
Gailey
Hatherton Junction
Lichfield
Huddlesford Junction
Telford
135
58-59
60-61
Autherley Junction
Hatherton Junction
Tamworth
Aldersley Junction
Wolverhampton
21
Fazeley Fazeley Junction
Glascote
Birmingham & Fazeley Canal
Wightwick
36-37
Walsall
45
56-57
Birmingham Canal
Sutton Coldfield
M6 TOLL
Kingsbury
Bridgnorth
Wombourne
Birmingham & Fazeley Canal
42-43
Dudley
40-41
Minworth
Coventry
34-35
West Bromwich
Curdworth Tunnel 57 yds
Halesowen
30-31
BIRMINGHAM
Stourbridge
6
13
118-119
Birmingham International
Haw Ju
Worcester & Birmingham Canal
155
Brandwood Tunnel 352 yds
116-117
Cov Bas
Kidderminster
King's Norton Junction
151
Grand Union Canal
Bewdley
Solihull
115
Stourport-on-Severn
144-145
M42
Hockley Heath
Knowle
Bromsgrove
Stratford-on-Avon Canal
146-147
Kenilworth
Kingswood Junction
Lapworth
112-113
Shrewley Tunnel 433 yds
Redditch
Warwick
Hatton 21
110-111
Budbrooke Junction
Droitwich
Alcester
Worcester
Stratford-upon-Avon

Mapping for the canal between the two markers can be found on the pages shown

90-91 Tunnel

Aqueduct 5 Lock (symbol points uphill)

Flight of locks (5=number of locks)

GENERAL INFORMATION FOR WATERWAYS USERS

INTRODUCTION

Boaters, walkers, fishermen, cyclists and gongoozlers (on-lookers) all share in the enjoyment of our quite amazing waterway heritage. British Waterways and the Environment Agency, along with other navigation authorities, are empowered to develop, maintain and control this resource. It is to this end that a series of guides, codes, and regulations have come into existence over the years, evolving to match a burgeoning – and occasionally conflicting – demand. Set out in this section are key points as they relate to everyone wishing to enjoy the waterways.

The *Boater's Handbook* is available from all navigation authorities and can be downloaded from www.aina.org.uk. It contains a complete range of safety information, boat-handling know-how, warning symbols and illustrations.

BRITISH WATERWAYS

British Waterways (BW) cares for 2,200 miles of the country's canals and rivers. *The Waterways Code* gives advice and guidance to visitors on how to enjoy the inland waterways safely. It, and the *Boater's Handbook*, are available from the Customer Service Centre or from www.waterscape.com/downloads. BW Customer Service Centre is staffed Mon–Fri, 08.00–18.00, Sat 09.00–13.00. The helpful staff will answer general enquiries and provide information about boat licensing, boating holidays and activities on the waterways. They can be contacted on 0845 6715530; enquiries@britishwaterways.co.uk; British Waterways Customer Service Centre, 64 Clarendon Road, Watford WD17 1DA. Visit www.waterscape.com for up-to-date information on almost every aspect of the inland waterways, from news and events to moorings.

Emergency Helpline Available from BW outside normal office hours on weekdays and throughout weekends. For emergency help, or to report something dangerous, such as serious damage to structures or water escaping, call 0800 47 999 47.

ENVIRONMENT AGENCY

The Environment Agency (EA) manages around 600 miles of the country's rivers, including the Thames and the River Medway. For general enquiries or to obtain a copy of the *Boater's Handbook*, contact EA Customer Services on 08708 506 506; enquiries@environment-agency.gov.uk. To find out about their work nationally (or to download a copy of the *Handbook*) and for lots of other useful information), visit www.environment-agency.gov.uk. The website www.visitthames.co.uk provides lots on information on boating, walking, fishing and events on the river.

Incident Hotline The EA maintain an Incident Hotline. To report damage or danger to the natural environment, damage to structures or water escaping, telephone 0800 80 70 60.

LICENSING – BOATS

The majority of the navigations covered in this book are controlled by BW and the EA and are managed on a day-to-day basis by local Waterway Offices (you will find details of these in the introductions to each waterway). All craft using the inland waterways must be licenced and charges are based on the dimensions of the craft. In a few cases, these include reciprocal agreements with other waterway authorities (as indicated in the text). BW and the EA offer an optional Gold Licence which covers unlimited navigation on the waterways of both authorities. Permits for permanent mooring on BW waterways are issued by BW.

Contact the BW Boat Licensing Team on 0845 6715530; www.britishwaterways.co.uk/licenseit; British Waterways Boat Licensing, PO Box 162, Leeds LS9 1AX.

For the Thames and River Medway contact the EA. River Thames: 0118 953 5650; www.environment-agency.gov.uk; Environment Agency, PO Box 214, Reading RG1 8HQ. River Medway: 01732 223222 or visit the website.

BOAT SAFETY SCHEME

BW and the EA operate the Boat Safety Scheme – boat construction standards and regular tests required by all licence holders on BW and EA waterways. A Boat Safety Certificate (for new boats, a Declaration of Conformity), is necessary to obtain a craft licence. BW also requires proof of insurance for Third Party Liability for a minimum of £1,000,000 for powered boats. The scheme is gradually being adopted by other waterway authorities. Contact details are: 01923 201278; www.boatsafetyscheme.com; Boat Safety Scheme, 64 Clarendon Road, Watford, Herts WD17 1DA. The website offers useful advice on preventing fires and avoiding carbon monoxide poisoning.

TRAINING

The Royal Yachting Association (RYA) runs one and two day courses leading to the Inland Waters Helmsman's Certificate, specifically designed for novices and experienced boaters wishing to cruise the inland waterways. For details of RYA schools, telephone 0845 345 0384 or visit www.rya.org.uk. The practical course notes are available to buy. Contact your local boat clubs, too. The National Community Boats Association (NCBA) run courses on boat-handling and safety on the water. Telephone 0845 0510649 or visit www.national-cba.co.uk.

LICENSING – CYCLISTS

Not all towpaths are open to cyclists. Maps on www.waterscape.com show the stretches of towpath open to cyclists, and local offices can supply more information. A cycle permit is usually required. Cycling along the Thames towpath is generally accepted, although landowners have the right to request that you do not cycle. Some sections of the riverside path, however, are designated and clearly marked as official cycle ways. No permits are required but cyclists must follow London's Towpath Code on Conduct at all times. For further information, to obtain a permit or a copy of the Towpath Code, contact BW Customer Services or visit www.waterscape.com.

TOWPATHS

Few, if any, artificial cuts or canals in this country are without an intact towpath accessible to the walker at least and the Thames is the only river in the country with a designated National Trail along its path from source to sea (for more information visit www.nationaltrail.co.uk). However, on some other river navigations, towpaths have on occasion fallen into disuse or, sometimes, been lost to erosion. The indication of a towpath in this guide does not necessarily imply a public right of way or mean that a right to cycle along it exists. Horse riding and motorcycling are forbidden on all towpaths.

INDIVIDUAL WATERWAY GUIDES

No national guide can cover the minutiae of detail concerning every waterway, and some BW Waterway Managers produce guides to specific navigations under their charge. Copies of individual guides (where available) can be obtained from the relevant BW Waterway Office or downloaded from www.waterscape.com/boatersguides. Please note that times – such as operating times of bridges and locks – do change year by year and from winter to summer. For a free copy of River Thames – a User's Guide visit www.visitthames.co.uk/forms.

STOPPAGES

BW and the EA both publish winter stoppage programmes which are sent out to all licence holders, boatyards and hire companies. Inevitably, emergencies occur necessitating the unexpected closure of a waterway, perhaps during the peak season. You can check for stoppages on individual waterways between specific dates on www.waterscape.com/stoppages, lockside noticeboards or by telephoning 01923 201401; for stoppages and river conditions on the Thames, visit www.visitthames.co.uk or telephone 0845 988 1188, press 1 following by 011131 for river conditions; 011132 for river works and lock closures.

NAVIGATION AUTHORITIES AND WATERWAYS SOCIETIES

Most inland navigations are managed by BW or the EA, but there are several other navigation authorities. For details of these, contact the Association of Inland Navigation Authorities on 0113 243 3125 or visit www.aina.org.uk. The boater, conditioned perhaps by the uniformity of our national road network, should be sensitive to the need to observe different codes and operating practices.

BW is a public corporation, responsible to the Department for Environment, Food and Rural Affairs in England and Wales, and is linked with an ombudsman. BW has a comprehensive complaints procedure and a free explanatory leaflet is available from Customer Services. Problems and complaints should be addressed to the local Waterway Manager in the first instance. For more information, visit their website.

The EA is the national body, sponsored by the Department for Environment, Food and Rural Affairs, to manage the quality of air, land and water in England and Wales. For more information, visit its website.

The Inland Waterways Association (IWA) campaigns for the use, maintenance and restoration of Britain's inland waterways, through branches all over the country. For more information, contact them on 01494 783453; iwa@waterways.org.uk; www.waterways.org.uk; The Inland Waterways Association, Island House, Moor Road, Chesham HP5 1WA. Their website has a huge amount of information of interest to boaters, including comprehensive details of the many and varied waterways societies.

STARTING OUT
Extensive information and advice on booking a boating holiday is available from the Inland Waterways Association, www.visitthames.co.uk and www.waterscape.com. Please book a waterway holiday from a licenced operator – only in this way can you be sure that you have proper insurance cover, service and support during your holiday. It is illegal for private boat owners to hire out their craft. If you are hiring a holiday craft for the first time, the boatyard will brief you thoroughly. Take notes, follow their instructions and don't be afraid to ask if there is anything you do not understand. BW have produced a short DVD giving basic information on using a boat safely. Copies are available from BW Customer Services (charge).

PLACES TO VISIT ALONG THE WAY
This guide contains a wealth of information, not just about the canals and rivers and navigating on them, but also on the visitor attractions and places to eat and drink close to the waterways. Opening and closing times, and other details often change; establishments close and new ones open. If you are making special plans to eat in a particular pub, or visit a certain museum it is always advisable to check in advance.

MORE INFORMATION
An internet search will reveal many websites on the inland waterways. Those listed below are just a small sample:
National Community Boats Association is a national charity and training provider, supporting community boat projects and encouraging more people to access the inland waterways. Telephone 0845 0510649; www.national-cba.co.uk.

National Association of Boat Owners is dedicated to promoting the interests of private boaters on Britain's canals and rivers. Visit www.nabo.org.uk.
www.canalplan.org.uk is an online journey-planner and gazetteer for the inland waterways.
www.canals.com is a valuable source of information on anything related to cruising the canals, with loads of links to canal and waterways related websites.
www.saveourwaterways.org is the website of Save Our Waterways, a campaign which embraces all waterways users and is dedicated to securing the long-term future of the inland waterways.
www.ukcanals.net lists services and useful information for all waterways users.

GENERAL CRUISING NOTES
Most canals and rivers are saucer shaped, being deepest at the middle. Few canals have more than 3-4ft of water and many have much less. Keep to the centre of the channel except on bends, where the deepest water is on the outside of the bend. When you meet another boat, keep to the right, slow down and aim to miss the approaching craft by a couple of yards. If you meet a loaded commercial boat keep right out of the way and be prepared to follow his instructions. Do not assume that you should pass on the right. If you meet a boat being towed from the bank, pass it on the outside. When overtaking, keep the other boat on your right side.

Some BW and EA facilities are operated by pre-paid cards, obtainable from BW and EA regional and local waterways offices, lock keepers and boatyards. Weekend visitors should purchase cards in advance. A handcuff/anti-vandal key is commonly used on locks where vandalism is a problem. A watermate/sanitary key opens sanitary stations, waterpoints and some bridges and locks. Both keys and pre-paid cards can be obtained via BW Customer Service Centre.

Safety
Boating is a safe pastime. However, it makes sense to take simple safety precautions, particularly if you have children aboard.
- Never drink and drive a boat – it may travel slowly, but it weighs many tons.
- Be careful with naked flames and never leave the boat with the hob or oven lit. Familiarise

yourself and your crew with the location and operation of the fire extinguishers.

- Never block ventilation grills. Boats are enclosed spaces and levels of carbon monoxide can build up from faulty appliances or just from using the cooker.
- Be careful along the bank and around locks. Slipping from the bank might only give you a cold-water soaking, but falling from the side of, or into a lock is more dangerous. Beware of slippery or rough ground.
- Remember that fingers and toes are precious! If a major collision is imminent, never try to fend off with your hands or feet; and always keep hands and arms inside the boat.
- Weil's disease is a particularly dangerous infection present in water which can attack the central nervous system and major organs. It is caused by bacteria entering the bloodstream through cuts and broken skin, and the eyes, nose and mouth. The flu-like symptoms occur two-four weeks after exposure. Always wash your hands thoroughly after contact with the water. Visit www.leptospirosis.org for details.

Speed

There is a general speed limit of 4 mph on most BW canals and 5 mph on the Thames. There is no need to go any faster – the faster you go, the bigger a wave the boat creates: if your wash is breaking against the bank, causing large waves or throwing moored boats around, slow down. Slow down also when passing engineering works and anglers; when there is a lot of floating rubbish on the water (try to drift over obvious obstructions in neutral); when approaching blind corners, narrow bridges and junctions.

Mooring

Generally you may moor where you wish on BW property, as long as you are *not causing an obstruction*. Do not moor in a winding hole or junction, the approaches to a lock or tunnel, or at a water point or sanitary station. On the Thames, generally you have a right to anchor for 24 hours in one place provided no obstruction is caused, however you will need explicit permission from the land owner to moor. There are official mooring sites along the length of the river; those provided by the EA are free, the others you will need to pay for. Your boat should carry metal mooring stakes, and these should be driven firmly into the ground with a mallet if there are no mooring rings. Do not stretch mooring lines across the towpath and take account of anyone who may walk past. Always consider the security of your boat when there is no one aboard. On tideways and commercial waterways it is advisable to moor only at recognised sites, and allow for any rise or fall of the tide.

Bridges

On narrow canals slow down well in advance and aim to miss one side (usually the towpath side) by about 9 inches. *Keep everyone inboard when passing under bridges and ensure there is nothing on the roof of the boat that will hit the bridge.* If a boat is coming the other way, that nearest to the bridge has priority. Take special care with moveable structures – the crew member operating the bridge should be strong and heavy enough to hold it steady as the boat passes through.

Going aground

You can sometimes go aground if the water level on a canal has dropped or you are on a particularly shallow stretch. If it does happen, try reversing *gently*, or pushing off with the boat hook. Another method is to get your crew to rock the boat from side to side using the boat hook, or move all crew to the end opposite to that which is aground. Or, have all crew leave the boat, except the helmsman, and it will often float off quite easily.

Tunnels

Again, ensure that everyone is inboard. Make sure the tunnel is clear before you enter, and use your headlight. Follow any instructions given on notice boards by the entrance.

Fuel

Hire craft usually carry fuel sufficient for the rental period.

Water

It is advisable to top up daily.

Lavatories

Hire craft usually have pump out toilets. Have these emptied *before* things become critical. Keep the receipt and your boatyard will usually reimburse you. The Green Blue, an organisation providing environmental advice for boating and watersports, has produced a series of maps locating pump out facilities within the UK. Visit www.thegreenblue.org.uk/youandyourboat for these and other advice.

Boatyards
Hire fleets are usually turned around on a Saturday, making this a bad time to call in for services.

VHF Radio
The IWA recommends that all pleasure craft navigating the larger waterways used by freight carrying vessels, or any tidal navigation, should carry marine-band VHF radio and have a qualified radio operator on board. In some cases the navigation authority requires craft to carry radio and maintain a listening watch. Two examples of this are for boats on the tidal River Ouse wishing to enter Goole Docks and the Aire & Calder Navigation, and for boats on the tidal Thames, over 45ft, navigating between Teddington Lock and Limehouse Basin. VHF radio users must have a current operator's certificate. The training is not expensive and will present no problem to the average inland waterways boater. Contact the RYA (see Training) for details.

PLANNING A CRUISE
Don't try to go too far too fast. Go slowly, don't be too ambitious, and enjoy the experience. Mileages indicated on the maps are for guidance only. A *rough* calculation of time taken to cover the ground is the lock-miles system:

Add the number of *miles* to the number of *locks* on your proposed journey, and divide the resulting figure by three. This will give you an approximate guide to the number of *hours* your travel will take.

TIDAL WATERWAYS
The typical steel narrow boat found on the inland waterways is totally unsuitable for cruising on tidal estuaries. However, the adventurous will inevitably wish to add additional 'ring cruises' to the more predictable circuits of inland Britain. Passage is possible in most estuaries if careful consideration is given to the key factors of weather conditions, tides, crew experience, the condition of the boat and its equipment and, perhaps of overriding importance, the need to take expert advice. In many cases it will be prudent to employ the skilled services of a local pilot. Within the text, where inland navigations connect with a tidal waterway, details are given of sources of advice and pilotage. It is also essential to inform your insurance company of your intention to navigate on tidal waterways as they may very well have special requirements or wish to levy an additional premium. This guide is to the inland waterways of Britain and therefore recognizes that tideways – and especially estuaries – require a different approach and many additional skills. We do not hesitate to draw the boater's attention to the appropriate source material.

LOCKS AND THEIR USE
A lock is a simple and ingenious device for transporting your craft from one water level to another. When both sets of gates are closed it may be filled or emptied using gates, or ground paddles, at the top or bottom of the lock. These are operated with a windlass. On the Thames, the locks are manned all year round, with longer hours from April to October. You may operate the locks yourself at any time.

If a lock is empty, or 'set' for you, the crew open the gates and you drive the boat in. If the lock is full of water, the crew should check first to see if any boat is waiting or coming in the other direction. If a boat is in sight, you must let them through first: do not empty or 'turn' the lock against them. This is not only discourteous, and against the rules, but wastes precious water.

In the diagrams the *plan* shows how the gates point uphill, the water pressure forcing them together. Water is flooding into the lock through the underground culverts that are operated by the ground paddles: when the lock is 'full', the top gates (on the left of the drawing) can be opened. One may imagine a boat entering, the crew closing the gates and paddles after it.

In the *elevation*, the bottom paddles have been raised (opened) so that the lock empties. A boat will, of course, float down with the water. When the lock is 'empty' the bottom gates can be opened and the descending boat can leave.

Remember that when going *up* a lock, a boat should be tied up to prevent it being thrown about by the the rush of incoming water; but when going *down* a lock, a boat should never be tied up or it will be left high and dry.

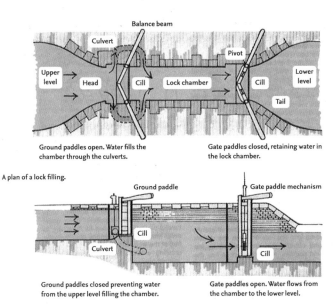

Ground paddles open. Water fills the chamber through the culverts.

Gate paddles closed, retaining water in the lock chamber.

A plan of a lock filling.

Ground paddles closed preventing water from the upper level filling the chamber.

Gate paddles open. Water flows from the chamber to the lower level.

An elevation of a lock emptying.

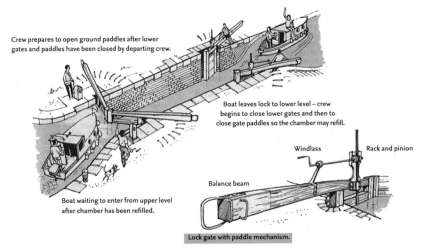

Crew prepares to open ground paddles after lower gates and paddles have been closed by departing crew.

Boat leaves lock to lower level – crew begins to close lower gates and then to close gate paddles so the chamber may refill.

Boat waiting to enter from upper level after chamber has been refilled.

Lock gate with paddle mechanism.

- Make safety your prime concern. *Keep a close eye on young children.*
- Always take your time, and do not leap about.
- Never open the paddles at one end without ensuring those at the other end are closed.
- Keep to the landward side of the balance beam when opening and closing gates.
- Never leave your windlass slotted onto the paddle spindle – it will be dangerous should anything slip.

- Keep your boat away from the top and bottom gates to prevent it getting caught on the gate or the lock cill.
- Never drop the paddles – always wind them down.
- Be wary of fierce *top gate* paddles, especially in wide locks. Operate them slowly, and close them if there is *any* adverse effect.
- Always follow the navigation authority's instructions, where given on notices or by their staff.

Crick (see page 74)

ASHBY CANAL

MAXIMUM DIMENSIONS

Length: 72'
Beam: 7'
Headroom: 6' 6"
Draught: 3' 6"

MILEAGE

MARSTON JUNCTION (Coventry Canal) to:
Burton Hastings: 3 miles
Hinckley Wharf: 6 miles
Stoke Golding Wharf: 8¾ miles
Dadlington: 10 miles

Shenton Aqueduct: 13 miles
Market Bosworth Wharf: 15 miles
Congerstone: 17¼ miles
Shackerstone: 18¼ miles
Snarestone Tunnel: 21 miles
HEAD OF NAVIGATION: 22 miles

No locks

MANAGER

01825 252000
enquiries.westmidlands@britishwaterways.co.uk

Looking at this canal on a map it appears to be very much out on a limb. In fact the Ashby Canal was originally intended to be a through route from the River Trent at Burton to the Coventry Canal near Bedworth, but this plan was repeatedly shelved. In 1792, however, an Ashby Canal Company was formed and a Bill promoted, mostly by the owners of Leicestershire limeworks and the new coalfields near Ashby de la Zouch, who decided that an outlet southwards was required from their various works. The problem that soon arose was that, while the proposed canal could be built level for 30 miles (following the 300ft contour) from the junction with the Coventry Canal at Marston Jabbett, near Bedworth, to Moira, the section north of Moira would require expensive and complicated works, including locks, reservoirs, pumping engines and possibly a tunnel. Part of this cost was, in fact, avoided by building an extensive system of tramroads to and around the various coalmines and limeworks. However, while the canal was still being built (by a succession of engineers – Jessop, Outram, Whitworth senior and junior, and Thomas Newbold), the new coalmines near Ashby Wolds were found to be less productive than had been hoped. This, combined with the fact that the canal was never extended north to the Trent, was instrumental in preventing the Ashby Canal from making a profit for 20 years. However, a new coal mine sunk at Moira in 1804 eventually produced coal of such excellent quality that it became widely demanded in London and southern England. The canal flourished at last.

In 1845 the Midland Railway bought up the Ashby Canal – with the approval of all concerned except the Coventry and Oxford canal companies, who stood to lose a lot in tolls if the coal traffic from Moira switched to rail carriage. These two companies managed to hamstring the Midland Railway so effectively over its management of the canal that, instead of switching to carriage by rail, the coal traffic from Moira continued along the canal at a substantial level through to the turn of the century. It is therefore hard to see what real benefit the railway company gained from buying the canal.

Subsidence from the coal mines near Measham (now stabilised with the completion of mining in the area) has caused great damage in this century to the canal that served them. This subsidence has brought about the abandonment of over 8 miles of the canal, so that the waterway now terminates just north of Snarestone, outside the coalfield. The last load to be carried along the canal was coal to Croxley (Herts), from Gopsall Wharf in 1970. Ambitious plans are in hand to re-open the waterway through to Moira, making use of the abandoned railway line in Measham. Already a new 1¼ mile section, complete with a lock in water, has been constructed beside Moira Furnace.

Burton Hastings

At Marston Junction the Ashby Canal branches east off the Coventry Canal. Under the bridge there is a box containing guides to the waterway produced by the Ashby Canal Association. As soon as it leaves Marston, the canal changes completely and dramatically. The industry and housing estates that had accompanied the Coventry Canal through the Nuneaton–Bedworth conurbation suddenly vanish to be replaced by green fields, farms and trees. In this way the character of the Ashby Canal is established at once: also the first of the typical stone-arched bridges occurs which, together with the shallow and relatively clear water, suggests a rurality far from the industrial Midlands. Only the power lines that criss-cross this stretch are a memory of the other world to the west. A long wooded cutting leads the canal towards Burton Hastings, a typical farming village. Then the canal turns north, setting a course for Hinckley passing, to the east of bridge 13, Stretton Baskerville, a 'lost' village and scheduled ancient monument. The A5 (Watling Street) and the A47 cross near Hinckley. There is no navigation on the Hinckley Wharf Arm, which is used as a boat club mooring. However there are good moorings west of bridge 16 and to the north and south of the marina complex beyond bridge 17 (but ask at the marina first). Keeping west of the town, the canal continues through the fine rolling farmland that typifies the Ashby Canal.

Boatyards

Ⓑ **Trinity Marinas** Wharf Farm, Coventry Road, Hinckley LE10 0NF (01455 896820; www.trinitymarinas.co.uk). ⛴ ⛴ ⚓ D E Pump out, gas, overnight and long-term mooring, wet dock, DIY facilities, chandlery, books, maps and gifts, telephone, toilets, showers, solid fuel, laundrette, café, restaurant and hotel. Boat licensing at marina office. *Emergency call-out.*

WALKING & CYCLING

The condition of the towpath has been greatly improved and erosion in the bridgeholes has been made good. This is a very rural waterway, so few sections of the towpath have an all-weather surface, making progress for walker and cyclist difficult in some areas during the winter months. Hinkley and Bosworth Borough Council publish four guides which detail walks that include sections of the canal. These are available from local Tourist Information Centres.

NAVIGATIONAL NOTES

The canal is still shallow in places although a robust dredging programme has done a great deal to improve things. Headroom under bridge 17 is very limited. Random mooring may be awkward due to shallow sides, so use the wharfs and recognised moorings.

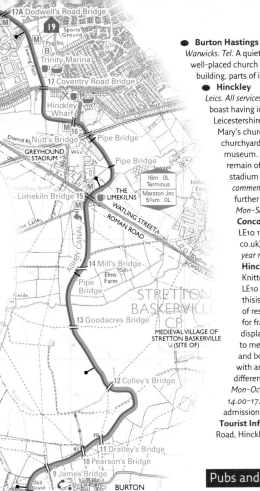

● Burton Hastings

Warwicks. Tel. A quiet village set on a hill in open farmland. The well-placed church dedicated to St Botolph is a Grade II listed building, parts of its construction dating back to the 14th C.

● Hinckley

Leics. All services. A hosiery manufacturing town that can boast having installed the first stocking machine in Leicestershire, in 1640. Buildings of interest include St Mary's church with the 'bleeding' tombstone in the churchyard; the Great Meeting Chapel (1722) and the museum. Only the bailey and part of the moat remain of the Norman castle. There is a greyhound stadium south of bridge 16 with racing *Wed and Sat* commencing at 19.30. Telephone 01455 634006 for further details. The shop on Coventry Road is open *Mon-Sat 05.30-21.00 & Sun 06.00-17.00;*

Concordia Theatre Stockwell Head, Hinckley LE10 1RE (01455 615005; www.concordiatheatre. co.uk). Small local theatre with performances *all year round.*

Hinckley and District Museum Framework Knitters Cottages, Lower Bond Street, Hinckley LE10 1QU (01455 251218; www.beehive. thisisleicestershire.co.uk). Established in a row of restored 17th-C thatched cottages once used for framework knitting, the museum houses displays on the town and area from prehistoric to medieval times. Also depicted are the hosiery and boot and shoe making industries together with annually changing exhibitions reflecting different aspects of local history. *Open Easter Mon-Oct, Sat and B Hol Mon 10.00-16.00, Sun 14.00-17.00.* Tearoom and cottage garden. Small admission charge.

Tourist Information Centre The Library, Lancaster Road, Hinckley LE10 0ET (01455 635106).

Pubs and Restaurants

♟ The Corner House Hotel Bulkington Lane, Bulkington, Bedworth CV12 9SB (02476 386159). South of bridge 5 on B4112. Large friendly pub orientated around family eating. Real ales. Food available *all day, every day.* Children welcome. Patio.

♟ The Lime Kilns Inn Watling Street, Hinckley LE10 3ED (01455 631158). Canalside at bridge 15. Old coaching house with a downstairs boaters' bar. A family pub serving real ale and bar food *L and E, daily* Children's menu. Canalside seating, garden and children's play area. *Open all day Sat, Sun in summer.*

♟ The Wharf Inn Coventry Road, Hinckley LE10 0NQ (01455 615830; www.wharf-inn.co.uk). East of bridge 17, near Hinckley Wharf. Real ales dispensed in a pub dating back to the 1700s. Children's room and outdoor play area. Garden, darts. Dogs (on a lead) welcome. *Occasional* summer barbecues, weather permitting. There is a variety of services close by including a good *general stores, fish & chips, PO, off-licence, Indian restaurant, takeaway, newsagent and garage.*

♟ ✕ The Watergate Restaurant Trinity Marinas, Wharf Farm, Coventry Road, Hinckley LE10 0NF (01455 896827; www.trinitymarinas.co.uk). Modern restaurant-cum-pub set in a marina complex, serving real ales, bar snacks (available *all day*) and an à la carte restaurant menu *L and E,* prepared from local produce wherever possible. Children welcome when dining. Canalside decking and beer garden. Regular quiz and live entertainment.

Stoke Golding

The canal now runs fairly directly to Stoke Golding where there is one of the finest churches in Leicestershire. Just to the west of Wharf Bridge 25 there is an excellent farm shop selling both home-produced meat and vegetables. There are no locks, but the typical Ashby accommodation bridges occur regularly. The Ashby Canal is remote and rural, an ironic contrast to its raison d'être, the Ashby coalfields. After Stoke Golding the contours cause the canal to meander carelessly, passing Dadlington, heading in a northerly direction towards Sutton Cheney Wharf (*showers and toilets*) and the Bosworth Battlefield Centre nearby.

Pubs and Restaurants

The Oddfellows Arms Main Street, Higham on the Hill CV13 6AE (01455 212322). Real ale and food served *L daily (not Mon or Tue) and E Wed–Sat*. Children welcome. Patio seating. Pub games. Varied entertainment *weekends*.

The Fox Inn Main Street, Higham on the Hill CV13 6AH (01455 212241). Friendly country pub serving real ales, with home-made bar snacks available *L and E Sun*. Children welcome during day. Beer garden.

The White Swan High Street, Stoke Golding, CV13 6HE (01455 212313; www.everards.co.uk). Real ale dispensed in a homely village local with friendly staff. Bar snacks available *L and E, daily*. Children and dogs welcome. Garden. Twice-monthly quiz, pub games and *summer* barbecues. Open *12.00–14.00 and 18.00–23.00 (Fri, Sat and Sun 16.30–23.00)*.

The George & Dragon Station Road, Stoke Golding CV136EZ (01455 213268). Inexpensive, interesting and varied food available *L and E, daily*. Real ale. Children welcome. Garden and children's play area. Book if eating *after 20.00*.

The Dog & Hedgehog The Green, Dadlington CV13 6JB (01455 212629; www.dogandhedgehog.co.uk). A most deceptive pub, tiny from the outside but able to seat upwards of 80 diners (*L and E, daily*) in its air-conditioned, ex-malthouse dining room and minstrels

gallery. A good selection of real ales available. Children well catered for. The 2-acre gardens are an extravaganza of floral colour. Booking advisable *E and Sun L*.

Café Wharfside Sutton Cheney Wharf, Wharf lane, Sutton Cheney CV13 0AL (01455 213838/07778 734073; www.ashbytrip.com). Friendly café serving tasty homemade dishes, tea, coffee, snacks and ices from breakfast through to tea. Also gifts, guides and souvenirs including Measham Ware. Muddy boots and well-behaved dogs on leads are welcomed. *Open daily 09.00 and closing Mon–Fri 17.00 (16.00 in winter) and Sat–Sun 18.00 (17.00 in winter)*.

The Hercules Inn Main Street, Sutton Cheney CV13 0AG (01455 292591; www.reallytasty.co.uk). Real ales and good-value bar meals and snacks available *L and E and B Hol Mon* – booking advisable for *Sun L*. Children welcome. Patio. Quiz *twice a month*.

The Royal Arms Main Street, Sutton Cheney CV13 0AG (01455 290263; www.royalarms.co.uk). An excellent range of real ales. Bar meals or à la carte food is available *L and E, daily*, served in the traditional pub restaurant. Children welcome. B & B.

WALKING & CYCLING
In Shenton Cutting, waymarked from Railway Bridge 34A, there is a wildlife walk and a bird-watching hide.

Boatyards

ⓑ **The Barge** Hinckley Lane, Higham on the Hill, Nuneaton (01455 234213). Long-term mooring.

ⓑ **Ashby Boat Company** The Canal Wharf, Stoke Golding, Nuneaton (01455 212671; www. ashbyboats.co.uk). 🛱 🛱 ⚓ D E Pump out, narrowboat hire, gas, day-hire craft, long-term mooring, chandlery, boat building and fitting out, boat sales and repairs, engine sales and repairs, tearoom, toilets, telephone. *Emergency call out*.

ⓑ **Ashby Canal Centre** Willow Park Marina, Stoke Golding, Nuneaton (01455 212636). ⚓ Short and long-term moorings, winter storage, crane, slipway, covered wet dock, boat brokerage, boat building and fitting out, boat painting, engine sales, DIY facilities, boat and engine repairs, chandlery, solid fuel, boat surveys, toilets.

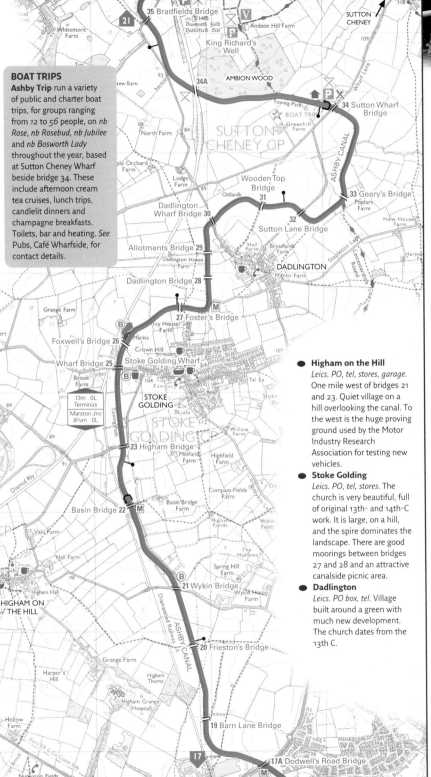

BOAT TRIPS

Ashby Trip run a variety of public and charter boat trips, for groups ranging from 12 to 56 people, on nb *Rose*, nb *Rosebud*, nb *Jubilee* and nb *Bosworth Lady* throughout the year, based at Sutton Cheney Wharf beside bridge 34. These include afternoon cream tea cruises, lunch trips, candlelit dinners and champagne breakfasts. Toilets, bar and heating. *See* Pubs, Café Wharfside, for contact details.

Higham on the Hill

Leics. PO, tel, stores, garage. One mile west of bridges 21 and 23. Quiet village on a hill overlooking the canal. To the west is the huge proving ground used by the Motor Industry Research Association for testing new vehicles.

Stoke Golding

Leics. PO, tel, stores. The church is very beautiful, full of original 13th- and 14th-C work. It is large, on a hill, and the spire dominates the landscape. There are good moorings between bridges 27 and 28 and an attractive canalside picnic area.

Dadlington

Leics. PO box, tel. Village built around a green with much new development. The church dates from the 13th C.

Market Bosworth

Just before Shenton Aqueduct there are good moorings for the Battlefield Centre. Shenton Park is passed on an embankment, and then the aqueduct carries the canal over the road to Shenton village. It continues towards Congerstone, with Market Bosworth and Carlton away to the east. There are good moorings between bridges 49 and 50, and north of bridge 51. Beyond Congerstone the navigation crosses the River Sence.

● **Shenton**

Leics. Tel. Estate village clustered around the Hall, a house of 1629 much rebuilt in the 19th C.

Battle of Bosworth Field 22 August 1485 Ambion Hill, Sutton Cheney. The battlefield where Richard III, last of the Plantagenets, was killed by Henry Tudor who thus became Henry VII. 3/4 mile walk from Shenton Embankment to the **Bosworth Battlefield Visitor Centre** Sutton Cheney CV13 0AD (01455 290429; www.leics.gov.uk). Award winning interpretation of the battle. Cafeteria (Battlefield Buttery 01455 291048), shop. Toilets. Visitor Centre *open Apr–Oct, Mon–Sat 11.00–17.00; Sun and B Hols 11.00–18.00; Nov and Dec, Sun 11.00–dusk, and Mar, Sat and Sun 11.00–17.00.* Charge. Footpaths *open all year in daylight hours.* Disabled access to Visitor Centre and Battlefield Trails.

Whitemoors Antique and Craft Centre Main Street, Shenton, Market Bosworth CV13 6BZ (01455 212250). Craft and antique centre. Tearooms. *Open all year (except Xmas Eve and Xmas Day), daily 11.00–17.00.*

● **Market Bosworth**

Leics. PO, tel, stores, chemist, bank, butcher, takeaways, garage. Almost a mile east of its wharf. Small market town remaining much as it was in the 18th C. Shop *open Mon–Sat 08.00–20.00 and Sun 09.00–18.00.*

Battlefield Line Shackerstone Station, Shackerstone CV13 0BS (01827 880754; www.battlefield-line-railway.co.uk). Preserved railway line. A ride can be linked in with a visit to the Bosworth Battlefield Visitor Centre. *See page 19* for further details.

Bosworth Water Trust Far Coton Lane, Wellsborough Road, near Nuneaton CV13 6PD (01455 291876; www.bosworthwatertrust. co.uk). Just to the west of Bosworth Wharf Bridge 42. Large leisure park with a 20-acre lake for water pursuits. Wetsuits and craft for hire. Changing rooms, toilets, showers and snack bar *open during main season.* Site *open all year, daily 10.00–dusk.* Charge.

Cadeby Experience The Old Rectory, Cadeby CV13 0AS (01455 290462). South east of Market Bosworth. The museum houses the Boston Collection of model and miniature railways and agricultural road vehicles. *Open on some Sats, telephone to confirm.* Donations.

● **Congerstone**

Leics. Tel. Scattered village.

Pubs and Restaurants

🍺 ✗ **The Black Horse** Market Place, Market Bosworth CV13 0LF (01455 290278). Old-world country pub dispensing real ales. Snacks and meals available *L and E, daily* in bar and restaurant. Children welcome. Patio area.

✗ **Victorian Tea Parlour** Wheatsheaf Courtyard, Market Place, Market Bosworth CV13 0LF (01827 880669). Off the courtyard. Step back in time and enjoy a trip down memory lane together with teas, coffees, snacks and light lunches. Children welcome. Pretty garden. *Open daily 11.00–17.00.*

🍺 **The Dixie Arms** Main Street, Market Bosworth CV13 0JW (01455 290218; www.dixiearmshotel.co.uk). 400-year-old hostelry in the town centre. Bar, restaurant and hotel *open L and E Tue–Sat*, dispensing real ales and food. Children and dogs welcome. Garden and big-screen TV.

🍺 **Ye Olde Red Lion Hotel** Park Street, Market Bosworth CV13 0LL (01455 291713; www.redlionmarketbosworth). Another 400-year-old hotel and public house in the town centre serving real ales. Home-made snacks and meals available *L and E (not Sun and Mon E).* Children and dogs welcome. Patio. Open fires *(winter only)* and pub games. Open *all day Sat.* B & B.

🍺 **The Gate Hangs Well** Barton Road, Carlton CV13 0DB (01455 291845). Small country pub with warm, cosy interior serving real ale and rolls and sandwiches *L (not Sun).* Children and dogs welcome *(dogs in conservatory area only).* Regular entertainment. Conservatory, garden and children's play area.

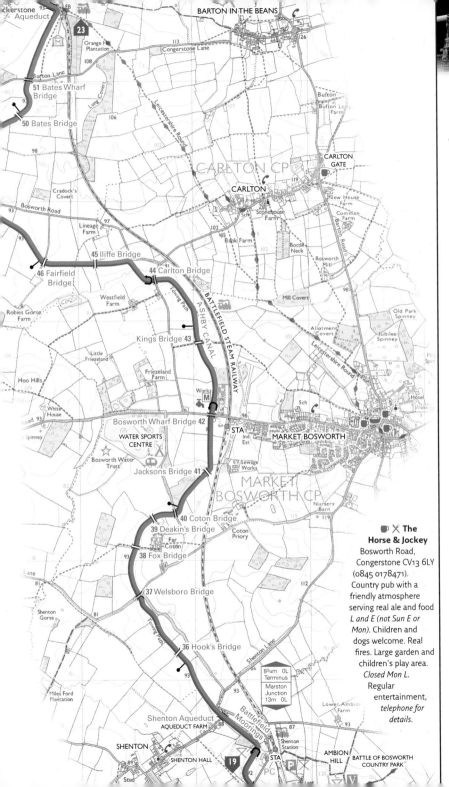

ckerstone Aqueduct

51 Bates Wharf Bridge

50 Bates Bridge

BARTON IN THE BEANS

Orange Hill Plantation

Congerstone Lane

Barton Lane

Long Covert

Leicestershire Round

CARLTON CP

CARLTON

CARLTON GATE

Bufton

Bufton Lodge Farm

Bosworth Road

Cradock's Covert

Lineage Farm

Westfield Farm

45 Iliffe Bridge

46 Fairfield Bridge

Robies Gorse Farm

Little Friezeland

Kings Bridge 43

Hoo Hills

White House Road

Bosworth Wharf Bridge 42

WATER SPORTS CENTRE

Bosworth Water Trust

Jacksons Bridge 41

40 Coton Bridge

39 Deakin's Bridge

Far Coton

38 Fox Bridge

Lane

37 Welsboro Bridge

Shenton Gorse

Towing Path

36 Hook's Bridge

Miles Ford Plantation

Shenton Aqueduct

AQUEDUCT FARM

SHENTON

SHENTON HALL

Stud

Stonehouse Farm

Bank Farm

Bottle Neck

Bosworth Mill

New House Farm

Common Farm

Barton Road

Mill Covert

BATTLEFIELD STEAM RAILWAY

ASHBY CANAL

Towing Path

Friezeland Farm

Works M

STA Ind Est

MARKET BOSWORTH

Sewage Works

MARKET BOSWORTH CP

Coton Priory

Nursery Barn

Allotment Covert

Leicestershire Round

Old Park Spinney

Jubilee Spinney

Hotel

Sch

Shenton Lane

8¾m 0L Terminus

Marston Junction 13m 0L

Battlefield Moorings

Shenton Station

STA

AMBION HILL

LOWER Ambion Farm

BATTLE OF BOSWORTH COUNTRY PARK

19

The Horse & Jockey

Bosworth Road, Congerstone CV13 6LY (0845 0178471). Country pub with a friendly atmosphere serving real ale and food *L and E (not Sun E or Mon)*. Children and dogs welcome. Real fires. Large garden and children's play area. *Closed Mon L.* Regular entertainment, *telephone for details.*

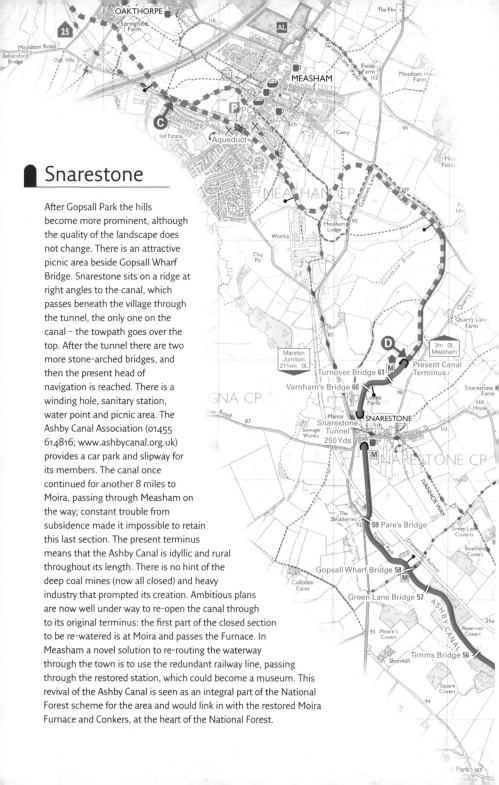

Snarestone

After Gopsall Park the hills become more prominent, although the quality of the landscape does not change. There is an attractive picnic area beside Gopsall Wharf Bridge. Snarestone sits on a ridge at right angles to the canal, which passes beneath the village through the tunnel, the only one on the canal – the towpath goes over the top. After the tunnel there are two more stone-arched bridges, and then the present head of navigation is reached. There is a winding hole, sanitary station, water point and picnic area. The Ashby Canal Association (01455 614816; www.ashbycanal.org.uk) provides a car park and slipway for its members. The canal once continued for another 8 miles to Moira, passing through Measham on the way; constant trouble from subsidence made it impossible to retain this last section. The present terminus means that the Ashby Canal is idyllic and rural throughout its length. There is no hint of the deep coal mines (now all closed) and heavy industry that prompted its creation. Ambitious plans are now well under way to re-open the canal through to its original terminus: the first part of the closed section to be re-watered is at Moira and passes the Furnace. In Measham a novel solution to re-routing the waterway through the town is to use the redundant railway line, passing through the restored station, which could become a museum. This revival of the Ashby Canal is seen as an integral part of the National Forest scheme for the area and would link in with the restored Moira Furnace and Conkers, at the heart of the National Forest.

- **Shackerstone**

Leics. Undeveloped and unchanged, Shackerstone is a farming village that reflects the pre-industrial feeling of the whole of the Ashby Canal. West of the village the canal flanks Gopsall Park; the house where Handel is reputed to have composed the *Messiah* was pulled down in 1951, and the park has since lost its original dignity and quality.

Battlefield Line Shackerstone Station, Shackerstone CV13 oBS (01827 880754; www.battlefield-line-railway.co.uk). Although the railway line that follows the Ashby Canal is now closed, the former Shackerstone Junction station (near canal bridge 52) has come to life again as a small railway museum (*open Sat 12.00–17.30, Sun and B Hol Mon 10.30–18.00*) and a depot for preserved steam locomotives which run 9-mile round trips to Shenton, via Market Bosworth, on *Sun (Mar–Oct); Sat (Apr–Oct) and Wed (Jul and Aug).* Diesel trains operate services on *Sat (Apr–Oct), Wed (May, Jun and Sep), Fri (Jun–Aug).* Victorian tearooms and on-train catering with bar. Souvenir shop. Charge. Can be linked in with a visit to the Bosworth Battlefield Centre.

- **Snarestone**

Leics. Tel. An 18th-C farming village built over the top of the canal, which passes underneath through the crooked tunnel (250yds).

Snibston Discovery Park Ashby Road, Coalville LE67 3LN (01530 510851; www.leics.gov.uk). An unique mixture of science, the environment and history together with brief glimpses into the future in an all-weather setting. Visitors can discover the wonders of technology through over 30 hands-on experiments and experience Leicestershire's rich industrial heritage. Four galleries embrace transport, engineering, extractives and textiles and fashion. Colliery tours, led by ex-miners, explore nearby mine buildings. The site includes 100 acres of landscaped grounds with nature reserve, fishing lakes, sculpture trail and picnic areas (indoor and outdoor). Site railway, coffee and gift shops. *Open daily 10.00–17.00. Closed Xmas and Boxing Day.* Charge. Whilst the Discovery Park is not adjacent to the canal it can make a very worthwhile (wet-weather) day out and is accessible by bus from Hinckley, Market Bosworth, Snarestone and Measham. From Snarestone and Measham buses (route no 97) run *in the morning Mon–Sat,* terminating in Memorial Square, Coalville – approx 800yds from the site entrance. Contact Traveline 0870 608 2608 (*open 07.00–22.30*) for further details. Bus details from Hinckley and Market Bosworth appear on previous pages.

Tourist Information Centre Snibston Discovery Park, Ashby Road, Coalville LE67 3LN (01530 813608). Opening hours as per the Discovery Park.

Pubs and Restaurants

🍺 **Rising Sun** Church Road, Shackerstone CV13 6NN (01827 880215). A range of real ales served in a wood-panelled bar in this old village pub. Food available *L and E, daily.* Children and dogs welcome. Conservatory and beer garden. Pool room.

🍺 ✗ **Globe Inn** Main Street, Snarestone DE12 7DB (01530 270272). A good selection of real ales served in a relaxed and friendly atmosphere. Boaters are welcomed and reasonably priced meals and snacks are available in both the bar and restaurant *E and all day Sat and Sun.* Children and dogs welcome (in the bar). Large garden and children's play area. *All day opening.*

NAVIGATIONAL NOTES

Headroom in Snarestone Tunnel decreases towards the northern portal. It is not safe for two boats to pass in the tunnel.

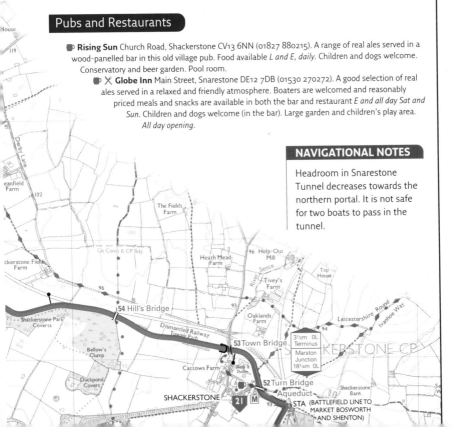

Moira

The 8-mile section of canal, beyond the present terminus at Snarestone, is under consideration for re-opening in three distinct sections; the most northerly, at Moira, being already completed. From the terminus, the first length (C–D on the map) is already the subject of a Transport and Works Act Order and substantially follows the line of the original navigation. However, it deviates outside Measham to make use of the alignment of the disused railway, making an aqueduct crossing over the High Street a likely outcome. This length then terminates before reaching the A42, the major obstacle in the way of the second section (B–C). Once under this dual carriageway, the waterway can largely follow its old, meandering course through to Donisthorpe where it may meet the third and already re-watered section (A–B) leading past Moira Furnace and into the basin beside Conkers. The countryside between Snarestone and Moira is a mixture of rolling Leicestershire arable land and the residues of extensive coal mining and clay extraction which are now the focus for imaginative landscaping, re-development and afforestation, as part of the National Forest.

● **Measham**
Leics. PO, stores, takeaway, chemist, library, fish & chips, garage. Thriving industrial centre even before the arrival of the canal, with coal pits at Oakthorpe and clay deposits that led to the development of a pottery and sanitary ware industry. Famed for its pottery, much prized amongst boating families.
Measham Museum 56 High Street, Measham DE12 7HZ (01530 273956). Follow the line of the old canal, from the present terminus at Snarestone, into Measham. Opposite St Lawrence's church. A uniquely personal history of a small community spanning 100 years as seen through the documents, artefacts and illustrations preserved by a former village doctor and his father. *Open Feb–Nov Tue 10.00–12.00 and 14.00–16.30, Sat 10.00–12.00.* Donations appreciated.
Measham Community Office 56 High Street, Measham DE12 7HZ (01530 273956). This is the base of Leicestershire County Council's Ashby Canal restoration project and of the Ashby Canal Trust (www.ashbycanaltrust.co.uk). There is a small exhibition on the canal and a leaflet is available on the current state of the canal restoration.

● **Oakthorpe**
Leics. PO, stores, takeaway. One-time mining village beside the Ashby Woulds Heritage Trail (*see* Walking & Cycling).

● **Donisthorpe**
Leics. 19th-C Perpendicular style church, constructed of grey sandstone, dedicated to St John the Evangelist. Another ex-mining village, now at the start of the isolated length of the newly re-watered canal and close to the Saltersford Valley Picnic Area.

● **Moira**
Leics. PO, stores. Source of the majority of the coal exported along the canal to Oxford, London and the Home Counties. The name derives from the Moira Estates in Ireland, owned by Baron Rawdon who developed the colliery, foundry and furnace in the area. Saline springs in the area also produced health-giving water but potential visitors were put off 'taking the waters' by the proximity of the coal mines and it was transported to Ashby-de-la-Zouch for final consumption.
Ashby Woulds Heritage Trail Moira (0116 265 7061). A 3-mile local history and heritage trail for walkers and cyclists connecting Conkers to Measham and laid out along the old trackbed of the Ashby and Nuneaton Joint Railway Line. Access points link attractions and numerous country sites.
Conkers Rawdon Road, Moira DE12 6GA (01283 216633; www.visitconkers.com). Ambitious project bringing the visitor close to nature in all its myriad forms. This hands-on experience, at the heart of the National Forest, offers a host of indoor and outdoor activities for all the family. *Open summer 10.00–18.00 and winter 10.00–17.00.*
Cycle Hire National Forest Cycle Hire (seasonal), Conkers, Moira (01283 558084); Just Bikes, 8 The Green, Ashby-de-la-Zouch (01530 415021); City Cycles, 61 Meadow Lane, Coalville (01530 812727).
Moira Furnace Furnace Road, Moira DE12 6AT (01283 224667; www.nwleicestershire.gov.uk). The furnace, completed in 1806, is a focus for a variety of hands-on exhibitions and outdoor attractions including a 150-year-old deciduous woodland plantation, lime kilns and a wildflower meadow, adventure playground, tea rooms and craft centre. The furnace itself had a short working life and so remains in superb condition today, providing an excellent means of accessing the industrial archaeology of this important area. Horse riding and cycling trails; regular special events and children's fun days; guided heritage walks. Furnace *open Apr–Aug, Tue–Sun 10.00–17.00; Sep–Mar, Wed–Sun 10.00–16.00.* Charge. *Site open all day, every day.* Free.

Traveline (0870 608 2 608). Comprehensive bus information *07.00–21.00*.

- **Ashby de la Zouch**

Leics. All services (exception station). Ashby is mentioned in the Doomsday Book as a settlement of approximately 100 people largely situated round the present site of St Helen's church. In 1160 a Norman nobleman, Alain de Parrhoet la Zouch, became lord of the manor by marriage so bestowing the somewhat striking addition to the town's name. During the 15th C, Ashby Manor was gifted to Lord Hastings by Edward IV and the town became the main seat of the Hastings family. The noble lord converted the manor house into a castle and extensively rebuilt St Helen's church. The Grammar School was founded in 1567 against a backdrop of growth and general prosperity as skilled craftsmen – swordsmiths, gold beaters, pewter workers, clockmakers and silversmiths – set up in 'courts' in the area of Market Street. Inevitably it was a Royalist garrison that occupied the castle during the Civil War under the command of Henry Hastings, later Lord Loughborough. It fell to the Parliamentarians in 1646 after a year-long siege and was all but destroyed. With the publication of Sir Walter Scott's classic romance in 1820, the castle regained something of its former prominence, this time as a romantic backcloth to Ivanhoe's victorious tournament and Robin Hood's arrow-splitting exploits. Two years later Ashby took on the mantle of Spa Town with the construction of the Ivanhoe Baths and the Royal (then Hastings) Hotel. Ironically enough, its fortunes were founded upon imported water, brought by canal from nearby Moira and discovered in the course of coal extraction. It was felt that mining was a somewhat less than salubrious companion to taking the waters! This was a relatively short-lived prosperity and following a steady decline, the Baths were closed in 1884. Today Ashby is both a centre for light industry and sought after as a residential area.

BOAT TRIPS

Joseph Wilkes based at Moira Furnace operates trips along the newly restored section of canal. Trips go through the new lock *at weekends* and along the pound to Donisthorpe *during the week*. Telephone 01283 224667 for further details.

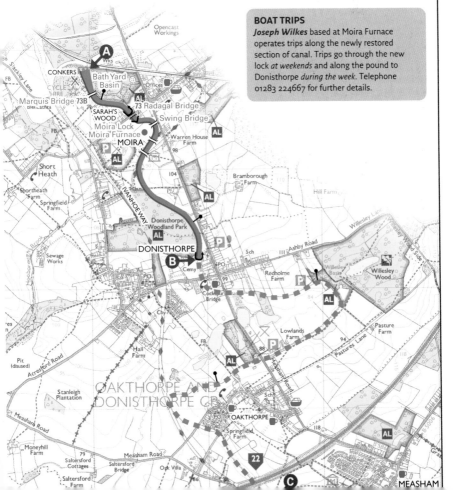

Ashby de la Zouch Museum North Street, Ashby de la Zouch LE65 1HU (01530 560090; www.ashbydelazouchmuseum.org.uk). A permanent display of the history of Ashby and its environs, archives of its rich heritage and a model of the castle as it was during the year-long siege of the Civil War. *Open Easter– Sep, Mon–Fri 11.00–13.00 and 14.00–16.00, Sat 10.00–16.00, Sun 14.00–16.00; winter by appointment only.* Disabled access. Small charge.

Ashby Castle South Street, Ashby de la Zouch LE65 1BR (01530 413343; www.english-heritage.org.uk). While some early remains date back to its 12th-C manor house origins, the most striking feature is the 75' Hastings Tower standing gaunt amongst the ruins. As the castle was designed to resist siege, this tower was connected by underground passage to the kitchens, which can still be explored today. *Open daily Apr–Sep 10.00–18.00; Oct 10.00–16.00; Nov–Mar, Wed–Sat 10.00–16.00.* Charge.

St Helen's Church Church Yard, Ashby de la Zouch LE65 1AA. In Perpendicular style, this church was built by Lord Hastings in 15th C on the site of an earlier Norman building. Enlarged and restored in 1880, it contains much of interest including a rare finger pillory (said to be used in the punishment of those misbehaving in church), glass from Ashby Castle chapel and a series of windows portraying the life of Christ.

Tourist Information Centre North Street, Ashby-de-la-Zouch LE65 1HU (01530 411767; www.nwleicester.gov.uk). *Open Mon–Fri 09.30–17.00 and Sat 09.30–16.00.*

● **Staunton Harold**
Leics. Tel. A hamlet of isolated farms, cottages and the Hall, two miles north of Ashby. There are early Saxon references to the manor of Staunton Harold which passed to the Normans following the Conquest of

1066. Later in the hands of the Ferrers family and subsequently held by the Shirleys. The Palladian style hall is now a Sue Ryder Home and is private.

Ferrers Centre for Arts and Crafts Staunton Harold, Ashby de la Zouch LE65 1RU (01332 863337; www.ferrerscentre.co.uk). Stable block now home to a thriving and diverse selection of craftsmen and women. Tea room and gift shop situated in the courtyard together with the Ferrers Gallery (01332 863337) who hold regular exhibitions and artist-led workshops. *Open Tue–Sun 11.00–17.00 (16.30 in winter).* Ground floor disabled access. Free.

Holy Trinity Church Staunton Harold, Ashby de la Zouch LE65 1RW (01332 863822; www.nationaltrust.org.uk). One of the few churches to have been built during the Commonwealth Period, in 1653. It contains a splendid painted ceiling, fine panelling and still has the original hangings, cushions and pews. *Open Apr–Oct, Wed–Sat 13.00–17.00 (or dusk); Oct Sat and Sun only.* Coffee shop at the Hall.

Calke Abbey Ticknall, Derby DE73 7LE (01332 863822; www.nationaltrust.org.uk). An extraordinary establishment: on the face of it another Baroque mansion from the early 18th C surrounded by extensive park and woodlands. It is in fact a time capsule depicting a grand country house in decline, the clock having stopped with the death of Sir Vauncey Harpur-Crewe in 1924. Since then little has altered either inside, or outside within the 750 acres of park, the stable block or Gothic-style church. Shop and information room. Restaurant. Disabled access including buggy driven by volunteers for access around the grounds. *Open Apr–Oct, Sat–Wed 13.00–17.30.* Telephone to confirm opening times. Charge.

WALKING & CYCLING

Although there is still a long way to go before the Ashby Canal is fully complete between Marston Junction and Moira, this is nevertheless a paradise for the walker and cyclist wishing to enjoy the countryside free from the motor car. Starting at the present canal terminus at Snarestone, a portion of the old waterway route can be walked into Measham. Where a stream makes the path impassable, go down onto Bosworth Road to the right, turn left and proceed to the crossroads and then turn left again. Rejoin the canal on your right near Measham Lodge and follow it into the village. To reach Moira by foot (or bicycle) join the Ashby Woulds Heritage Trail (*see* details in text) in Measham. The Ashby Canal Restoration Project (01530 273956) publish an excellent free walking guide (number 5 in the series) which details a series of walks based on, or around, the northern section of the waterway – Snarestone-Moira. Also available from local TICs. *A Family Cycling Guide* (free) is published by North West Leicestershire District Council (www.nwleicestershire.gov.uk) and details a variety of local routes, together with publications that cover cycling further afield in north west Leicestershire. For the most part these are off-road cycleways or include substantial traffic-free sections. Another excellent leaflet from North West Leicestershire DC, this time for the walker, is *Exploring the Ashby Woulds – A Guided Walk and Things To Do*. Free. Hinckley TIC 01455 635106 stock the comprehensive *Hinkley & Bosworth Visitor Guide* which is also available from Leicester TIC 0906 294 1113 (www.goleicestershire.com). Free.

The Mustard Seed High Street, Measham DE12 7HR (01530 272784). Teas, coffees and home-made snacks and light meals available *Mon–Sat (not Wed) 09.30–14.00.* Children welcome.

White Hart 13 Bosworth Road, Measham DE12 7LG (01530 270459). Traditional and friendly pub serving real ale. Children welcome. Beer garden. Log fires. Pub games and large-screen TV.

Swan Inn High Street, Measham DE127JB (01530 270518). Attractive pub serving real ale and food *L and E.* Children welcome. Beer garden.

Hollybush Inn Main Street, Oakthorpe, Swadlincote DE127RB (01530 270943). Large rambling establishment – the oldest building in the village. This pub serves real ale and a wide and appetising range of English and continental food *L and E (L weekends only).* Children and dogs (in bar) welcome. Garden and children's play area.

Shoulder of Mutton 64 Church Street, Oakthorpe, Swadlincote DE12 8EZ (01530 270436). Friendly, village pub serving real ales and food *L and E.* Outside patio. Children welcome.

Mason Arms 1 Church Street, Donisthorpe, Swadlincote DE12 7PX (01530 270378). An attractive exterior and a friendly welcome inside. This hostelry dispenses real ales and home-made traditional pub food *L and E, daily.* Dogs welcome in the bar. Garden. Darts.

Railway 3 Ashby Road, Moira, Swadlincote DE12 6DJ (01283 217453). Small, welcoming local dispensing real ale and bar snacks *all day.* Children and dogs welcome. Patio seating. Quiz *at weekends.* Darts, dominoes, crib and pool.

Moira Furnace Tearooms Furnace Lane, Moira, Swadlincote DE12 6AT (01283 224667). Serving a variety of home-made lunches, teas and snacks in a relaxed and friendly atmosphere. Children welcome. *Open Mon–Fri 09.30–17.00; Sat, Sun and B Hols 10.00–18.00.*

Conkers Millennium Avenue, Rawdon Road, Moira, Swadlincote DE12 6GA (01283 216633; www. visitconkers.com). Traditional English fayre and snacks available in each of two fully licensed, lakeside restaurants, *The Olive Tree* and *The Waterside.* Children welcome. *Open daily 10.00–17.00 (later in summer).*

Plough Inn The Green, Ashby de la Zouch LE65 1JU (01530 412817; www.theploughashby.co.uk). Serves an excellent and ever-changing range of real ales together with good value, home-made food available *L.* Pub games and open fires in *winter.* Outside seating and disabled access. Charity quiz *last Thu of month.* Open all day. B & B.

La Zouch 2 Kilwardby Street, Ashby de la Zouch LE65 2FQ (01530 412536; www.lazouch.com). A family run restaurant serving an English/French style table d'hôte and à la carte menu *E,* together with morning coffee, snacks and light meals *L.* Also traditional *Sun* roasts. Children welcome. Disabled access. *Open Tue–Sat 10.00–16.00 and 18.30–23.00, Sun 12.00–16.00. Closed Mon and B Hols.*

Tudor Court Tearooms 51A Market Street, Ashby de la Zouch LE65 1AG (01530 417610). Snacks, lunches and cream teas in a charming tearoom or outside under parasols in verdant surroundings. All food is home made. Children welcome. *Open Mon–Sat 08.00–17.00; B Hols 10.00–16.30.*

White Hart 82 Market Street, Ashby de la Zouch LE65 1AP (01530 414531). Unadulterated, 17th-C hostelry, complete with well and bear pit. Good selection of real ales and traditional, home-made food *available Mon–Thu 12.00–20.00 and Fri–Sun 12.00–16.00. Sun* roasts a speciality. Children and dogs (on a lead) welcome. Patio (with heaters). Open fires in *winter.* Quiz *Tue,* live music *Sun. Open all day.*

Smisby Arms Main Street, Smisby, Nr Ashby de la Zouch LE65 2UA (01530 412677). Set in a peaceful hamlet 2 miles north of Ashby. Traditional village local serving real ales and an appetising range of food *L and E (not Sun E).* Young children not encouraged. Pub quiz *Sun.* Open fires in *winter.*

Saracen's Head Heath End Lane, Heath End LE65 1RJ (01332 862323). Traditional Victorian village local, well off the beaten track but handy for thirsty walkers trekking twixt Staunton Harold and Calke. Draught Bass dispensed from a jug. No machines. Pub games, open fires, quarry tile floors and scrubbed tables. Outside seating.

BIRMINGHAM CANAL NAVIGATIONS (BCN) – MAIN LINE

MAXIMUM DIMENSIONS
Length: 70'
Beam: 7' 0"
Headroom: 6' 6"

MANAGER
01827 252000
enquiries.westmidlands@britishwaterways.co.uk

MILEAGES

Birmingham Canal new main line

BIRMINGHAM Gas Street to:
SMETHWICK JUNCTION (old main line): 2⅞ miles
BROMFORD JUNCTION: 4⅞ miles
PUDDING GREEN JUNCTION
(Wednesbury Old Canal): 5⅝ miles
TIPTON FACTORY JUNCTION
(old main line): 8¾ miles
DEEPFIELDS JUNCTION
(Wednesbury Oak loop): 10 miles
(Bradley Workshops: 2¼ miles)
HORSELEY FIELDS JUNCTION
(Wyrley & Essington Canal): 13 miles
Wolverhampton Top Lock: 13½ miles
ALDERSLEY JUNCTION
(Staffordshire & Worcestershire Canal): 15⅛ miles
Locks: 24

Birmingham Canal old main line

SMETHWICK JUNCTION to:
SPON LANE JUNCTION: 1½ miles
OLDBURY JUNCTION
(Titford Canal, 6 locks): 2½ miles
BRADESHALL JUNCTION
(Gower Branch, 3 locks): 3½ miles
Aqueduct over Netherton Tunnel Branch: 4⅜ miles
TIPTON JUNCTION (Dudley Canal): 5½ miles
FACTORY JUNCTION (new main line): 6 miles
Locks: 9

Netherton Tunnel Branch

WINDMILL END JUNCTION to:
DUDLEY PORT JUNCTION: 2⅞ miles
No locks

Wednesbury Old Canal

PUDDING GREEN JUNCTION to:
RYDER'S GREEN JUNCTION: ⅝ mile
No locks

Walsall Canal

RYDER'S GREEN JUNCTION to:
Ryder's Green Bottom Lock: ¼ mile
DOEBANK JUNCTION: 1⅜ miles
WALSALL JUNCTION: 6⅞ miles
Locks: 8

Walsall Branch Canal

WALSALL JUNCTION to:
BIRCHILLS JUNCTION (Wyrley &
Essington Canal): ⅞ mile
Locks: 8

Wyrley & Essington Canal

HORSELEY FIELDS JUNCTION to:
SNEYD JUNCTION: 6¼ miles
BIRCHILLS JUNCTION (Walsall Branch Canal): 8 miles
PELSALL JUNCTION (Cannock Extension): 12⅞ miles
Norton Canes Docks: 1½ miles
CATSHILL JUNCTION: 15⅜ miles
OGLEY JUNCTION (Anglesey Branch): 16⅜ miles
Anglesey Basin and Chasewater: 1½ miles
No locks

Daw End Branch

CATSHILL JUNCTION to:
LONGWOOD JUNCTION (Rushall Top Lock): 5¼ miles
No locks

Rushall Canal

LONGWOOD JUNCTION to:
RUSHALL JUNCTION: 2¾ miles
Locks: 9

Tame Valley Canal

DOEBANK JUNCTION to:
RUSHALL JUNCTION: 3½ miles
Perry Barr Top Lock: 5½ miles
SALFORD JUNCTION: 8½ miles
Locks: 13

British Waterways have developed a dedicated anti-vandal water conservation key for the BCN; it differs from the T-shaped key used on other parts of the system and is required for most BCN lock flights. Charge. The keys can be obtained from the West Midlands Waterways Unit (above); Farmer's Bridge; Gas Street; and the Toll Office at The Bratch.

The Birmingham Canal Company was authorised in 1768 to build a canal from Aldersley on the Staffordshire & Worcestershire Canal to Birmingham. With James Brindley as engineer the work proceeded quickly. The first section, from Birmingham to the Wednesbury collieries, was opened in November 1769, and the whole 22½-mile route was completed in 1772. It was a winding, contour canal, with 12 locks taking it over Smethwick, and another 20 (later 21) taking it down through Wolverhampton to Aldersley Junction. As the route of the canal was through an area of mineral wealth and developing industry, its success was immediate. Pressure of traffic caused the summit level at Smethwick to be lowered in the 1790s (thus cutting out six locks – three on either side of the summit), and during the same period branches began to reach out towards Walsall via the Ryder's Green Locks, and towards Fazeley. Out of this very profitable and ambitious first main line there grew the Birmingham Canal Navigations, more commonly abbreviated to BCN.

As traffic continued to increase so did the wealth of the BCN. The pressures of trade made the main line at Smethwick very congested and brought grave problems of water supply. Steam pumping engines were installed in several places to recirculate the water, and the company appointed Thomas Telford to shorten Brindley's old main line. Between 1825 and 1838 he engineered a new main line between Deepfields and Birmingham, using massive cuttings and embankments to maintain a continuous level. These improvements not only increased the amount of available waterway (the old line remaining in use), but also shortened the route from Birmingham to Wolverhampton by 7 miles.

Railway control of the BCN meant an expansion of the use of the system, and a large number of interchange basins were built to promote outside trade by means of rail traffic. This was of course quite contrary to the usual effect of railway competition upon canals. Trade continued to grow in relation to industrial development and by the end of the 19th C it was topping 8½ million tons per annum. A large proportion of this trade was local, being dependent upon the needs and output of Black Country industry. After the turn of the century this reliance on local trade started the gradual decline of the system as deposits of raw materials became exhausted. Factories bought from further afield and developed along the railways and roads away from the canals. Yet as late as 1950 there were over a million tons of trade and the system continued in operation until the end of the coal trade in 1967 (although there was some further traffic for the Birmingham Salvage Department), a pattern quite different from canals as a whole. Nowadays there is no recognisable commercial traffic – a dramatic contrast to the roaring traffic on the newer Birmingham motorways.

As trade declined, so parts of the system fell out of use and were abandoned. In its heyday in 1865, the BCN comprised over 160 miles of canal. Today just over 100 miles remain, and much has been done in recent years to tidy these up. This is now having a noticeable effect. Where once there were the old and run-down relics of industry, there is now much new housing, and stylish industrial estates. Of course some of the older vestiges of industry can still be found, and we hope that their most charming manifestations are kept for future generations to see and enjoy. But overall (and noting the exceptions and inevitable run-down areas) it is a fascinating environment. Just do not treat it like the remoter parts of Cheshire and Shropshire – it will always be subjected to the stresses of inner-city life, and you must always exercise caution. But it remains an area of retreat for the harassed city dweller and a new area of exploration for the canal traveller.

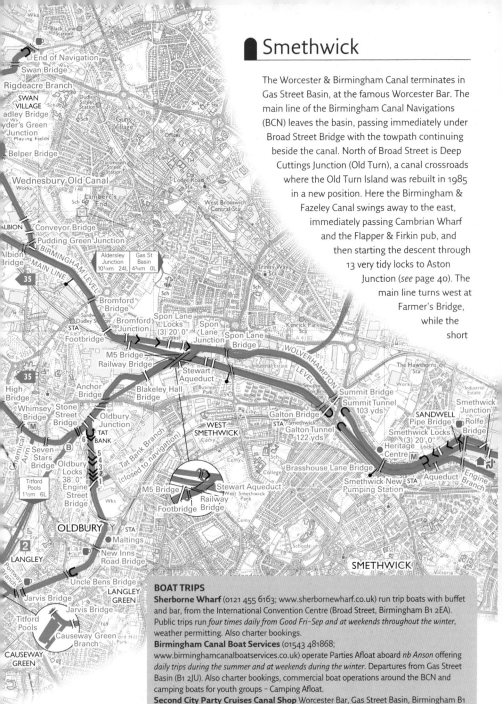

Smethwick

The Worcester & Birmingham Canal terminates in Gas Street Basin, at the famous Worcester Bar. The main line of the Birmingham Canal Navigations (BCN) leaves the basin, passing immediately under Broad Street Bridge with the towpath continuing beside the canal. North of Broad Street is Deep Cuttings Junction (Old Turn), a canal crossroads where the Old Turn Island was rebuilt in 1985 in a new position. Here the Birmingham & Fazeley Canal swings away to the east, immediately passing Cambrian Wharf and the Flapper & Firkin pub, and then starting the descent through 13 very tidy locks to Aston Junction (*see page 40*). The main line turns west at Farmer's Bridge, while the short

Aldersley Junction	10¼m 24L	Gas St Basin	4¾m 0L

BOAT TRIPS

Sherborne Wharf (0121 455 6163; www.sherbornewharf.co.uk) run trip boats with buffet and bar, from the International Convention Centre (Broad Street, Birmingham B1 2EA). Public trips run *four times daily from Good Fri–Sep* and *at weekends throughout the winter*, weather permitting. Also charter bookings.

Birmingham Canal Boat Services (01543 481868; www.birminghamcanalboatservices.co.uk) operate Parties Afloat aboard *nb Anson* offering *daily trips during the summer* and *at weekends during the winter*. Departures from Gas Street Basin (B1 2JU). Also charter bookings, commercial boat operations around the BCN and camping boats for youth groups – Camping Afloat.

Second City Party Cruises Canal Shop Worcester Bar, Gas Street Basin, Birmingham B1 2JU (0121 236 9811; www.secondcityboats.co.uk). *Nb Europe* and *nb Dragonfly* operate from *Mar–Sep* running ½ *hr and 1 hr public trips* together with *day trips* to the Black Country Museum and Cadbury World. Also charter bookings.

Oozell's Street loop goes to the south, quickly disappearing behind new apartments. This loop, which now houses a boatyard and moorings, and the others further along, are surviving parts of Brindley's original contour canal, now known as the Birmingham Canal Old Main Line. The delays caused by this prompted the Birmingham Canal Company to commission Telford to build a straighter line, the Birmingham Canal New Main Line. This was constructed between 1823 and 1838, and when completed reduced Brindley's old 22½-mile canal to 15 miles. The Oozell's Street loop reappears from the south, and then, after two bridges, the Icknield Port loop leaves to the south. This loop acts as a feeder from Rotton Park Reservoir and rejoins after ¼ mile at another canal crossroads – the Winson Green or Soho loop, which leaves the main line opposite the Icknield Port loop. This last loop is the longest of the three, running in a gentle arc for over a mile before rejoining the main line again. It was the only loop to have a towpath throughout its length until the recently completed towpath on the Oozell's Street loop. At its eastern end is Hockley Port, formerly railway-owned but now used for residential moorings. There are houseboats, a community hall, dry docks and workshops. The main line continues towards Smethwick Junction. Here there is a choice of routes: Brindley's old main line swings to the right, while Telford's new main line continues straight ahead – the old line is the more interesting of the two. The two routes run side by side, but the old line climbs to a higher level via the three Smethwick Locks. Here there were two flights of locks side by side. Beyond the junction, Telford's new line enters a steep-sided cutting. This 40ft-deep cutting enabled Telford to avoid the changes in level of the old line and thus speed the flow of traffic. The two routes continue their parallel courses, the one overlooking the other, until the lower line passes under the Telford Aqueduct. This elegant single span cast iron structure carries the Engine Branch, a short feeder canal that leaves the old line, crosses the new line and then turns back to the south for a short distance. This arm is named after the first Boulton & Watt steam pumping engine to be bought by the Birmingham Canal Company. This continued to feed the old summit level for 120 years. It was then moved to Ocker Hill for preservation and demonstrations, until the 1950s, when it was finally retired. The sides of the cutting are richly covered with wild flowers and blackberry bushes, and the seclusion of the whole area has turned it into an unofficial nature reserve. The old pumping station at Brasshouse Lane has been restored after years of disuse as part of the new Galton Valley Canal Park development. A Tangyes Engine has been installed to replace the original. The New Main Line continues through natural wilderness to Galton Tunnel. Telford's Galton Bridge crosses the cutting in one magnificent 150ft cast iron span. This bridge is preserved as an ancient monument. The old and the new Birmingham canal lines continue their parallel course, and soon the pleasant semi-rural isolation of the cutting ends, to be replaced by a complex meeting of three types of transport system. The M5 motorway swings in from the east, carried high above the canal on slender concrete pillars; the railway stays close beside Telford's new line; and the canals enter a series of junctions that seem to anticipate modern motorway practice. The new line leaves the cutting and continues in a straight line through industrial surroundings. It passes under Stewart Aqueduct and then reaches Bromford Junction. Here a canal sliproad links the old and the new lines via the three Spon Lane Locks, joining the new at an angle from the east. Note the unusual split bridge at Spon Lane top lock, which was rebuilt in 1986. The old line swings south west following the 473ft contour parallel to the M5, crossing the new line on Stewart Aqueduct. Thus canal crosses canal on a flyover. Spon Lane Locks, the linking sliproad, survive unchanged from Brindley's day and are among the oldest in the country. The old and the new lines now follow separate courses. The old line continues below the motorway to Oldbury Locks Junction. Here the short Titford Canal climbs away to the south via the six Oldbury Locks; this canal serves as a feeder from Titford Pools to Rotton Park Reservoir. After the junction the old line swings round to the north west and continues on a parallel course to the new line once again. After Bromford Junction the new line continues its straight course towards Wolverhampton. At Pudding Green Junction the main line goes straight on; the Wednesbury Old Canal forks right to join the Walsall Canal, which in turn joins the Tame Valley Canal at Doebank Junction.

WALKING & CYCLING

Much of Birmingham's 100-mile network of canals offers excellent opportunities for walkers and cyclists, and provides the chance to explore a side of the city well away from the obvious tourist attractions and close to the area's industrial roots. From a more formal approach, Birmingham is a crossroads for the National Cycle Network with Route 5 approaching from Kings Norton via Worcester & Birmingham Canal. Route 81 follows the Birmingham Level Main Line from the city to Wolverhampton, to eventually head into Mid Wales. Several excellent routes lead out from the city centre along traffic-free or contraflow cycle lanes. Further details are contained in *CycleCity's Birmingham Cycling Map – City Centre and Suburbs* and is available from Sustrans (0845 1130065; www.sustrans.org.uk). Charge. On the main line the south side tow path is no longer usable between Rolfe Bridge and Bromford Junction.

NAVIGATIONAL NOTES

Since the Titford Canal is the highest level on the BCN, it is advisable to telephone the BW Waterway Unit (01827 252000; enquiries.westmidlands@britishwaterways.co.uk) to check that there is adequate water before you visit the canal. You will need a dedicated BCN water conservation key for Oldbury Locks in order to access this canal.

Boatyards

Ⓑ**Sherborne Wharf** Sherborne Street, Birmingham B16 8DE (0121 455 6163; www.sherbornewharf.co.uk). On the Oozell's Street Loop. 🚽 🛢 🗜 D E Pump out, gas, day-hire boats, overnight mooring, long-term mooring, wet docks, winter storage, chandlery, boat repairs, engine sales and repairs, books, maps and gifts, DIY facilities, electrical hook-up, solid fuel, toilets, showers, laundrette, large supermarket nearby. *Emergency call out.*

● **The Titford Canal**

Built in 1837 as part of the original Birmingham Canal scheme, acting as a feeder to Spon Lane, the Titford Canal served Causeway Green. This must have been a very busy canal in its heyday, with many branches, wharves and tramways connecting it to the surrounding mines and engineering works. Today it survives in shortened form and has the distinction of being the highest navigable part of the BCN with a summit level above Oldbury Locks of 511ft. The locks are sometimes referred to as the Crow – a branch which left the canal above the third lock and served the alkali and phosphorus works of a local industrialist and benefactor Jim Crow. The last surviving recirculatory pumphouse can be seen by the top lock. It is hoped that BW, in partnership with the local Canal Society, can raise funds for its restoration. The waterway now terminates at the wide expanse of water of Titford Pools

Tourist Information Centre The Rotunda, 150 New Street, Birmingham B2 4TA (0121 202 5099; www.beinbirmingham.com). *Open Mon–Sat 09.30–17.30, Sun 10.30–16.30.*

Pubs and Restaurants

In a large city such as Birmingham there are many fine pubs and restaurants. As a result of the development of the area adjoining the canal, between Gas Street Basin and Cambrian Wharf, there are now approaching two dozen eating and drinking establishments. This choice is further expanded by walking south along Broad Street, from Broad Street Bridge, at Gas Street Basin. However beyond the canalside the enterprising boater (walker and cyclist) might like to seek out some of the City's more diverse hostelries:

The Flapper & Firkin Cambrian Wharf, Kingston Row, Birmingham B1 2NU (0121 236 2421). Real ale in a student-type pub, together with food available *L and E*. Children welcome *until 19.00*. Outside terrace seating by the basin. Live music. *Open all day.*

The Figure of Eight 236-239 Broad Street, Birmingham B1 2HG (0121 633 0917). Sensibly priced real ale in a pub handy for Gas Street Basin. Food available *all day, every day.* Outside seating. Disabled access. *Open all day.*

The Anchor 308 Bradford Street, Birmingham B5 6ET (0121 622 4516). Edwardian pub tucked away behind the Digbeth coach station. Food available *daily (until 20.00 weekdays and 18.00 weekends)* together with real ales, German and Belgian draught beers and real cider. Also an excellent range of bottled beers from far and wide. Outside seating. *Open all day.*

The Gunmaker's Arms Bath Street, Birmingham B4 6HG (0121 236 1201).

Comfortable, two-roomed pub serving real ales and food *L and E, Mon–Fri.* Outside seating. *Closed Sun E.* Live bands *occasionally.*

Darwins 57 Grosvenor Street West, Birmingham B16 8HJ (0121 643 6064). Near Tesco's. Traditional two-roomed city pub, with a wide ranging clientele, dispensing real ales together with food *L and E, daily.* Children welcome *until 21.00.* Skittles, darts and pool. *Tue evening* entertainment.

The Black Eagle 16 Factory Road, Hockley B18 5JU (0121 523 4008; www.blackeaglepub.co.uk). North of Hockley Port. Bar and restaurant serving real ales and food *L and E (not Sun E).* Children welcome. Outside seating. Booking advisable for meals.

The Olde Windmill 84 Dudley Road, Winson Green B18 7QN (0121 455 6907). East of Lee Bridge, opposite the hospital. Real ales served in a compact, traditional old pub. Food available *L, daily.* Children welcome *until 16.00.* Beer garden and pub games. *Open all day.*

The Bridge 91 Station Road, Oldbury B69 4LU (0121 544 6467). A range of real ales dispensed in the old HP&D brewery tap. Friendly, welcoming atmosphere. Meals and bar snacks available *L and E (until 20.00), daily.* Pool, karaoke and live music. *Open all day.*

The Whiteheath Tavern 400 Birchfield Lane, Whiteheath, Oldbury B69 1AD (0121 552 3603). Just west of Titford Pools, near M5 junction 2. Real ale in a pub close to Titford Pools. Children welcome at lunchtime. Traditional pub games.

Dudley

At Bradeshall Junction the Gower Branch links the two lines, descending to the lower level of the new line through three locks. To the south west of Tipton Junction is the branch leading to the Black Country Museum and the Dudley Tunnel. This branch connects with the Dudley Canal, the Stourbridge Canal, and thus with the Staffordshire & Worcestershire Canal. The old line turns north at the junction, rejoining the new line at Factory Junction. At Albion Junction the Gower Branch turns south to join the old line at Bradeshall. At Dudley Port Junction the Netherton Tunnel Branch joins the main line. The Netherton Tunnel Branch goes through the tunnel to Windmill End Junction (note the west side towpath through the tunnel is closed); from here boats can either turn south down the old Dudley Canal to Hawne Basin, or west towards the Stourbridge Canal, and thus to the Staffordshire & Worcestershire Canal. North of Dudley Port the new line crosses a main road on the Ryland Aqueduct. Continuing its elevated course the new line reaches Tipton, where there are moorings with shops close by, and a small basin. The new line climbs the three Factory Locks and immediately reaches Factory Junction, where the old line comes in from the south.

Pubs and Restaurants

The Old Court House Lower Church Lane, Tipton DY4 7PG (0121 520 2865). North east of Dudley Port Station. Real ales and food available *L and E, daily* in a pub that used to be the holding cells for the police station across the road. Children and dogs welcome. Outside seating. Karaoke *Fri.*

✕ **The Bottle & Glass Inn** Black Country Living Museum, Tipton Road, Dudley DY1 4SQ (0121 557 9643; www.bclm.co.uk). Real ale in a wonderful old pub, moved to the site. Snacks available *all day. Open 10.00–16.00.* More substantial refreshment available in the adjoining Stables Restaurant and 1930s fish & chip shop.

The Port 'N' Ale 178 Horsley Heath, Tipton DY4 7DS (0121 532 2805). North east of Dudley Port railway station. One of the rare, genuine free houses left dispensing an excellent range of real ales and two traditional ciders. Children's room, outside seating and traditional pub games.

The Barge & Barrel Factory Road, Tipton DY4 9AJ (0121 520 6962). A rock and blues bar, serving real ale, and inexpensive bar meals *L (not Sat and Sun).* Children welcome *until 21.00.* Outside seating. Bands weekly and rock discos Fri and Sat. Moorings.

BOAT TRIPS
Aaron Manby operates trips from outside the Malthouse Stables outdoor pursuits centre, Hurst Lane, Tipton DY4 9AB (0121 520 7861; www.laws.sandwell.gov.uk). With a capacity of 33 this boats offers full or half day charters. Modified to accommodate wheelchair users.

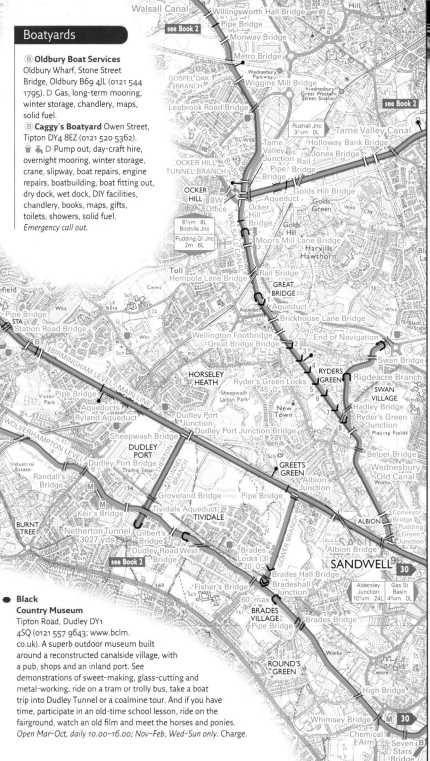

Boatyards

Ⓑ**Oldbury Boat Services**
Oldbury Wharf, Stone Street
Bridge, Oldbury B69 4JL (0121 544
1795). D Gas, long-term mooring,
winter storage, chandlery, maps,
solid fuel.

Ⓑ**Caggy's Boatyard** Owen Street,
Tipton DY4 8EZ (0121 520 5362).
🚽 ⚓ D Pump out, day-craft hire,
overnight mooring, winter storage,
crane, slipway, boat repairs, engine
repairs, boatbuilding, boat fitting out,
dry dock, wet dock, DIY facilities,
chandlery, books, maps, gifts,
toilets, showers, solid fuel.
Emergency call out.

● **Black
Country Museum**
Tipton Road, Dudley DY1
4SQ (0121 557 9643; www.bclm.
co.uk). A superb outdoor museum built
around a reconstructed canalside village, with
a pub, shops and an inland port. See
demonstrations of sweet-making, glass-cutting and
metal-working, ride on a tram or trolly bus, take a boat
trip into Dudley Tunnel or a coalmine tour. And if you have
time, participate in an old-time school lesson, ride on the
fairground, watch an old film and meet the horses and ponies.
Open Mar–Oct, daily 10.00–16.00; Nov–Feb, Wed–Sun only. Charge.

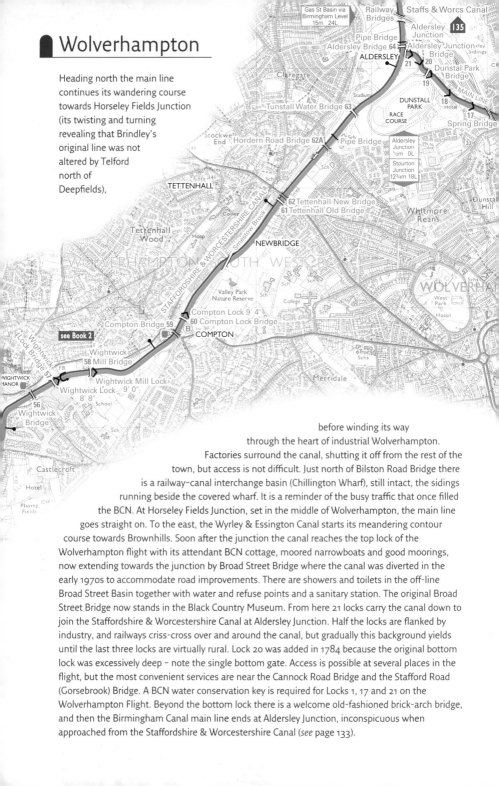

Wolverhampton

Heading north the main line continues its wandering course towards Horseley Fields Junction (its twisting and turning revealing that Brindley's original line was not altered by Telford north of Deepfields),

before winding its way through the heart of industrial Wolverhampton. Factories surround the canal, shutting it off from the rest of the town, but access is not difficult. Just north of Bilston Road Bridge there is a railway–canal interchange basin (Chillington Wharf), still intact, the sidings running beside the covered wharf. It is a reminder of the busy traffic that once filled the BCN. At Horseley Fields Junction, set in the middle of Wolverhampton, the main line goes straight on. To the east, the Wyrley & Essington Canal starts its meandering contour course towards Brownhills. Soon after the junction the canal reaches the top lock of the Wolverhampton flight with its attendant BCN cottage, moored narrowboats and good moorings, now extending towards the junction by Broad Street Bridge where the canal was diverted in the early 1970s to accommodate road improvements. There are showers and toilets in the off-line Broad Street Basin together with water and refuse points and a sanitary station. The original Broad Street Bridge now stands in the Black Country Museum. From here 21 locks carry the canal down to join the Staffordshire & Worcestershire Canal at Aldersley Junction. Half the locks are flanked by industry, and railways criss-cross over and around the canal, but gradually this background yields until the last three locks are virtually rural. Lock 20 was added in 1784 because the original bottom lock was excessively deep – note the single bottom gate. Access is possible at several places in the flight, but the most convenient services are near the Cannock Road Bridge and the Stafford Road (Gorsebrook) Bridge. A BCN water conservation key is required for Locks 1, 17 and 21 on the Wolverhampton Flight. Beyond the bottom lock there is a welcome old-fashioned brick-arch bridge, and then the Birmingham Canal main line ends at Aldersley Junction, inconspicuous when approached from the Staffordshire & Worcestershire Canal (*see page 133*).

NAVIGATIONAL NOTES

1 A BCN water conservation key is needed to operate Tipton Factory Locks.
2 Bradeshall Bridge, on the Gower Branch (page 35) has an air draught of 6' 6".

see Book 2

Wyrley & Essington Canal

Wood End

Wards Bridge
Nordley Hill

Pinfold Bridge

Church Bridge

Offices

Pol Sta

Rookery Bridge

New Cross
Hospital

Wednesfield Junction
New Cross Bridge

Site of Bentley Canal

New Bentley Bridge

Neachells

Ind

Gorsebrook Bridge
Pipe Bridge
Stour Valley Viaduct
Fox's Lane Bridge
Jordans Bridge

Wolverhampton
Locks
(21) 132' 0"

Park Village

Lby & Baths

HEATH TOWN

Heath Town Bridge

WYRLEY & ESSINGTON CANAL

Cannock Road Bridge
Springfield
Deans Road Bridge
Molineux

Little's Lane Bridge
Rail Bridge

PTON

WOLVERHAMPTON

8m 0L
Birchills Jnc

Broad Street Bridge
Civic Centre

STA

Mill Street Bridge

Swan Garden Bridge
Horseley Fields Junction
Horseley Fields Bridge   Rail Bridge

Walsall Street Bridge

Pipe Bridge
Chillington Wharf
Bilston Road Bridge

The Royal Station
Hosp

WOLVERHAMPTON LEVEL

East Park

Speedway Stadium

Mkt

Cable Street Bridge

MONMORE GREEN

Stow Heath

College

Pipe Bridge   Dixon Street Bridge

Priestfield

Catchems Corner Bridge   Freezeland

Rough Hills

Pipe Bridges

MAIN LINE

Jibbet Lane Bridge

Millfields Bridge

MILLFIELDS

ingshall

BOAT TRIPS
Nb Stafford is a 42-seat boat operating public trips *on first Sun of the month*. Also booked charter trips. Telephone 01902 789522 for further details.

5m 21L
Aldersley Junction

Gas St Basin
10m 3L

34

SPRING VALE

Lan

WOLVERHAMPTON LEVEL

LADYMOOR
Highfields Road Bridge

72B

Pubs and Restaurants

In a town such as Wolverhampton there are many pubs to choose from. Below are a selection for the enterprising to seek out:

🍺 **The Feathers** Molineux Street, Wolverhampton WV1 1RY (01902 426924). By the football ground. Small friendly local renowned for its garden. Real ale, and food *L Mon-Fri*. Children welcome. Pub games. Karaoke *Sat. Open all day Mon-Sat*.

🍺 **The Clarendon** Chapel Ash, Wolverhampton WV3 0TN (01902 420587). A41, just to the west of the town centre. Offers real ale and food *all day every day*. Also breakfasts *08.00-L* and takeaway sandwich bar. Outside seating. *Open all day*.

🍺 **The Combermere Arms** 90 Chapel Ash, Wolverhampton WV3 0TY (01902 421880). Real ale served in a terraced house look-alike: both cosy and intimate. Open fires and garden. Food *L Mon-Fri*. Children welcome.

🍺 **The Great Western** Sun Street, Wolverhampton WV10 0DJ (01902 351090). Real ale, railway memorabilia and good local cooking *L (not Sun)*. Children welcome at lunchtime if eating, dogs welcome in the evening. Garden.

🍺 **Posada** 48 Lichfield Street, Wolverhampton WV1 1JJ (07967 185830). Grade II listed building with its striking tiled frontage. A good range of real ales and snacks *L Mon-Fri* are always available. *Open all day except Sun*.

🍺 **The Tap & Spile** 35 Princess Street, Wolverhampton WV1 1HD (01902 713319). An open bar and two snugs in a city centre pub dispensing an excellent range of real ales and home-made food *L and E Mon-Fri*. Also real cider and traditional pub games. Disabled access. *Open all day, every day*.

Boatyards

ⓑ **Associated Cruisers** Lock Street, Little's Lane, Wolverhampton (01902 423673). Sign writer and boat painter.

ⓑ **Oxley Marine** The Wharf, Oxley Moor Road, Wolverhampton (01902 789522; www.oxleymarine.co.uk). 🚽 D Pump out, gas, overnight and long-term mooring, winter storage, slipway, boat and engine sales and repairs, DIY facilities, *emergency call out*. Licensed bar *each evening*, snacks.

Malthouse Stables, Tipton Green (see page 34)

BIRMINGHAM & FAZELEY CANAL

MAXIMUM DIMENSIONS

Length: 70'
Beam: 7'
Headroom: 6' 6"

MILEAGE

FARMER'S BRIDGE JUNCTION
(Birmingham Canal) to:
  ASTON JUNCTION (Digbeth Branch): 1½ miles

SALFORD JUNCTION
(Tame Valley Canal): 3¼ miles
Minworth Top Lock: 6¼ miles
Curdworth Tunnel: 8½ miles
Bodymoor Heath Bridge: 11½ miles

FAZELEY JUNCTION (Coventry Canal): 15 miles
Hopwas: 17¾ miles
Whittington Brook: 20½ miles

Locks: 38

MANAGER

01827 252000
enquiries.westmidlands@britishwaterways.co.uk

The Birmingham & Fazeley Canal was authorised in 1784, after a great deal of opposition from the well-established Birmingham Canal Company (who very soon merged with it), as a link between Birmingham and the south east. Until then, London-bound goods from Birmingham had to go right round by the River Severn. Naturally, the canal was useless until the Coventry Canal had at least reached Fazeley, but the new Birmingham & Fazeley Company ensured – even before its enabling Act was passed – that the other canals important to its success were completed. Thus at Coleshill in 1782 the Oxford Canal Company agreed to finish its line to Oxford and the Thames; the Coventry Canal Company agreed to extend its line from Atherstone to Fazeley; the new Birmingham & Fazeley Company agreed to build its proposed line and continue it along the defaulting Coventry route from Fazeley to Whittington Brook; and the Trent & Mersey Company pledged to finish the Coventry's line from Whittington Brook to Fradley Junction on the Trent & Mersey Canal.

This rare example of cooperation among canal companies paid off when, in 1790, the great joint programme was finished and traffic immediately began to flow along the system. The Birmingham & Fazeley Company employed John Smeaton to build their canal: he completed it in 1789. The flights of narrow locks at Farmer's Bridge and Aston became very congested, especially after the Warwick canals had joined up with the Birmingham & Fazeley Canal at Digbeth; two new canals were built to bypass this permanent obstacle, one on each side. The Tame Valley Canal and the Birmingham & Warwick Junction Canal were opened in 1844, and traffic flowed more smoothly. After this the Birmingham & Fazeley Canal became more attractive to carriers and it continued to be an important link route. It still provides this link, but is now worthy of exploration in its own right.

Birmingham

Turning north east off the main line of the Birmingham Canal brings you to Cambrian Wharf. There is a BW Customer Service Centre here (01827 252000). From this point the Farmer's Bridge flight of 13 locks fall steeply away from the heart of Birmingham. Aston Junction marks the start of the Aston Flight, which falls through 11 locks to Salford Junction. The Ashted Flight drops through six locks to Typhoo Basin, and on to Bordesley Junction. All shops are readily available alongside the B & F beyond Salford; the bridge carrying the A452 across the canal at Tyburn is one convenient access point.

Ackers Adventure Activity Centre Golden Hillock Road, Small Heath, Birmingham B11 2PY (0121 772 5111; www.ackers-adventure.co.uk). Alongside the Grand Union canal at Small Heath. This non-profit making charity, run for the benefit of the community, offers a wide range of outdoor activities for all ages and abilities – everything from skiing and snowboarding to climbing, canoeing, archery and operating four-wheel-drive vehicles. Also a nature area. Charge. Telephone for further details.

Alexandra Theatre, Station Street, Birmingham B5 4DS (0121 643 5536; www.alexandratheatre.org.uk). One of the top touring theatres in the country featuring a wide range of entertainment from West End musicals to comedies and concerts.

Aston Hall Trinity Road, Aston, Birmingham B6 6JD (0121 327 0062; www.bmag. org.uk). Built between 1618 and 1635, this one of the last great houses to be constructed in the spectacular Jacobean style and is decorated and furnished to reflect the lifestyle of a wealthy gentleman.

[Map: ERDINGTON, GRAVELLY HILL, Birches Green, Tyburn Bridge, TYBURN, Berwood Bridge, Butler's Bridge, Brace Factory Bridge, Wood Lane Bridge, Pipe Bridge, BROMFORD, Bromford Bridge No 2, Bromford Bridge No 1, Troutpool Bridge, New Troutpool Bridge, Erdington Hall Bridge, River Tame, Pipe Bridge, Star City, NECHELLS, M6, 42]

There is the 136' Long Gallery and a magnificent carved oak staircase. It has been home to Charles I (albeit for a single night) and James Watt junior, son of the famous steam engineer. Drinks, snacks and souvenirs. *Open Apr–Oct, Tue–Sun & B Hol Mons 11.30–16.00.* Free.

Aston Villa Stadium Tours Aston Villa Football Club, Villa Park, Birmingham B6 6HE (0121 327 5353; www.avfc.co.uk). A chance to take a look behind the scenes of one of the world's oldest football clubs. *Open Mon–Fri 10.30–14.30, Sat 10.30 & Sun 11.00–13.00.* Tours last approx 2 hours and are subject to availability and matches. No tours *Thu.* Charge.

Barber Institute of Fine Arts The University of Birmingham, Edgebaston, Birmingham B15 2TS (0121 414 7333; www.barber.org.uk). A fine collection, donated to the university complete with the impressive gallery building, and embracing works of art from Old Masters through to modern paintings, drawings and sculpture, including major works by Bellini, Poussin, Rubens, Gainsborough, Rossetti, Monet, Degas and Magritte. There really is something here for everyone. Also a regular programme of exhibitions, concerts, lectures and events. *Open Mon–Sat 10.00–17.00, Sun 12.00–15.00.* Free (donations welcome).

NAVIGATIONAL NOTES

The lock keeper at Farmer's Bridge is on duty *07.30–17.00 Mon–Thu (until 16.30 Fri).* Telephone 0121 236 1607.

Pubs and Restaurants

🍺 **The Flapper & Firkin** Cambrian Wharf, Kingston Row B1 2NU (0121 236 2421). Real ale in a student-type pub, together with food available *L and E*. Children welcome *until 19.00.* Outside terrace seating by the basin. Live music *Thu*, DJ *Fri and Sat*. Open all day.

🍺 **The Malt House** 75 King Edwards Road, Brindley Place B1 2NX (0121 633 4171).

Overlooking Deep Cuttings Junction, this pub serves real ale and food *12.00–20.00 daily*. Children welcome *until 19.00.* Handy for the Sea Life Centre.

🍺 **The James Brindley** Gas Street Basin, Bridge Street B1 2JR (0121 644 5971). Modern pub overlooking Gas Street Basin. Bar meals are served *L and E (not Sat E)*. Children welcome. Outside seating. Jazz *Sat and Sun* lunchtimes.

Curdworth

Most of the factories on this section ignore the canal, although the Cincinnati works are a laudable exception: landscaped lawns and gardens run down from the buildings to the water's edge. Minworth Locks (anti-vandal key needed) start the descent towards Fazeley, and gradually the canal loses the industry that has accompanied it from Birmingham. Curdworth is passed in a tree-lined cutting: the church tower here has been visible for some time. The cutting continues beyond Curdworth Bridge, and enters a short tunnel (57yds), with the towpath alongside. From now until Fazeley the canal makes its passage in complete isolation through the empty fields, only the 11 locks falling down to Fazeley Junction breaking its journey. The lack of hedges in this area is very noticeable and only those by the towpath seem to have survived. As the canal swings north, hedges and trees thankfully reappear, and after Bodymoor Heath trees line the canal on both sides for two miles. By the bottom lock there is a swing bridge (kept open) which contributes to what is a pretty canal scene. Flooded gravel pits, and the bird life they attract, now constitute the Kingsbury Water Park – the Visitor Centre is east of Bodymoor Heath Bridge, across the motorway.

- **Tyburn**
  Warwicks. PO, tel, stores. A mixture of factories and houses.
- **Minworth**
  Warwicks. PO, tel, stores. A mainly residential area on the city outskirts, totally dominated by roads. There is a handy transport café close to Hansons Bridge.
- **Curdworth**
  Warwicks. PO, tel, stores, garage. Now set in the shadow of the motorway, and not far from the sewage works, Curdworth still manages to cling to a village identity. The squat church is partly Norman, c. 1170; note the finely carved Norman font, with images of standing men, a monster and a lamb.
- **Bodymoor Heath**
  Warwicks. Tel. A scattered village which has found a new lease of life with the creation of Kingsbury Water Park. Occasional 18th-C buildings survive as a memory of the pre-industrial

Midlands, with the Dog & Doublet being one such fine example.

Kingsbury Water Park Bodymoor Heath Lane, Bodymoor Heath, Sutton Coldfield B76 0DY (01827 872660; www.warwickshire.gov.uk/countryside). A 600-acre landscaped park containing 30 lakes and pools, created from gravel pits worked over the last 50 years. Walks, nature trails, fishing, horse riding, sailing, power-boating and windsurfing. Visitor Centre and coffee shop. Excellent programme of events *Apr–Sep* (modest charge per event). There is also a children's farm at Broomey Croft, with goats, sheep and ponies. Open *08.00–16.00 daily*, later closing times in *Jun, Jul and Aug*. Telephone 01827 873844 for details. Charge, tearoom.

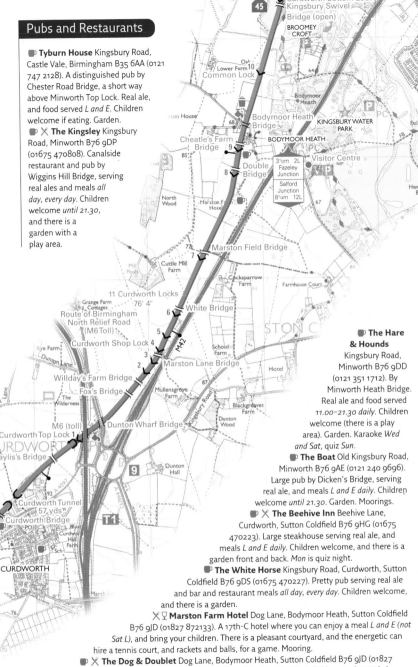

Pubs and Restaurants

🍺 **Tyburn House** Kingsbury Road, Castle Vale, Birmingham B35 6AA (0121 747 2128). A distinguished pub by Chester Road Bridge, a short way above Minworth Top Lock. Real ale, and food served *L and E*. Children welcome if eating. Garden.

🍺 ✕ **The Kingsley** Kingsbury Road, Minworth B76 9DP (01675 470808). Canalside restaurant and pub by Wiggins Hill Bridge, serving real ales and meals *all day, every day*. Children welcome *until 21.30*, and there is a garden with a play area.

🍺 **The Hare & Hounds** Kingsbury Road, Minworth B76 9DD (0121 351 1712). By Minworth Heath Bridge. Real ale and food served *11.00-21.30 daily*. Children welcome (there is a play area). Garden. Karaoke *Wed and Sat*, quiz *Sun*.

🍺 **The Boat** Old Kingsbury Road, Minworth B76 9AE (0121 240 9696). Large pub by Dicken's Bridge, serving real ale, and meals *L and E daily*. Children welcome *until 21.30*. Garden. Moorings.

🍺 ✕ **The Beehive Inn** Beehive Lane, Curdworth, Sutton Coldfield B76 9HG (01675 470223). Large steakhouse serving real ale, and meals *L and E daily*. Children welcome, and there is a garden front and back. *Mon* is quiz night.

🍺 **The White Horse** Kingsbury Road, Curdworth, Sutton Coldfield B76 9DS (01675 470227). Pretty pub serving real ale and bar and restaurant meals *all day, every day*. Children welcome, and there is a garden.

✕ 🍷 **Marston Farm Hotel** Dog Lane, Bodymoor Heath, Sutton Coldfield B76 9JD (01827 872133). A 17th-C hotel where you can enjoy a meal *L and E (not Sat L)*, and bring your children. There is a pleasant courtyard, and the energetic can hire a tennis court, and rackets and balls, for a game. Mooring.

🍺 ✕ **The Dog & Doublet** Dog Lane, Bodymoor Heath, Sutton Coldfield B76 9JD (01827 872374). Smart and handsome red-brick canalside pub by Cheatles Farm Bridge, serving real ale. Varied menu and specials *L and E*. Children welcome. Canalside garden with good views, and a barbecue. Mooring. B & B. Look out for George, the 'car park ghost'.

Fazeley

Continuing north, the canal runs through quiet and attractive open farmland, flanked on both sides by oak trees, their roots often projecting into the water. The isolation of the canal ends at Drayton Bassett where the A4091 swings in to run parallel as far as Fazeley. By Drayton Bassett is a curious footbridge, a marvellous folly, and immediately after it a second swing bridge. The countryside then gives way to the outskirts of Fazeley, which are quickly followed by a handsome mill building and the junction with the Coventry Canal, overlooked by an imposing canal house. The Birmingham & Fazeley Canal continues to the north west, although its route is subsumed as part of the Coventry Canal.

● **Drayton Bassett**
Staffs. PO, tel, stores, fish & chips. The village is set ½ mile to the west of the canal. The best feature is the charming and totally unexpected Gothic-style footbridge over the canal. Its twin battlemented towers would look quite commanding but for their ridiculously small size. This bridge is unique, and there seems to be no explanation for its eccentricity, thus greatly increasing its attraction.
Drayton Manor Family Theme Park B78 3TW. Alongside the canal, off the A4091 at Drayton Manor Bridge (08708 725252; www.draytonmanor.co.uk). 24hr recorded information for general enquiries on (01827) 287979. Formerly the site of the house of Sir Robert Peel's father, built 1820–35. The now-vanished house was designed by Sir Robert Smirke and the garden, 15 acres of wood and parkland, was originally laid out by William Gilpin. It has an extensive series of exciting rides, including Storm Force Ten, and amusements. *Open late Mar–Oct, 10.00–late afternoon.* Charge. Caravan and camping site.
● **Fazeley**
Staffs. PO, tel, stores, garage. Its importance as a road and canal junction determines the character of Fazeley; it is a small, industrial centre that has grown up around the communication network. From the canal the town appears more attractive than it really is. Useful as a supply centre.
● **Fazeley Junction**
Staffs. The Birmingham & Fazeley Canal joins the Coventry Canal here. Originally the Coventry Canal was to continue westwards to meet the Trent & Mersey Canal at Fradley; however, the Coventry company ran out of money at Fazeley, and so the Birmingham & Fazeley Canal continued on to Whittington (this section is covered within the Coventry Canal, for continuity). The Trent & Mersey Company then built a linking arm from Fradley to Whittington, which was later bought by the Coventry Company, thus becoming a detached section of their canal. The junction has been tastefully restored, with good moorings and a canalside seat made from a balance beam, overlooked by a fine navigation office. It was at Fazeley, in the 1790s, that Robert Peel, father of the prime minister, in partnership with Joseph Wilkes, transformed the area, building mills and wharves, chapels and watercourses, and making it a centre of industry that was to last until the depression of the mid-19th C. Just to the south of the canal junction is the Bourne Brook Cut, which has its source in reservoirs to the north of Watling Street and originally supplied the bleach and dye works here. A little further south of the junction, by the Birmingham & Fazeley Canal, is Fazeley Mill, built in 1886 as a tape mill and which has continued as such largely unaltered. Just beyond the next bridge, on the opposite side of the canal, is one of the best surviving mills of the Richard Arkwright pattern, built in 1791 with three storeys and 19 bays. In Coleshill Street a fine terrace of 20 workers' houses can still be seen.

Boatyards

ⓑ **Fazeley Mill Marina** Coleshill Road, Fazeley, Tamworth B78 3SE (01827 261138). 🛎 🛠 D Pump out, gas, overnight and long-term mooring, engine repairs, toilets and showers, solid fuel.
ⓑ **Debbie's Day Boats** Coleshill Road, Fazeley, Tamworth B78 3RY (01827 262042). 🛠 Gas, day-hire boats, long-term mooring, boat and engine repairs. *Emergency call out.*
ⓑ **BW Fazeley** Peel's Wharf, Lichfield Street, Fazeley, Tamworth B78 3QZ (01827 252000; enquiries.hg@britishwaterways.co.uk). 200yds west of the junction. 🛎 🛎 🛠

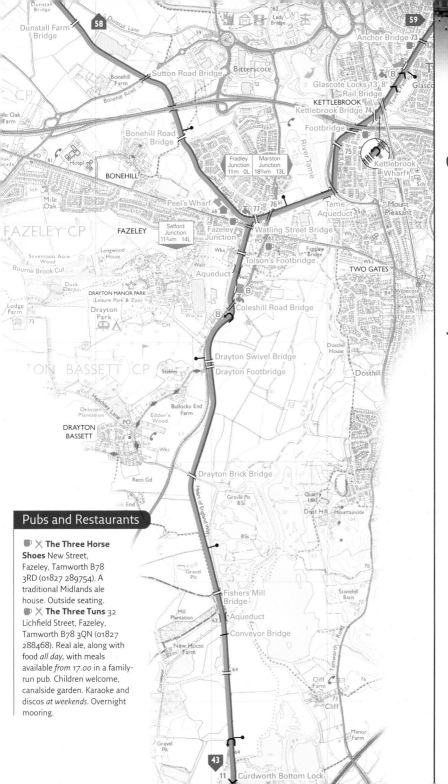

Pubs and Restaurants

🍺 ✕ **The Three Horse Shoes** New Street, Fazeley, Tamworth B78 3RD (01827 289754). A traditional Midlands ale house. Outside seating.

🍺 ✕ **The Three Tuns** 32 Lichfield Street, Fazeley, Tamworth B78 3QN (01827 288468). Real ale, along with food *all day*, with meals available *from 17.00* in a family-run pub. Children welcome, canalside garden. Karaoke and discos *at weekends*. Overnight mooring.

45

Cruising past Hartshill Yard (see *page 54*)

COVENTRY CANAL

MAXIMUM DIMENSIONS

Length: 72'
Beam: 7'
Headroom: 6' 6"

MILEAGE

COVENTRY BASIN to:
HAWKESBURY JUNCTION (Oxford Canal): 5½ miles

MARSTON JUNCTION (Ashby Canal): 8¼ miles

Boot Wharf, Nuneaton: 10½ miles
Hartshill: 14 miles
Atherstone Top Lock: 16½ miles
Polesworth: 21½ miles
Alvecote Priory: 23¼ miles
Glascote Bottom Lock: 25½ miles

FAZELEY JUNCTION (Birmingham & Fazeley Canal): 27 miles
Hopwas: 29¾ miles
Whittington Brook: 32½ miles
Huddlesford Junction: 34 miles

FRADLEY JUNCTION (Trent & Mersey Canal): 38 miles

Locks: 13

MANAGER

01827 252000
enquiries.westmidlands@britishwaterways.co.uk

The Coventry Canal, whose enabling Act of Parliament was passed in 1768, was promoted by pit owners such as the Parrotts of Hawkesbury and the Newdigates of Arbury with two main objectives: to connect the fast-growing town of Coventry with the new trade route called the Grand Trunk, now the Trent & Mersey Canal; and to provide Coventry with cheap coal from Bedworth coalfield, 10 miles to the north.

The first, long-term objective was not achieved for some years until the company had overcome financial difficulties, but – wisely – the stretch between Coventry and Bedworth was completed early on, so that the profitable carriage of local coal was quickly established along the canal, in 1769.

By the time the canal reached Atherstone in 1771, all the authorised capital had been spent and James Brindley, the original engineer of the canal, had been sacked. For these reasons – and because of the interminable wrangle with the Oxford Canal Company, whose scheme to link Coventry with southern England had followed hard upon the original Coventry scheme – the Coventry Canal did not reach Fazeley, nearly 12 miles short of its intended terminus at Fradley, until 1790.

By this time, the Birmingham & Fazeley Canal had been built, extending along the Coventry Canal's original proposed line to Whittington Brook, from where the Grand Trunk Canal Company carried it north to Fradley. The Coventry Company later bought this section back, which explains the fact that there is now a detached portion of the Coventry Canal from Whittington Brook to Fradley Junction (look out for the marker stone).

In 1790, the Oxford Canal was also completed through to Oxford and thus to London via the Thames. The profits of the Coventry Canal rose quickly, and rose even higher when the Grand Junction Canal was completed in 1799, shortening the route to London by 60 miles. Other adjoining canals contributed to the Coventry Canal's prosperity: the Ashby, the Wyrley & Essington and the Trent & Mersey. The extension of the Grand Junction Canal via Warwick to Birmingham naturally dismayed the Coventry, but the numerous locks – and high tolls on the stretch of the Oxford Canal between Braunston and Napton Junctions – ensured that a lot of traffic to and from Birmingham still used the slightly longer route via the Coventry and Birmingham & Fazeley Canals, especially after the Oxford Canal was shortened by 14 miles between Braunston and Longford.

The continuous financial success of the Coventry Canal could be attributed both to its being part of so many long-distance routes and to the continued prosperity of the coal mines along its way. Extensive landscaping and reclamation, along with extensive rebuilding, have made this an extremely attractive and interesting route.

Coventry

The Coventry Canal begins at the large Bishop Street Basin, opened in 1769, near the town centre. It is an interesting situation on the side of a hill, overlooked by tall buildings and attractive old wooden canal warehouses; the warehouses date from 1914, although there were, of course, earlier such buildings on the site. They once stored grain, food and cement, and were well restored in 1984. The old Weighbridge Office is now a shop and information centre, looking out over the basin towards the Vaults, which were used to store coal. The canal leaves the terminus through bridge 1, a tiny structure designed to be easily closed with a wooden beam each evening: indeed at one time no boats were allowed to stay in the basin overnight (it is now an excellent mooring). There was once a toll house here. To the west of this bridge is Canal House, built for the local trader Alderman Clarke. The canal company purchased the house in 1809 and it was used for successive canal managers until 1947, when the last manager of the Coventry Canal, John Kaye, purchased it upon his retirement. It is now owned by the City Council. The canal now begins to wind through what were busy industrial areas towards Hawkesbury: it is in places quite narrow, and often flanked by buildings. Just beyond bridge 2 are 'Cash's Hundred Houses', an elegant row of weavers' houses, where the living accommodation was on the lower two floors, with the top storey being occupied by looms, driven by a single shaft from a steam engine. There never were 100 houses: only 48 were built, and of these only 37 remain. The canal then, after various contortions, continues towards Hawkesbury, passing through the outskirts of Coventry. Before it ducks under the motorway, just beyond bridge 10, you will notice that the canal is wider: this was the site of the original junction between the Oxford and Coventry Canals. It was known as Longford Junction. Hawkesbury Junction, their present meeting, contains all the elements expected of such a notable place: plenty of traditional boats, interesting buildings including a fine engine house, a splendid pub and useful facilities for boaters. To the east of the junction is Hawkesbury Hall (private), at one time the home of mine owner and sponsor of the Coventry Canal, Richard Parrott. The towpath between Coventry and Hawkesbury is decorated with some excellent sculptures, as the Canal Art Trail.

● **Coventry**
West Midlands. PO, tel, stores, garage, station, cinema, theatre.
Recorded as Couentrev in the Domesday Book, Coventry's modern history begins with the foundation of a Benedictine priory by Leofric and his wife Godgyfu in 1043, but its fame came with Lady Godiva, who in legend rode naked through the streets, to divert Leofric's anger from the town. This episode is first recorded in the *Flores Historiarum* of 1235. Following the Norman invasion, the town became second in commercial importance to London. Largely destroyed during World War II, it is today a modern and well-planned city, although a restored row of medieval buildings can be visited in Spon Street, in the west of the city centre. The origin of the popular phrase 'to send to Coventry', meaning to cold-shoulder or ignore, is uncertain, but there is no reason to connect it with the present population, who seem generally warm and friendly.

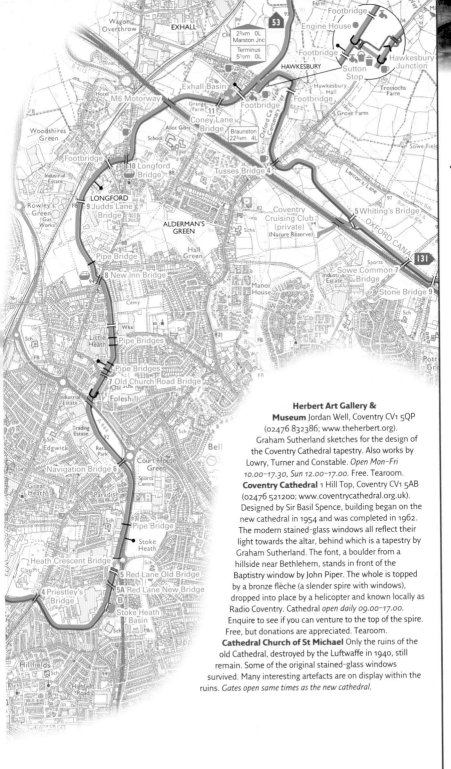

**Herbert Art Gallery &
Museum** Jordan Well, Coventry CV1 5QP
(02476 832386; www.theherbert.org).
Graham Sutherland sketches for the design of
the Coventry Cathedral tapestry. Also works by
Lowry, Turner and Constable. *Open Mon–Fri
10.00–17.30, Sun 12.00–17.00.* Free. Tearoom.
Coventry Cathedral 1 Hill Top, Coventry CV1 5AB
(02476 521200; www.coventrycathedral.org.uk).
Designed by Sir Basil Spence, building began on the
new cathedral in 1954 and was completed in 1962.
The modern stained-glass windows all reflect their
light towards the altar, behind which is a tapestry by
Graham Sutherland. The font, a boulder from a
hillside near Bethlehem, stands in front of the
Baptistry window by John Piper. The whole is topped
by a bronze flèche (a slender spire with windows),
dropped into place by a helicopter and known locally as
Radio Coventry. Cathedral *open daily 09.00–17.00.*
Enquire to see if you can venture to the top of the spire.
Free, but donations are appreciated. Tearoom.
Cathedral Church of St Michael Only the ruins of the
old Cathedral, destroyed by the Luftwaffe in 1940, still
remain. Some of the original stained-glass windows
survived. Many interesting artefacts are on display within the
ruins. *Gates open same times as the new cathedral.*

Museum of British Road Transport Millennium Place, Hales Street, Coventry CV1 1PN (02476 234270; www.transport-museum.com). Walk south from the canal basin. Reputedly the largest display of British-made transport in the world, with over 200 cars, 90 motorbikes and 230 cycles on view. There are also period street scenes, royal vehicles and the Blitz Experience. You can also see the awesome *Thrust SSC*, world land-speed record holder, and take an audio-visual run at over 600 mph. *Open daily 10.00–17.00.* Free. Café on site.

Tourist Information Centre 5 Priory Row, Coventry CV1 5EX (02476 227264; www.visitcoventryandwarwickshire.co.uk).

● **Longford Bridge**
West Midlands. Stores, off-licence, chandlery. It was here, between 1769 and 1865, that members of the nearby Salem Baptist Chapel were baptised in the canal.

● **Hawkesbury Junction**
Hawkesbury Junction is also known as Sutton's Stop, after the name of the toll clerks here. It was always a busy canal centre, and remains so today, with plenty of narrowboats permanently moored at the junction. There are also other things to see: a fine canal pub, a stop lock and a disused engine house. The latter used to pump water up into the canal from a well. Its engine was installed in 1821, having been previously employed for nearly 100 years at Griff Colliery, a few miles up the canal towards Nuneaton. This Newcomen-type atmospheric steam engine, called Lady Godiva, is now in Dartmouth Museum. It ceased work in 1913. Sephtons House and Boatyard once faced the junction: it was here, in 1924, that *nb Friendship* was built. This boat can now be seen at the Boat Museum, Ellesmere Port. The western side of the canal has now been engulfed in a vast area of housing.

BOAT TRIPS
Nb Coventrian is a 38-seater boat based at Swan Lane Wharf and used as floating classroom for local children. Also available for private charter, for parties and trips. Details from 02476 258864.

Boatyards

ⓑ **Club Line Cruisers** Swan Lane Wharf, Swan Lane, Stoke Heath, Coventry CV2 4QN (02476 258864). 🛒 🛢 ⚓ D Pump out, gas, narrowboat hire, long-term mooring, slipway, boat and engine repairs, toilets, books and maps.

WALKING & CYCLING
The towpath is in good condition for walkers throughout, and the stretch between Coventry and Hawkesbury is now enlivened as the Canal Art Trail. Cyclists will find parts of the towpath bumpy.

A. K. A. SUTTON'S STOP
Hawkesbury Junction was more commonly known to the boat people as Sutton's Stop. It took this name from a family called Sutton who, during the 1800s, were the toll clerks here.
The Greyhound overlooks the junction now as it did then. Corn, oats and maize used to be stored around the back of the pub, as feed for the towing horses. It was often the children's job to bag this up for a trip, lowering the sacks down using a small hand crane.

Pubs and Restaurants

✕ **Country Crust Tearooms** Canal Basin, St Nicholas Street, Coventry CV1 4LY (02476 633477). Excellent cooked breakfasts, light meals, coffee and tea. Outside seating. *Open Mon–Fri 09.30–16.30.*

🍺 **The Admiral Codrington** St Columba's Close, Coventry CV1 4BX (02476 258520). By the canal basin. Children welcome *until 19.00.* Garden. Occasional karaoke, discos and quiz nights.

🍺 ✕ **The Royal Hotel** Old Church Road, Little Heath, Coventry CV6 7DU (02476 686152). Near bridge 7. Friendly local, serving snacks *L.* Children's room and garden.

🍺 ✕ **The Greyhound** Hawkesbury Junction, Longford CV6 6DF (02476 363046). A fascinating pub beside the junction, decorated with canal memorabilia, warmed by log fires in *winter.* Meals served in the bar or restaurant *L and E.* A choice of real ale is available. Canalside garden. Moorings.

🍺 **The Boat Inn** Blackhorse Road, Longford, Near Coventry CV6 6DL (02476 361438). A fine friendly pub with unspoilt rooms and a cosy lounge, just a 3-minute walk north west of the junction. Real ale. Children welcome. Garden for the *summer* and a real fire for the *winter.* Quiz *Mon.*

Engine house at Hawkesbury

Nuneaton

Leaving Hawkesbury Junction, the canal passes through Bedworth in a long cutting: the town seems to be composed mainly of vast housing estates, but these make little impression upon the canal. At Marston Junction the Ashby Canal (*see* page 16) branches to the east through pleasant countryside, while the Coventry Canal bends due west for a short way before resuming its course towards Nuneaton to the north. There is a pleasant short stretch of open fields, giving a welcome breathing space, before the canal once again enters the suburbs, this time of Nuneaton. There are good moorings and easy access to facilities by Boot Bridge (bridge 20). The canal takes a route around the town, marked by a succession of housing estates and well-tended allotments.

● **Nuneaton**
Warwicks. PO, tel, stores, garage, station, cinema. A typical Midlands town. On the site of the Griff Colliery canal arm are the hollows said to be the origin of the Red Deeps in the *Mill on the Floss* by George Eliot, who was born here in 1819.
Nuneaton Museum & Art Gallery
Riversley Park, Coton Road, Nuneaton CV11 5TU (02476 350720; www.nuneatonandbedworth.gov.uk). Archaeological specimens of Nuneaton from prehistoric to medieval times, and also items from the local earthenware industry. Geological and mining relics, ethnography from Africa, Asia, America and Oceania. Paintings, prints and watercolours. Personalia collection of the novelist George Eliot. *Open Tue–Sat 10.30–16.30, Sun 14.00–16.30. Closed Mon except B Hols.* Free. Tearoom (*open daily*) on site.
Arbury Hall Nuneaton CV10 7PT (02476 382804). Two miles south west of the canal off B4102.

Originally an Elizabethan house, it was gothicised by Sir Roger Newdigate in 1750–1800 under the direction of Sanderson Miller, Henry Keene and Couchman of Warwick. Fine pictures, furniture, china and glass. The Hall is in a beautiful park setting. *Open Easter–last Sun in Sep, B Hol Sun and Mon only; house 14.00–17.00, gardens 14.00–18.00.* Charge.
Tourist Information Centre Nuneaton Library, Church Street, Nuneaton CV11 4DR (02476 384027; www.warwickshire.gov.uk).
● **Chilvers Coton**
Warwicks. PO, tel, stores. A suburb of Nuneaton. Its church dates from 1946 and was designed by H. N. Jepson and built by German prisoners-of-war.
● **Bedworth**
Warwicks. PO, tel, stores. The most impressive parts of this town are its church by Bodley and Garner, 1888–90, and the almshouses built in 1840. Good shops.

Pubs and Restaurants

🍺 **The Boot Inn** Boot Wharf, Bridge Street, Chilvers Coton CV10 7BB (02476 385635). Real ale in a pub with a large bar and quiet lounge. The enclosed garden has toys for the children and barbecues are held in *summer.* Meals available *L and E.* Post box outside. Live music *Tue.*
🍺 **The Fleur de Lys** Coventry Road, Chilvers Coton CV11 4NL (02476 382366). Two minutes' walk down

the hill from bridge 19a. There is a large bar and pleasant lounge in this friendly pub. Food *L and E.* Children welcome. Garden. Regular *weekend* live music.
🍺 **The King William** Coton Road, Chilvers Coton CV11 5TS (02476 348308). About ¹/₄ mile north east from bridge 19a. Traditional pub serving real ale.

BIRD LIFE
The *Nuthatch* is recognised by its rounded, short-tailed appearance and its habit of descending tree trunks head-downwards, a trait unique in Britain to this species. The Nuthatch has blue-grey upperparts, a black eyestripe, white cheeks and orange-buff underparts. The chisel-like bill is used to prise insects from tree bark and to hammer open acorns wedged in bark crevices. This woodland species has a falcon-like call. It nests in tree holes, often plastering the entrance with mud to reduce its diameter.

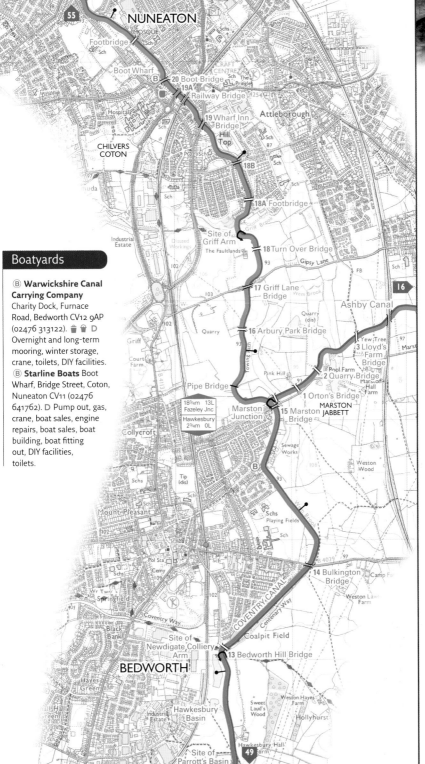

Boatyards

Ⓑ **Warwickshire Canal Carrying Company** Charity Dock, Furnace Road, Bedworth CV12 9AP (02476 313122). 🚿 🚽 D Overnight and long-term mooring, winter storage, crane, toilets, DIY facilities.

Ⓑ **Starline Boats** Boot Wharf, Bridge Street, Coton, Nuneaton CV11 (02476 641762). D Pump out, gas, crane, boat sales, engine repairs, boat sales, boat building, boat fitting out, DIY facilities, toilets.

Hartshill

Continuing north west out of Nuneaton, the canal winds along the side of a hill into a landscape which is curiously exciting. What were once quarries and spoil heaps are now landscaped, with many transformed into nature reserves. The largest mountain of waste, built with spoil from the old Judkins Quarry, is known as Mount Judd, or locally 'Jees'. This distinctly man-made landscape is broken up with unexpected stretches of open countryside, with fine views away to the north across the Anker valley. The canal passes below the town of Hartshill: the attractive buildings in the British Waterways yard are crowned by a splendid clock tower, and those travelling on the canal will want to slow right down to enjoy the mellow architecture and old dock. The canal then continues towards Mancetter, leaving the quarry belt and moving into open rolling country backed by thick woods to the west. The railway closes from the east as the canal approaches Atherstone.

WALKING & CYCLING
From Hartshill Yard you can walk south west to the Fox & Hounds, through Hartshill Hayes Country Park, then north by Mancetter Quarries, Quarry Farm, Purley Park and The Outwoods to Atherstone. After refreshment in the pub it is an easy return along the canal.

● **Hartshill**
Warwicks. PO, tel, stores, garage. Once a mining community, Hartshill has now been swallowed up by Nuneaton, and as such its interest lies mainly in its past. The Romans recognised its strategic importance. There is evidence that they settled here, as both kilns and fragments of pottery have been unearthed. Hugh de Hardreshull chose it as a site for his castle in 1125, the view from the ridge enabling him to see as far as the distant peaks of Derbyshire on a clear day. Below, on the plains, can be counted the towers and steeples of 40 churches. Hartshill's most famous claim is that it was the birthplace of the poet Drayton in 1563, a friend of both Ben Johnson and Shakespeare. Drayton's greatest work was *Polyolbion*, a survey of the country with a son for each county. He died in 1631 and was buried in Westminster. There are fine walks over Hartshill Green to Oldbury Camp, a Bronze Age hill-fort covering 7 acres. Hartshill's shops are a 15-minute walk from the canal.

Hartshill Yard Hartshill, Nuneaton (01283 790236). Part of the yard contains a 19th-C carpenters' workshop and blacksmiths' forge. Visits are by appointment *for groups only* – telephone for details.

● **Mancetter**
Warwicks. PO, tel, stores, garage. About ½ mile east of bridge 36. The church dates from the 13th C, but its best feature is the large collection of 18th-C slate tombstones displaying all the elegance of Georgian incised lettering. There are some almshouses of 1728 in the churchyard, and across the road another row with pretty Victorian Gothic details. The manor, south of the church, is rather over-restored. It was from this house, in 1555, that Robert Glover was led when the Bishop of Lichfield ordered his arrest. A victim of the reign of Mary Tudor, he was seized and taken to the stake, where he was executed alongside a poor cap-maker from Coventry.

Pubs and Restaurants

🍺 ✕ **Stag & Pheasant** The Green Avenue, Hartshill, Nuneaton CV10 0SW (02476 393173). About a ¹/₂-mile walk up the lane behind Hartshill Yard, this family-run village-green pub has outside seating and a family room. Real ale. Restaurant food, *L and E*.

🍺 **Malt Shovel** 39 Grange Road, Hartshill, Nuneaton CV10 0SS (02476 392501) 1000 yards south west of bridge 31. Real ale is available and meals (including Indian and Chinese, and *Sun* roasts) are served *all day*.

Beer garden and children's play area. Darts and juke box.

🍺 **The Maid of the Mill** 85 Coleshill Road, Atherstone CV9 2AB (01827 716517). South of bridge 41. Locals' and boaters' pub. Real ale is served and there is outside seating. PO opposite, and fish & chips next door.

🍺 **The Barge & Bridge** 79 Coleshill Road, Atherstone CV9 2AB (01827 717707). North of bridge 42. Traditional locals' pub. Real ale is available. Meals served *L and E*. Outside seating, and children are welcome. *Occasional* entertainment.

Boatyards

ⓑ **Valley Cruises** Springwood Haven, Mancetter Road, Nuneaton CV10 0RZ (02476 393333; www.valleycruises.co.uk).

ⓑ **Springwood Haven Marina** Springwood Haven, Mancetter Road, Nuneaton CV10 0RZ (02476 393676; www.springwoodhaven.co.uk).

🔒 🛠 D Pump out, gas, narrowboat hire, overnight and long-term mooring, narrowboat slipway, boat repairs, engine sales and repairs, boat fitting out, chandlery, toilets, solid fuel.

BW Hartshill Yard Clock Hill, Hartshill (02476 392489). 🛠

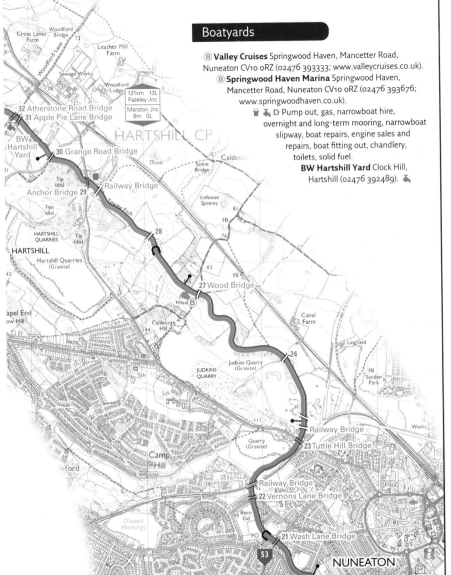

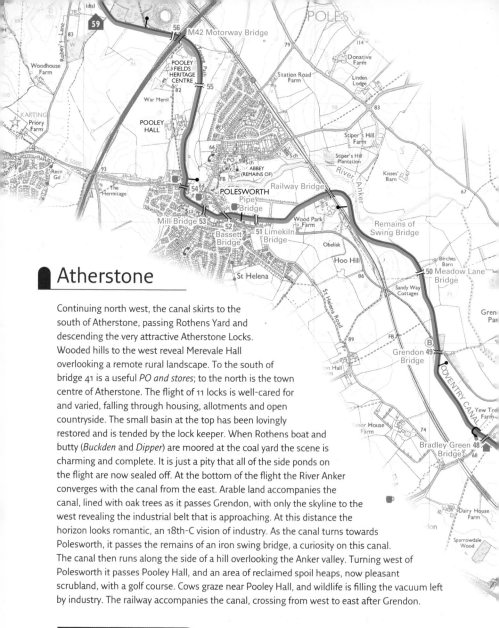

Atherstone

Continuing north west, the canal skirts to the
south of Atherstone, passing Rothens Yard and
descending the very attractive Atherstone Locks.
Wooded hills to the west reveal Merevale Hall
overlooking a remote rural landscape. To the south of
bridge 41 is a useful *PO and stores*; to the north is the town
centre of Atherstone. The flight of 11 locks is well-cared for
and varied, falling through housing, allotments and open
countryside. The small basin at the top has been lovingly
restored and is tended by the lock keeper. When Rothens boat and
butty (*Buckden* and *Dipper*) are moored at the coal yard the scene is
charming and complete. It is just a pity that all of the side ponds on
the flight are now sealed off. At the bottom of the flight the River Anker
converges with the canal from the east. Arable land accompanies the
canal, lined with oak trees as it passes Grendon, with only the skyline to the
west revealing the industrial belt that is approaching. At this distance the
horizon looks romantic, an 18th-C vision of industry. As the canal turns towards
Polesworth, it passes the remains of an iron swing bridge, a curiosity on this canal.
The canal then runs along the side of a hill overlooking the Anker valley. Turning west of
Polesworth it passes Pooley Hall, and an area of reclaimed spoil heaps, now pleasant
scrubland, with a golf course. Cows graze near Pooley Hall, and wildlife is filling the vacuum left
by industry. The railway accompanies the canal, crossing from west to east after Grendon.

Boatyards

ⓑ **A.G. & R.A. Rothen** Top Lock Wharf, Coleshill Road, Atherstone CV9 1BW (01827 717884). D Coal and gas.
Canal carrying.

ⓑ **Barry Hawkins Narrowboats** Baddesley Basin, Hooley Lane, Atherstone CV92EH (01827 711762;
www.barryhawkinsnarrowboats.co.uk). D Pump out, gas, overnight and long-term mooring, winter storage, boat
sales, engine sales and repairs, boat building, chandlery, solid fuel, books, maps, and gifts. *Emergency call out*.

ⓑ **Narrowcraft** Grendon Dock, Atherstone CV10 (01827 898585). D Pump out, gas, overnight and long-term
mooring, winter storage, boat sales, boat and engine repairs, DIY facilities, chandlery, solid fuel, toilets, books,
maps, and gifts. Clubhouse and restaurant.

Atherstone
Warwicks. PO, tel, stores, garage, station, cinema. A pleasant town, with a strong 18th-C feeling, especially in the open market place in front of the church.
Merevale Atherstone CV9 2HG. A large battlemented house, high to the west, is Merevale Hall, an early 19th-C mock Tudor mansion. To the west are the remains of the 12th-C abbey and the very pretty 13th-C church which contains fine stained glass, monuments and brasses.

Grendon
Warwicks. ½ mile north east of bridge 48. Grendon is just a small church set in beautiful parkland. The woods and rolling fields are a last refuge before the industrial landscape that precedes Tamworth.

Polesworth
Warwicks. PO, tel, stores, garage, fish & chips, station. The splendid gatehouse and the clerestory are all that remain of the 10th-C abbey, where Egbert, first Saxon King of England, built a nunnery.

Pubs and Restaurants

Old Red Lion Hotel Long Street, Atherstone CV9 1BB (01827 713156; www.atherstoneredlion.co.uk). Friendly residential hotel serving real ale. Bar snacks *L and E, daily,* restaurant meals *E only.* Conservatory and library. Children welcome. B & B.

The Kings Head Old Watling Street, Atherstone CV9 2PA (01827 717945). Real ale, along with bar and à la carte meals *L and E.* Special meals for OAPs. Children welcome. Outside seating, mooring. Live music *once a month.*

Market Tavern 21 Market Street, Atherstone CV9 1BB (07786 836303). 18th-C pub located in the historic market square. Real ale can be enjoyed here. Outside seating.

The Black Swan Watling Street, Grendon, Atherstone CV9 2PY (01827 713640). Real ale, and meals from an English and Indian menu *L and E.* Children welcome, and there is a soft toy activity centre for children. Garden, mooring.

The Bulls Head Tamworth Road, Polesworth, Tamworth B78 1JH (01827 893022). West of bridge 54. Real ale, and meals *L and E (not Sun E or Mon).* Children welcome if eating.

Fosters Yard Hotel 12 Market Street, Polesworth, Tamworth B78 1HW (01827 899313). South of bridge 53. Tall listed building, with oak beams, an open fire and a skittle alley, also incorporating a Balti restaurant (01827 33034). Real ale and meals *L and E.* Children welcome. Entertainment *Sat.* Moorings 100yds away at the bridge.

The Royal Oak Grendon Road, Polesworth, Tamworth B78 1NU (01827 331025). South of bridge 52. Traditional pub offering real ale. Food served *12.00–19.00 daily.* Children welcome. Outside seating on the patio. Live music alternate; quiz and poker alternate *Tue.*

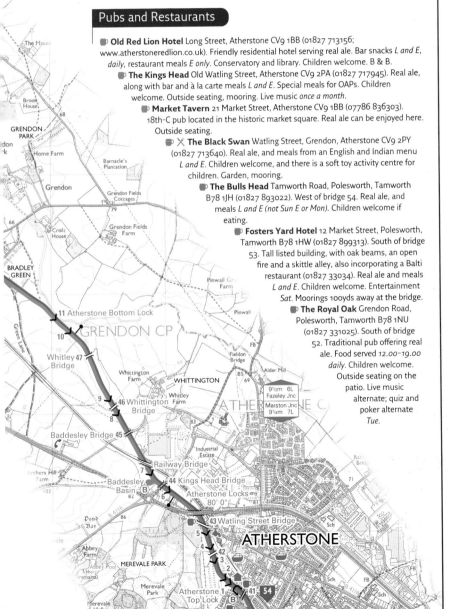

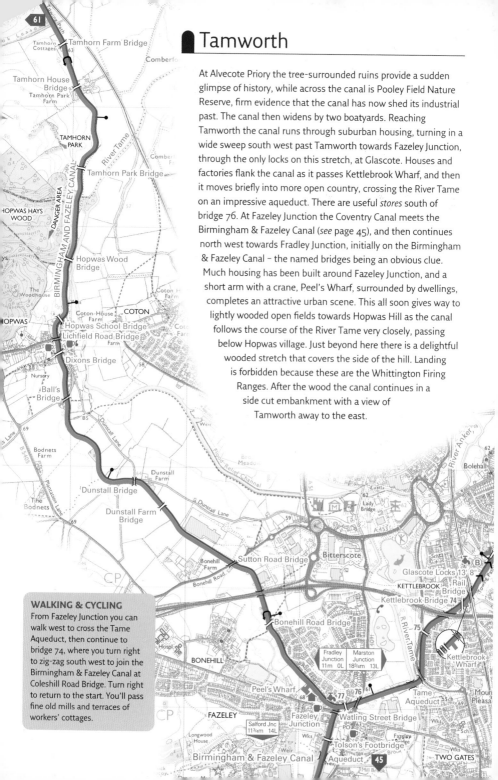

Tamworth

At Alvecote Priory the tree-surrounded ruins provide a sudden glimpse of history, while across the canal is Pooley Field Nature Reserve, firm evidence that the canal has now shed its industrial past. The canal then widens by two boatyards. Reaching Tamworth the canal runs through suburban housing, turning in a wide sweep south west past Tamworth towards Fazeley Junction, through the only locks on this stretch, at Glascote. Houses and factories flank the canal as it passes Kettlebrook Wharf, and then it moves briefly into more open country, crossing the River Tame on an impressive aqueduct. There are useful *stores* south of bridge 76. At Fazeley Junction the Coventry Canal meets the Birmingham & Fazeley Canal (*see page 45*), and then continues north west towards Fradley Junction, initially on the Birmingham & Fazeley Canal – the named bridges being an obvious clue. Much housing has been built around Fazeley Junction, and a short arm with a crane, Peel's Wharf, surrounded by dwellings, completes an attractive urban scene. This all soon gives way to lightly wooded open fields towards Hopwas Hill as the canal follows the course of the River Tame very closely, passing below Hopwas village. Just beyond here there is a delightful wooded stretch that covers the side of the hill. Landing is forbidden because these are the Whittington Firing Ranges. After the wood the canal continues in a side cut embankment with a view of Tamworth away to the east.

WALKING & CYCLING

From Fazeley Junction you can walk west to cross the Tame Aqueduct, then continue to bridge 74, where you turn right to zig-zag south west to join the Birmingham & Fazeley Canal at Coleshill Road Bridge. Turn right to return to the start. You'll pass fine old mills and terraces of workers' cottages.

Amington
Staffs. PO, tel, stores, garage. To the south of bridge 68 is the Canal Craft Shop, where you can have Buckby canalware painted to order.

Tamworth
Staffs. PO, tel, stores, garage, station, cinema. Tamworth was originally a Saxon settlement, although only earthworks survive from this period.

Tamworth Castle The Holloway (off Castle Street), Tamworth B79 7NA (01827 709626; www.tamworthcastle.co.uk). With a Norman motte, an Elizabethan timbered hall and Jacobean apartments, it is a splendid mélange of styles. *Open mid Feb–Oct, Tue–Sun 12.00–17.15 (restricted opening in winter).* Charge.

Tourist Information Centre 29 Market Street, Tamworth B79 7LR (01827 709581).

Fazeley Junction
Staffs. PO and stores in Fazeley.

Hopwas
Staffs. PO, tel, stores. A pretty and tidy village with a green, built on the side of a hill. Anyone walking should look out for the danger flags for Whittington Firing Ranges.

Boatyards

Ⓑ **Narrowcraft** Grendon Dock, Atherstone (01827 898585; www.narrowboat.co.uk). Ⓓ Pump out, gas, overnight and long-term mooring, winter storage, boat sales, boat and engine repairs, DIY facilities, chandlery, solid fuel, toilets, books, maps, and gifts. Clubhouse and restaurant.

Ⓑ **Alvecote Marina** Robey's Lane, Alvecote B78 1AS (01827 892764). Hire base.

Ⓑ **S.M. Hudson** Glascote Basin Boatyard, Basin Lane, Tamworth B77 2AH (01827 311317). Ⓓ Gas, long-term mooring, winter storage, boat and engine sales and repairs, boat building.

Ⓑ **BW Fazeley Office** Peel's Wharf, Lichfield Street, Fazeley, Tamworth B78 3QZ (01827 252000). 200yds west of the junction.

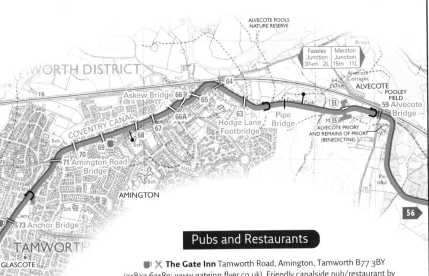

Pubs and Restaurants

🍺 ✕ **The Gate Inn** Tamworth Road, Amington, Tamworth B77 3BY (01827 63189; www.gateinn.flyer.co.uk). Friendly canalside pub/restaurant by bridge 69, serving real ale. Home-cooked meals *L and E*. Children welcome in the family room, or if dining. Garden with children's play area. Quiz *fortnightly on Mon*. PO box in the car park. Moorings.

🍺 ✕ **The Three Tuns** 32 Lichfield Street, Fazeley, Tamworth B78 3QN (01827 288468). Real ale, along with food *all day*, with Indian meals available *from 17.00* in a family-run pub. Children welcome, canalside garden. Overnight mooring.

🍺 **The Tame Otter** Hints Road, Hopwas, near Tamworth B78 3AB (01827 53361). Canalside pub serving real ale. Food *all day, every day*. Children welcome. Garden and moorings.

🍺 **The Red Lion** Lichfield Road, Hopwas, Near Tamworth B78 3AF (01827 62514). A canalside pub with an extensive garden, offering real ale. Home-cooked food, with steaks a speciality, served *from 10.00*. Children welcome, and there is a play area.

Whittington and Fradley Junction

Between Whittington Bridge and Bridge 78 the canal changes from being the Birmingham & Fazeley Canal to the Coventry Canal (*see* Introduction, page 47). A stone marks the actual point. At Huddlesford the remains of the eastern end of the Wyrley & Essington Canal, now referred to as the Lichfield Canal and presently used only for moorings, branches to the south west. This route, which extends west to Ogley Junction on the Anglesey Branch of the BCN, is the subject of an energetic and effective restoration campaign. Problems of obstruction by the new M6 Toll road have been overcome with the installation of an aqueduct, but much still remains to be done. The Coventry Canal then runs northwards through flat, open country towards Fradley Junction. There are no locks, but a swing bridge announces your arrival at Fradley. Here the Coventry Canal meets the Trent & Mersey Canal, overlooked by The Swan, a famous canal landmark.

● **Fisherwick**
Staffs. Tel. A small hamlet overlooking the canal.
● **Whittington**
Staffs. PO, tel, stores, garage, chemist, Chinese takeaway, off-licence. The village centre is to the west of Whittington Bridge; shops are best approached from bridge 78.
● **Lichfield**
Staffs. PO, tel, stores, garage, cinema, station. Two miles south west along the A38. Although not on the canal, Lichfield is well worth a visit.
Art Gallery The Friary, Lichfield Library, Lichfield WS13 6QG (01543 510700; www.staffordshire.gov.uk). *Open Mon, Wed and Fri 09.30–17.00, Tue and Thu 09.30–19.00 and Sat 09.00–13.00. Closed Sun.* Admission free.
Tourist Information Centre Lichfield Garrick, Castle Dyke, Lichfield WS13 6HR (01543 308211; www.visitlichfield.com).

● **Huddlesford**
Staffs. PO box. At Huddlesford Junction the Wyrley & Essington Canal used to join the Coventry. Long abandoned, the first ¼ mile is used for moorings and the remainder is scheduled for restoration, with much work already done.
● **Fradley**
Staffs. PO, tel, stores. A small village set to the east of the canal, and well away from the junction. It owed its prosperity to the airfield which is not used as such any more.
● **Fradley Junction**
Staffs. PO box, tel, garage. A long-established canal centre where the Coventry Canal joins the Trent & Mersey Canal. There is a boatyard, a British Waterways Information Centre and café, moorings, a boat club and a popular pub – all in the middle of a five-lock flight.

Boatyards

Ⓑ **Streethay Wharf** Streethay Basin, Streethay, Lichfield WS13 8RJ (01543 414808; www.streethaywharf.co.uk). 🚽 🛢 D Pump out, gas, day-hire craft, overnight and long-term mooring, winter storage, wet dock, slipway, crane, boat and engine sales and repairs, boat building, telephone, toilets, showers, chandlery, solid fuel, laundrette, DIY facilities. *Emergency call out.*
Ⓑ **Tom's Moorings** Streethay Basin, Streethay,

Lichfield WS13 8RJ (01543 414808). 🛢 Pump out, gas, overnight and long-term mooring.
Ⓑ **BW Waterways Office** Fradley Junction, Alrewas, Burton-on-Trent DE13 (01283 790236). 🚽 🚽 🛢 Overnight mooring, long-term mooring, toilets.
Ⓑ **Swan Line Cruisers** Fradley Junction, Alrewas, Burton-on-Trent DE13 7DN (01283 790332). 🛢 D Pump out (*not Sat*), gas, narrowboat hire, overnight mooring, boat and engine sales and repairs, chandlery, books and maps, gifts, groceries.

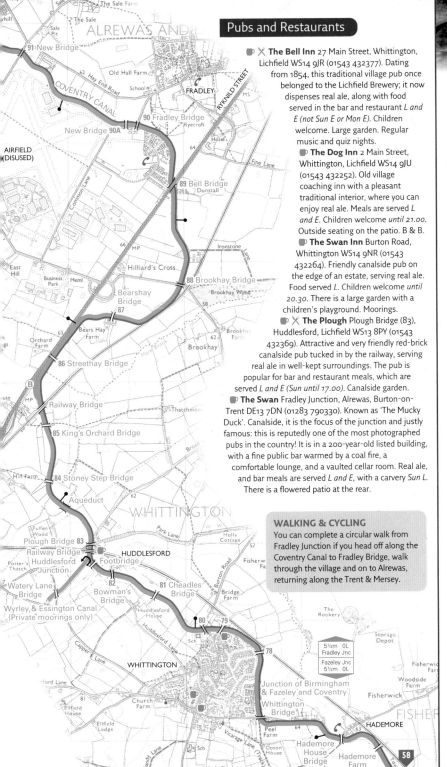

Pubs and Restaurants

The Bell Inn 27 Main Street, Whittington, Lichfield WS14 9JR (01543 432377). Dating from 1854, this traditional village pub once belonged to the Lichfield Brewery; it now dispenses real ale, along with food served in the bar and restaurant *L and E (not Sun E or Mon E)*. Children welcome. Large garden. Regular music and quiz nights.

The Dog Inn 2 Main Street, Whittington, Lichfield WS14 9JU (01543 432252). Old village coaching inn with a pleasant traditional interior, where you can enjoy real ale. Meals are served *L and E*. Children welcome *until 21.00*. Outside seating on the patio. B & B.

The Swan Inn Burton Road, Whittington WS14 9NR (01543 432264). Friendly canalside pub on the edge of an estate, serving real ale. Food served *L*. Children welcome *until 20.30*. There is a large garden with a children's playground. Moorings.

The Plough Plough Bridge (83), Huddlesford, Lichfield WS13 8PY (01543 432369). Attractive and very friendly red-brick canalside pub tucked in by the railway, serving real ale in well-kept surroundings. The pub is popular for bar and restaurant meals, which are served *L and E (Sun until 17.00)*. Canalside garden.

The Swan Fradley Junction, Alrewas, Burton-on-Trent DE13 7DN (01283 790330). Known as 'The Mucky Duck'. Canalside, it is the focus of the junction and justly famous: this is reputedly one of the most photographed pubs in the country! It is in a 200-year-old listed building, with a fine public bar warmed by a coal fire, a comfortable lounge, and a vaulted cellar room. Real ale, and bar meals are served *L and E*, with a carvery *Sun L*. There is a flowered patio at the rear.

WALKING & CYCLING

You can complete a circular walk from Fradley Junction if you head off along the Coventry Canal to Fradley Bridge, walk through the village and on to Alrewas, returning along the Trent & Mersey.

EREWASH CANAL

MAXIMUM DIMENSIONS
Length: 72'
Beam: 10' 6"
Draught: 2' 6"
Headroom: 7' 4"

MANAGER
01636 704481
enquiries.emidlands@britishwaterways.co.uk.

MILEAGE
TRENT LOCK to:
Sandiacre Lock: 3¼ miles
Hallam Fields Lock: 5½ miles
LANGLEY MILL: 11¾ miles

Locks: 15

The Erewash Canal is one of five canals built towards the end of the 18th C to carry coal from the pits of the Nottinghamshire/Derbyshire coalfield to the towns of the East Midlands. The construction of the canal was supported by local merchants and landowners who were keen to profit from the coal deposits of the Erewash Valley, as were the local colliery owners who could see the financial benefits of widening their markets. Completed in 1779 at a cost of £21,000 by the engineer John Varley, the canal involved the construction of 14 locks which took the navigation up 109ft from Trent Lock to Langley Mill. Begun in 1778, its 11¾ mile course was open to navigation by the following summer. As £23,000 had been raised in £100 shares in order to finance the project, the capital outlay was low. Abundant trade from local collieries, brickworks and ironworks made the canal one of the most prosperous in the country. The monopoly that the company had over transport in the area along with the high demand for coal meant that the £100 shares had risen to an incredible £1300. The enormous success of the Erewash Canal encouraged the promotion and construction, during the following decade, of the Cromford, Nottingham, Derby and Nutbrook canals. However, by 1834 the Canal Company was in trouble. High tolls plus the competition presented by the railways were taking trade away from the navigation. The Company reduced its tolls in an attempt to regain trade, but the railway system was expanding rapidly in the area and the Canal Company was unable to compete. The surrounding canals were bought up by the railway companies which further added to the problems of the Erewash Canal. The railway companies were happy to see these neighbouring waterways fall into disuse, thus putting an end to through traffic. By 1932 the Erewash Canal Company admitted defeat and was bought up by the Grand Union Canal Company. Having also bought the Loughborough and Leicester navigations, it was their intention to revitalise the network by creating a through navigation from the coalfields of Derbyshire to London. Sadly their attempts failed.

Nationalisation of the canals in 1947 brought the Erewash Canal under the administration of the British Transport Commission and in 1962 this body closed to navigation the upper section from Gallows Inn to Langley Mill. The need to supply water to the lower section for navigation and industry, however, meant that the upper section had still to be maintained and boats were allowed to navigate it upon application to the Commission and subsequently to its successor, the British Waterways Board. With the cessation of narrowboat carrying in 1963, such boats had been few, but the growing interest in pleasure boating resulted in more and more craft venturing up the canal from the popular River Trent. With increased use the canal gradually improved and the news that the major portion of it was to be designated a remainder waterway in the impending 1968 Transport Act was received locally with dismay. A public meeting led to the formation of the Erewash Canal Preservation and Development Association (ECPDA), a body consisting of representatives of boating and fishing interests, residents and local authorities. The need to convince local authorities of the value of the canal as an amenity was recognised at a very early stage and the association's efforts eventually met with success when, in 1972, Derbyshire and Nottinghamshire County Councils agreed to share the cost, with the then British Waterways Board, of the restoration of the canal to cruising waterway standards. This ambition was achieved in February 1983 when the canal was upgraded and boaters can now enjoy the entire course of the waterway. Further improvements are already afoot due to the continued involvement of the Erewash Initiative, a joint project involving British Waterways, Erewash Borough Council and Groundwork Erewash.

Shipley Lock (see page 69)

Long Eaton

The Erewash Canal leaves the Trent Navigation at Trent Lock. There is a useful supermarket just above Dockholme Lock, on the offside. North of the big concrete bridge carrying the A52 at Sandiacre is a delightfully landscaped free overnight mooring.

NAVIGATIONAL NOTES

1 Trent Lock should always be left *full*, with the top gates open, except when there is much traffic about. This will ensure that any flotsam coming down the canal is able to escape over the bottom gates.
2 The sanitary station at Sawley Locks should only be accessed from the backwater moorings on the river below the Lock.

● **Trent Lock**
An important waterway junction and a long-established boating centre. Boats navigating the Trent in this rather complicated area should beware of straying too near Thrumpton Weir.

● **Long Eaton**
Derbs. All services.
West Park Leisure Centre Wilsthorpe Road, Long Eaton NG10 4AA (0115 946 1400; www.erewash. gov.uk). *Open Mon, Wed, and Fri 07.30–22.30; Tue and*

Thu 06.30–22.30; Sat 06.30–21.00; and Sun 07.30–22.00. Charge.
Lock Cottage Sandiacre NG10 5LA. The last remaining toll house on the Erewash Canal. *Open Sun 14.30–17.00 throughout the summer and on B Hols.*

● **Derby Canal**
The closure of the Derby Canal ended Derby's link with the navigable waterways which dated back to the time when the Danes sailed up the River Derwent to found the settlement of Deoraby.

WALKING & CYCLING

The towpath is in excellent condition throughout the whole navigation and is suitable for both walking and cycling. The Nutbrook Trail is an off-road cycleway that runs from Long Eaton to Shipley and makes use of both canal towpath and abandoned railway track.

Pubs and Restaurants

✗ **Lock House Tearooms** Trent Lock (on the Erewash Canal), Lock Lane, Long Eaton NG10 2FY (0115 972 2288). Exquisite decoration, canal memorabilia, a waterways tableau in the entrance hall and menu boards which are in themselves a work of art all contribute to making this something special. The menu embraces seasonal specials: a wide range of teas and coffees, home-made cakes and scones, salads and hot toasties and jacket potatoes – not to mention the biggest Knickerbocker Glory this side of the Trent. *Open Wed-Fri 10.00-17.00 (winter 16.00) and Sat-Sun 10.00-18.00 (winter 17.00).* Also traditional canal art, giftware, antiques and collectables.

🍺 **Navigation Inn** Trent Lock, Long Eaton NG10 2FY (0115 973 2984). Large, popular, family pub with a garden and play area. Real ales and a wide range of reasonably priced food available *L and E, daily.* Moorings.

🍺 **Steamboat Inn** Trent Lock (on the Erewash Canal), Long Eaton NG10 2FY (0115 9463955). Built by the canal company in 1791, when it was called the Erewash Navigation Inn, it is now an upmarket canalside pub and restaurant. Real ale available. Food served *all day* from bar and à la carte restaurant. Children welcome *until 20.00.* Live music *Thu* and *regular* quiz nights.

🍺 **The Barge Inn** 177 Tamworth Road, Long Eaton NG10 1DH (0115 973 5265). Formerly the Old Ale House. Real ales. Bar meals available *Wed and Thu 12.00- 15.00, Fri and Sat 12.00-17.00, Sun 12.00-14.00.* Children welcome. Outside seating. Quiz night *Thu.* Skittle alley.

🍺 **The Hole in the Wall** Regent Street, Long Eaton NG10 2DL (0115 973 4920). Real ales. Meals *L and E, daily.* Children and dogs welcome. Garden.

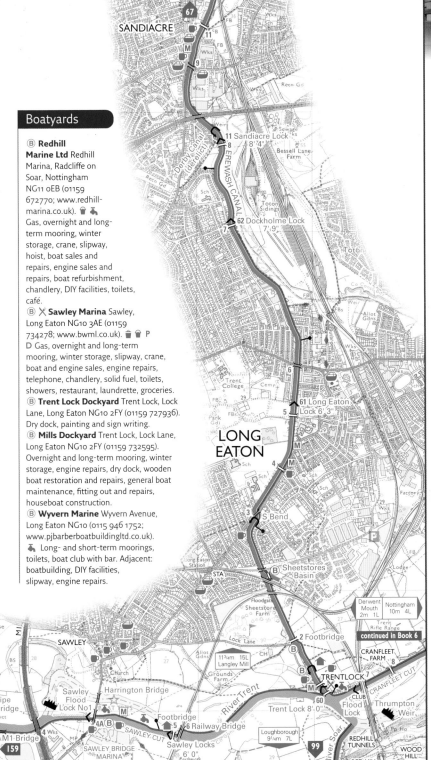

Boatyards

(B) **Redhill Marine Ltd** Redhill Marina, Radcliffe on Soar, Nottingham NG11 0EB (01159 672770; www.redhill-marina.co.uk). Gas, overnight and long-term mooring, winter storage, crane, slipway, hoist, boat sales and repairs, engine sales and repairs, boat refurbishment, chandlery, DIY facilities, toilets, café.

(B) ✕ **Sawley Marina** Sawley, Long Eaton NG10 3AE (01159 734278; www.bwml.co.uk). P D Gas, overnight and long-term mooring, winter storage, slipway, crane, boat and engine sales, engine repairs, telephone, chandlery, solid fuel, toilets, showers, restaurant, laundrette, groceries.

(B) **Trent Lock Dockyard** Trent Lock, Lock Lane, Long Eaton NG10 2FY (01159 727936). Dry dock, painting and sign writing.

(B) **Mills Dockyard** Trent Lock, Lock Lane, Long Eaton NG10 2FY (01159 732595). Overnight and long-term mooring, winter storage, engine repairs, dry dock, wooden boat restoration and repairs, general boat maintenance, fitting out and repairs, houseboat construction.

(B) **Wyvern Marine** Wyvern Avenue, Long Eaton NG10 (0115 946 1752; www.pjbarberboatbuildingltd.co.uk). Long- and short-term moorings, toilets, boat club with bar. Adjacent: boatbuilding, DIY facilities, slipway, engine repairs.

SANDIACRE

67
11

11 Sandiacre Lock
8' 4"

Bessell Lane Farm

62 Dockholme Lock
7' 9"

Toton Sidings

LONG EATON

61 Long Eaton Lock 6' 3"

S Bend

Sheetstores Basin

SAWLEY

2 Footbridge

11¾m 15L Langley Mill

CRANFLEET FARM

continued in Book 6

Derwent Mouth 2m 1L Nottingham 10m 4L

Trent Rifle Range

TRENTLOCK

Sawley Flood Lock No1

Harrington Bridge

CLUB

Thrumpton Weir

Trent Lock 8' 0"

Flood Lock

Pipe Bridge

M1-Bridge

159

Footbridge 5 6 Railway Bridge

SAWLEY CUT

Sawley Locks 6' 0"

Loughborough 9¼m 7L

99

REDHILL TUNNELS

RED HILL

WOOD HILL

Ilkeston

At Stanton Gate the M1 motorway looms up and then crosses the canal on its way to Leeds and points north. The outskirts of Ilkeston appear on the left side while, across the shallow Erewash valley, the course of the disused Nottingham Canal appears from the east, twisting along the contours of the hillside. Like the Erewash Canal, its course is generally northerly, but the two waterways do not meet until Langley Mill. Meanwhile the Erewash Canal passes extensive low-lying playing fields before reaching the pub at Gallows Inn Lock with *PO, stores, takeaways, laundrette and garages to the west of the navigation*. North of Gallows Inn Lock, the canal passes housing estates on one side and water meadows and a main line railway on the other. The town of Ilkeston is on the hillside on the west side of the canal. In spite of its proximity to these built-up areas, the canal is relatively unspoiled and surprisingly rural.

● **Sandiacre**
Derbs. PO, tel, stores, butcher, takeaway, chemist, off-licence, bank, garage. Services are all conveniently near the canal, but there is not much of interest in these outskirts, apart from the handsome Springfield Mill by the canal and the church, which is set on a rise called Stoney Clouds (clearly visible from the canal at Pasture Lock). The mill was built by Ernest Terah Hooley of Risley Hall in 1888. It houses four separate spiral staircase towers, each catering for an individual lace company. The canal was used for the transportation of the raw materials needed by the lace industry and for the finished articles. There are fine views over the industrial valley from the church which features some original Norman work inside, including carvings. Outside is an old tombstone bearing a skull and crossbones. The font is 600 years old.

● **Ilkeston**
Derbs. All services (except station). A market and textile town, with a compact main square. Pedestrianised areas make this a pleasant place to stroll. The parish church of St Mary dates from 1150 and has an unusual 14th-C stone screen. The annual three-day funfair is held in the Market Place in *Oct*.
Erewash Museum High Street, off East Street, Ilkeston DE7 5JA (0115 907 1141; www.erewash.gov.uk). Set in a late 18th-C house, the museum tells the story of the local and social history of the Erewash area as well as housing permanent displays of an Edwardian period kitchen and wash

house and an exhibition of children's toys. *Open Tue, Thu–Sat and B Hols 10.00-16.00. Closed Xmas Day, New Year and Jan.* Free.

● **Cossall**
Notts. Tel. Cossall is a refreshing contrast to Ilkeston, an attractive village built on top of a hill, spreading gently down to the Nottingham Canal. D.H. Lawrence used it as his background for Cossethay in *The Rainbow*. A narrow street winds among the houses, all of which seem to be surrounded by pretty gardens. The little church contains an oak screen made by village craftsmen; in the churchyard is a memorial to a soldier killed at Waterloo. Next to the church is Church Cottage, once the home of Louie Burrows to whom Lawrence was engaged. She was the model for the character of Ursula Brangwen.

● **Nutbrook Canal**
This little branch off the Erewash Canal used to lead for 4½ miles almost parallel to the Erewash Canal and slightly west of it. It still flows into the Erewash Canal upstream from Stanton Lock and parts of it are in water. The canal opened in 1795 at a cost of £22,800. Colliery owners Edward Miller-Mundy and Sir Henry Hunloke employed Benjamin Outram as engineer. It was in fact mining subsidence which caused much of the canal to be derelict by 1895 when it fell into disuse. Two of the three reservoirs which supplied the canal with water are still in evidence at Shipley. The short section that used to pass through the old Stanton Ironworks was filled in in 1962 and is now quite untraceable.

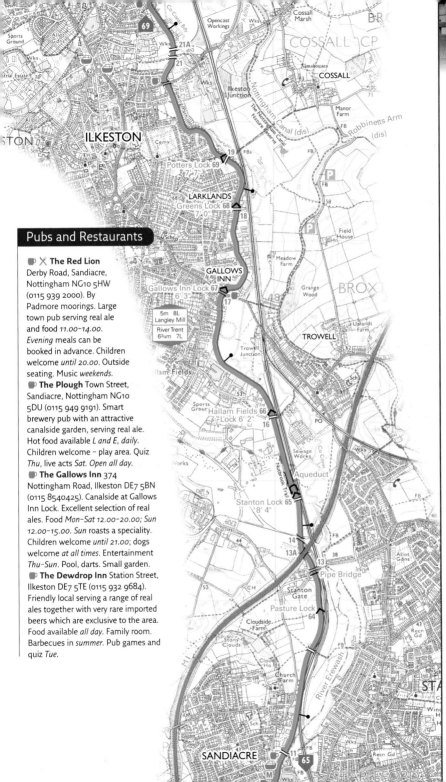

Pubs and Restaurants

🍺 ✕ **The Red Lion** Derby Road, Sandiacre, Nottingham NG10 5HW (0115 939 2000). By Padmore moorings. Large town pub serving real ale and food *11.00–14.00*. *Evening* meals can be booked in advance. Children welcome *until 20.00*. Outside seating. Music *weekends*.

🍺 **The Plough** Town Street, Sandiacre, Nottingham NG10 5DU (0115 949 9191). Smart brewery pub with an attractive canalside garden, serving real ale. Hot food available *L and E, daily*. Children welcome – play area. Quiz *Thu*, live acts *Sat. Open all day*.

🍺 **The Gallows Inn** 374 Nottingham Road, Ilkeston DE7 5BN (0115 8540425). Canalside at Gallows Inn Lock. Excellent selection of real ales. Food *Mon–Sat 12.00–20.00; Sun 12.00–15.00. Sun* roasts a speciality. Children welcome *until 21.00*; dogs welcome *at all times*. Entertainment *Thu–Sun*. Pool, darts. Small garden.

🍺 **The Dewdrop Inn** Station Street, Ilkeston DE7 5TE (0115 932 9684). Friendly local serving a range of real ales together with very rare imported beers which are exclusive to the area. Food available *all day*. Family room. Barbecues in *summer*. Pub games and quiz *Tue*.

Langley Mill

The northernmost section of the Erewash Canal is more isolated than the rest, and is definitely more rural and attractive. There are two splendid old canal buildings beside Shipley Lock – one was a stable and the other a slaughterhouse for worn-out canal horses. Just above the lock, the River Erewash creeps under the canal, which is carried above it on a very small aqueduct. Beyond the next pleasant rural stretch is Langley Mill, where the canal terminates at the Great Northern Basin beyond the final lock. Boatmen who have navigated the whole of the Erewash to this point are able to obtain a head of navigation plaque or a certificate. See notice in the basin for further details.

● Great Northern Basin

This restored basin, officially reopened in 1973, once formed the junction of the Erewash, Cromford and Nottingham canals. A feeder enters here from Moorgreen Reservoir. Since it passed through a coalfield on its way to the basin, it brought down a lot of coal silt – which over the years filled up the Great Northern Basin. Now the Erewash Canal Preservation & Development Association has restored the basin and lock, so that boats may reach a good mooring site with an enjoyable pub beside it. The Nottingham canal can never be restored here, for its closure was necessitated by mining subsidence – although lengths of the waterway are still in water, away from Langley Mill. The Cromford Canal, however, has nudged its way onto the BW priority list for restoration promoted by The Friends of the Cromford Canal (01773 833425; www.cromfordcanal.org.uk). It was originally engineered by William Jessop and Benjamin Outram, its 14½ mile length being completed in 1793. One of its chief instigators had been Richard Arkwright who had come to Cromford in 1771 and built the world's first successful water-powered cotton spinning mill. The canal was used for transporting raw cotton and textile yarn as well as coal, iron, lead and building stone. Jessop was joined by James Green in engineering the Nottingham Canal. Running from Langley Mill to the River Trent at Nottingham, it involved 20 locks including a flight of 14 at Wollaton. The stretch from Langley Mill to Lenton had to be abandoned in 1937 but the remaining section through to the River Trent is still in use. Both canals pass through an interesting mixture of heavily industrial surroundings and quiet open countryside. The northern 5 miles of the Cromford Canal, from Ambergate to Cromford (a length still in water) is strongly recommended to all walkers, country lovers and especially industrial archaeologists. Explorers will find all kinds of exciting things, including two aqueducts and a fine old pumping station, regularly in steam.

● Langley Mill

Derbs. PO, tel, stores, chemist, takeaways, station, garage. Near the head of the Erewash Canal, with the little Erewash river going past it.

● Eastwood

Notts. PO, tel, stores, banks, takeaways, farm shop, chemist, off-licence, fish & chips, garage. Up on the hill east of the Great Northern Basin, this mining town is best known as the childhood home of D.H. Lawrence. He was born at 8a Victoria Street, and the early part of Sons and Lovers is set in the town. The cemetery contains the Lawrence family graves. Lawrence's own headstone was brought from Vence in France and is now on display in the local library. A meeting at the Sun Inn in 1843, between local coal owners and iron masters, led to the construction of the Midland Railway.

D.H. Lawrence Birthplace Museum 8a Victoria Street, Eastwood NG16 3AW (01773 763312). Birthplace of the novelist, poet and playwright, David Herbert Lawrence. The house has been restored to reflect the lifestyle of a working-class Victorian family. There is also a video presentation of the author's Eastwood days. Also available from the museum is a leaflet entitled The Blue Line Trail which guides you around Eastwood's Lawrentian connections. Open daily, Apr-Oct 10.00-17.00; Nov-Mar 10.00-16.00. Charge.

Eastwood Library Wellington Place, Nottingham Road, Eastwood NG16 (01773 712209; www.nottinghamshire.gov.uk). The library houses a display of letters, books and first editions connected with D.H. Lawrence. Open Mon, Tue, Thu 09.30-19.00, Fri 09.30-18.00, Sat 09.30-16.00. Closed all day Wed. Free.

Heritage Centre Mansfield Road, Eastwood NG16 3DZ (01773 717353). Set in the mining company offices where Lawrence would have collected his wages. The displays tell you about Lawrence himself, the social history of the area and its changing community. Opening times as per Birthplace Museum. Charge.

Tourist Information Centre Market Place, Ripley DE5 3BT (01773 841488; www.visitambervalley.co.uk). Open Mon-Fri 09.30-17.30, Sat 09.30-15.00. This office produces an excellent guide to the Cromford Canal featuring both a complete walk along its 15-mile course, from the Great Northern Basin to its terminus at Cromford, and shorter circular walks taking in specific highlights. There is much of interest to visit in the Amber valley, to the north west of Langley Mill, all of which is very accessible by bus or train. So before navigating the waterway contact the TIC for their comprehensive information pack.

Boatyards

Ⓑ **Langley Mill Boat Co** Great Northern Basin, Derby Road, Langley Mill NG16 4AA (01773 760758). 🏠 🏠 ♿ D Pump out, gas, overnight mooring, long-term mooring (by arrangement), winter storage, boat repairs, engine repairs, boat building and fitting out, dry dock, DIY facilities, solid fuel, toilets, laundrette.

Ⓑ **ECPDA** Great Northern Basin, Derby Road, Langley Mill NG16 4AA (01773 779699; www. erewashcanal.org.uk). Moorings in Great Northern Basin.

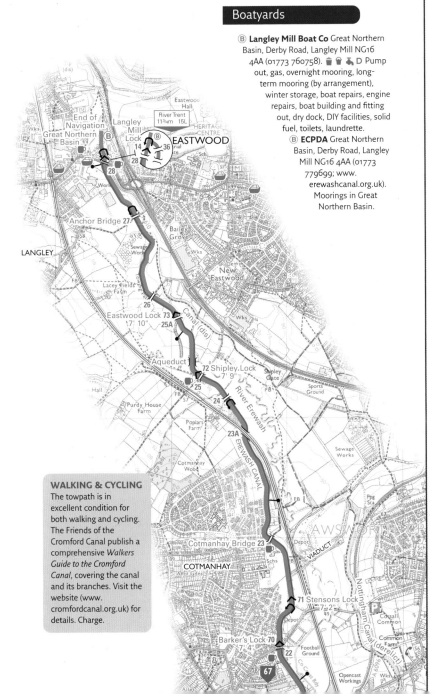

WALKING & CYCLING

The towpath is in excellent condition for both walking and cycling. The Friends of the Cromford Canal publish a comprehensive *Walkers Guide to the Cromford Canal*, covering the canal and its branches. Visit the website (www. cromfordcanal.org.uk) for details. Charge.

Pubs and Restaurants

The Bridge 107 Awsworth Road, Ilkeston DE7 8JF (0115 932 9903). Canalside pub with a large garden and adventure playground. Popular in season, this establishment has a welcoming, friendly atmosphere and dispenses real ales. Filled cobs available *at weekends*. Children welcome *until 20.00*, dogs *until closing time*. Large garden with children's play area. Moorings below Barker's Lock.

The Bridge Inn Bridge Street, Cotmanhay DE7 8RD (0115 932 2589). Small canalside local serving real ale. Children and dogs welcome. Garden with swings. Traditional pub games. Moorings.

The Great Northern Derby Road, Langley Mill NG16 4AA (01773 713834). At Great Northern Basin (the railway company was once owner of the canal). An excellent local pub serving real ale and traditional pub food *L and E*, *daily*. Children and dogs welcome. Canalside garden. Moorings.

The Derby Arms High Street, Heanor DE75 7EX (01773 713508). Real ale in a traditional drinkers' pub. Children welcome. Garden and pub games.

GERMANS COTTON ON

Before the arrival of Richard Arkwright and his partners in August 1771, the area around Cromford was a scattered community of families who earned their livings in the lead mines. By Christmas of that year Arkwright was already utilising the waters of a local lead mine drain, the Cromford Sough, and of the Bonsall Brook, to power what was soon to become the world's first successful water-powered cotton spinning mill. By 1777 there were two mills in Cromford and further developments were soon to take place in Derby and Matlock Bath. New housing built to accommodate the workers in Cromford featured an additional upper storey which acted as a workroom. Visiting industrialists from New England were entertained in the new Greyhound Hotel. So impressed were they with the developments in Cromford that they returned to America and used Sir Richard's mills as a model for their own. By 1783 continental Europe was catching up with the rest of the world when its first water-powered cotton spinning mill was erected near Ratingen, Germany. Johann Gottfried Brägelmann created his very own cotton new town and named it Cromford in recognition of Arkwright's innovation.

Trent Lock (see page 65)

GRAND UNION CANAL – LEICESTER SECTION AND THE RIVER SOAR

MAXIMUM DIMENSIONS

Norton Junction to Foxton Junction
Length: 72'
Beam: 7'
Headroom: 7'

Market Harborough to Leicester
Length: 72'
Beam: 13'
Headroom: 7'

Leicester West Bridge to River Trent
Length: 72'
Beam: 14' 4"
Headroom: 7' 6"

MILEAGE

NORTON JUNCTION to:
Crick: 5 miles
Welford Arm: 15½ miles
Market Harborough Arm: 23¼ miles
Blaby: 36 miles
Leicester West Bridge: 41¼ miles
Cossington Lock: 49 miles
Barrow upon Soar: 53¼ miles
Loughborough Basin: 57¼ miles
Zouch Lock: 60½ miles
RIVER TRENT: 66¼ miles

Locks: 59

MANAGER

Norton Junction to Kings Lock 38
(including the Welford Arm and the
Market Harborough Arm): 01908 302500
enquiries.southeast@britishwaterways.co.uk
Kings Lock 38 to the Trent: 01636 704481
enquiries.emidlands@britishwaterways.co.uk

The River Soar is a tributary of the River Trent and is approximately 40 miles long. It runs mainly through Leicestershire, rising at Smockington Hollow on the Warwickshire border. For most of the way from Aylestone (just south of Leicester) to the Trent, the Soar forms the Leicester section of the Grand Union Canal.

In 1634 Thomas Skipworth of Cotes attempted to make the River 'portable for barges and boats up to the town of Leicester' by means of a grant from King Charles I in return for 10 per cent of the profits. This scheme was a failure. But, after several other attempts, prominent citizens of Loughborough secured an Act of Parliament in 1776, and the River Soar Navigation (Loughborough Canal) was opened two years later, bringing great prosperity to the town. The continuation of the navigation up to Leicester (the Leicester Canal) was built under an Act passed in 1791. Its opening was marked by the arrival in Leicester of two boats loaded with provisions from Gainsborough on 21 February 1794. The engineers concerned with construction of the River Soar Navigation were John Smith and John May (Loughborough Canal) and William Jessop (Leicester Canal). With the completion of the Grand Junction Canal between Brentford and Braunston, a connection was soon established between this and the River Soar Navigation, built to the narrow gauge, thwarting the Grand Junction's scheme for a system of wide canals.

The Loughborough Navigation was one of the most prosperous canals in England, by virtue of its position in relation to the Nottinghamshire/Derbyshire coalfield and the Erewash Canal. However, railway competition took its usual toll, and although trade revived when the Grand Union Canal purchased the Loughborough and Leicester navigations in 1931, the improvement proved temporary. It remains a pretty, rural river and is much enjoyed by those on pleasure craft.

Norton Junction

Leaving Norton Junction there is a quiet, meandering mile through light woods and rolling fields before the motorway and railway take over; the canal passes the back door of the Watford Gap service area. The noise and bustle of the motorway and main railway line intrude, accentuating the sedate pace of those using the original of the three transport systems. The Watford Gap motorway service station (south of bridge 6) is by no means inaccessible from the towpath and could provide the boater with *24hr* sustenance and provisions. Otherwise the Leicester Section of the Grand Union Canal is very attractive, quiet and in no hurry to reach Foxton. It wanders through rolling, hilly country, riverlike with constant changes of direction that guide it gently north eastwards. It avoids villages and civilisation generally; only the old wharves serve as a reminder of the canal's function. The slow course of the navigation, its relative emptiness and its original plan combine to make it very narrow in places; reeds, overhanging trees and shallow banks quite often do not allow two boats to pass. After negotiating Watford Locks and reaching the summit level of 412ft there is nothing strenuous to look forward to, as this level continues for the next 20½ miles. Four of these locks form a staircase – adopt a 'one up, one down' procedure, and use both ground and side paddles when going either up or down. At Watford the waterway swings east away from the M1 for good. The locks and Crick Tunnel with its wooded approaches offer canal excitement to contrast with the quiet of the landscape.

NAVIGATIONAL NOTES

1 Watford locks are open *daily*. The locks open *from 08.00* but the time of the last boat through depends on the time of year. From *end Apr–end Sep, last boat into lock is 18.15*; *during Oct and mid-Mar–end Apr 16.15*; *from Nov–mid Mar 14.45*. The exact times are variable depending when Easter falls, therefore, it is advisable to contact the lock keeper.
2 Local branches of the IWA have produced a guide to the Leicester Arm obtainable from various lockside positions (using a Watermate key) or from the IWA's Northampton Branch website (http://northampton.waterways.org.uk and select 'Local Links').

● **Welton**
Northants. PO box, tel. The village climbs up the side of a steep, winding hill, which makes it compact and attractive, especially around the church.

● **Watford**
Northants. PO box, tel. Set in the middle of wooded parkland, Watford gives the impression of being a private village. The church and Watford Court dominate, and luckily the M1 has made no impact. The 13th-C church contains some interesting monuments. The Court is partly 17th-C, although there are Victorian additions. The rich brown stone used throughout the village adds to the feeling of unity. Bread and milk are available from the lock keeper's cabin at Watford top lock.

● **Crick Tunnel**
1528yds long, the tunnel was opened in 1814. All tunnels built in this area suffered great problems in construction. Quicksands caused the route of the tunnel to be changed and greatly affected work. Stephenson found similar difficulties when building the nearby Kilsby Tunnel for the London to Birmingham railway.

Pubs and Restaurants

▶ ✕ **The New Inn** Watling Street, Buckby Wharf, Long Buckby NN6 7PW (01327 844747; www.gillies-inns.com). Canalside, at Buckby Top Lock. Cosy alcoved free house, serving real ale and a range of inexpensive meals and snacks *all day, every day*. Children welcome. Canalside seating and patio. Darts, dominoes and large screen TV. Moorings. *Open all day.*

✕ ♀ **The Thai Garden** Station Road, Watford Gap, Northampton NN6 7UL (01327 703621). Authentic Thai Cuisine and bar. *Open every day 12.00–14.00 and 18.00–late.*

WALKING & CYCLING

The towpath along the entire Grand Union Leicester Section, including both arms, is variable and little used in places and can be followed by foot and bicycle (although in places bank erosion will require the cyclist to dismount for safety). However, to the north, where it follows the course of the River Soar, numerous water meadows and their attendant hedges throw up regular obstacles in the form of gates and stiles. These pose a bigger problem for cyclists than for walkers. *See* page 71 for information on negotiating Crick Tunnel.

Boatyards

Ⓑ **Weltonfield Narrowboats**

Welton Hythe, Daventry NN11 2LG (01327 842282; www.weltonfield.co.uk). Beside bridge 2. 🛒 D E Pump out, gas, overnight mooring, long-term mooring, winter storage, wet dock, slipway, chandlery, solid fuel, books, maps, boat building and repairs, boat sales, engine sales and repairs, brokerage, toilets. *Emergency call out.*

Crick Tunnel 1528 yds

Field House Farm
74
Welford Road
Old Tunnel Farm
Tunnel Farm
Bungalow Farm
Limes Farm
10
9A
The Old Lodge
M45
17
Home Farm
WATFORD GAP
Cattle Grid
9
Kilsby Road
Burnums Farm
Long Spinney
Barley Spinney
8 Kilsby Road Bridge
Cattle Grid
FORD
Park House
7 Ashby's Bridge
M1 Bridge
Jurassic Way
Bluebell Spinney
Watford Locks
52'6"
Staircase 3 – 6
Bottom Lock 1
Jurassic Way
Sewage Farm
PO
Watford
Foxholes
WATLING STREET ROMAN ROAD
Cricket Field
Watford Lodge
6 Welton Station Bridge
WATFORD GAP MOTORWAY SERVICES
Brockhill Lodge
5A
GRAND UNION CANAL LEICESTER SECTION
Langborough Barn
Langborough Clump
Welton Lodge Farm
60' max
5 Watling Street Bridge
Welton House Farm
Marina
3 Ball's Bridge
Ryehill Lodge
Sewage Works
Greenhill Farm
Oaklands Farm
Home Farm
WELTON
Welton House
Welton Place
Crockwell Hill
Welton Grange

Braunston Turn	Gayton Junction
4¼m 6L	12½m 7L

Ⓑ Marina Ⓜ

15½m 7L Welford Arm
Cornerhill Spinney
Crockwell Farm
103
To Birmingham
GRAND UNION CANAL – MAIN LINE
9
Norton Junction
10 Top Lock No 7
Thrupp Grounds
11 Watling Street Bridge
continued in Book 1
8
12
13
Long Buckby Wharf
To London
Grand Union Canal
Welton Manor

Yelvertoft

Leaving Crick Tunnel the navigation dodges the village and passes the site of an old wharf, followed by a large marina. After skirting Crack's Hill, a curious tree-topped mound, the canal wanders to the east in a series of loops which cause it to miss both Yelvertoft and Winwick, the only villages in the section. Hills surround the course of the canal, encouraging its meandering. At one point it passes under the same road three times in under a mile. Occasional woods add to the pleasure of the isolation. After Winwick, a vague north east course is resumed, passing the long-abandoned village of Elkington. There are no locks, but a regular procession of brick-arched bridges serves as a reminder that it is still a canal.

Jurassic Way

Woods Farm

Pages Lodge Farm **76**

30

29A

ELKING

Heygate's Lodge 29

Heygate Lodge

Cot

Elkington Bridge 28
Elkington Farm Cottage

Farm

YELVERTOFT FIELDSIDE COVERT

27 Mountain Barn Bridge

Mountain Barn

26 Clay Barn Bridge

WINWICK MANOR FARM

Chester's Bridge 25

Barn Ground Spinney

Bush C Spinn

Larch Spinney

24 Smart's Bridge

WINW

Flint Hill Farm
Pit (dis)

20

Darker's Bridge 23

New House Farm

WINWICK GRANGE

School

FB

YELVERTOFT

Skew Bridge 19

eep Dip

112

116

18

21

22

Haddon Road Bridge

Flinthill

GRAND UNION CANAL

129   16

17

Foxes Farm

Crackshill Farm

15

CRACK'S HILL

14

Crick Road

13 Crick Lodge Bridge

The Bungalow

118

Abattoir

Factory 129

Marina

B

Nursery

CRICK

Crick Wharf

Sch

132

12

B

11

132

136

Cottage Farm

PO

10½m 0L
Welford Arm
Norton Jnc
5m 7L

CP

154

73 Crick Tunnel
1528 yds

Field Ho Farm

Boatyards

Ⓑ **ABNB** Crick Wharf, West Haddon Road, Crick NN6 7XT (01788 822115/07721 378653; www.abnb.co.uk). Boat sales.

Ⓑ **Crick Wharf** West Haddon Road, Crick NN6 7XT (0116 236 6279/07765 405794; www.crickwharf.co.uk). 🔧

Ⓑ **Crick Marina** West Haddon Road, Crick NN6 7SQ (01788 824034; www.crickmarina.com). 🚿 🚽 🔧 D (E by arrangement) Pump out, gas, solid fuel, overnight mooring, dry dock, boat repairs, toilets, laundrette.

Ⓑ **D. & J. Narrowboats** The Boatshed, Crick Wharf, West Haddon Road, Crick NN6 7XT (01788 822611; www.djnarrowboats.co.uk). Boat building and fitting out.

- **Crick**
  Northants. PO, tel, stores, off-licence. A large village built around the junction of two roads. There are several attractive stone houses, and the large church has managed to escape restoration. It contains much decorative stonework and a circular Norman font. There is an intriguing second-hand shop *open Wed, Fri and Sat 14.00–18.00* that could well warrant a visit.
- **Yelvertoft**
  Northants. PO, tel, stores, off-licence, butcher, garage. Set back from the canal, the village is built round a wide main street, terminated in the east by the church. Sadly, many of the original thatched roofs have been replaced.
- **Winwick**
  Northants. Tel. One mile south east of bridge 23. The 16th-C Manor House, built of richly decorated brick and with an ornamental Tudor gateway, is the major building in this neat, sleepy, village.

WALKING & CYCLING

Walkers and cyclists bypassing Crick Tunnel need to take the short track on the right of the tunnel mouth and, on joining the minor road, turn left. Follow this into the village and turn right down Boathorse Lane. When the road bends sharply to the left walkers may follow the footpath straight ahead (signposted to West Haddon), cross a field along the hedgerow (still following the waymarking to West Haddon) and, having negotiated the stile, bear left diagonally, downhill across the next field following the line of the drainage pits to the sign in the hedge, which is immediately above the northern tunnel cutting. Cyclists are advised to follow the road through the village, bearing right and rejoining the canal at bridge 12.

Pubs and Restaurants

Edwards of Crick West Haddon Road, Crick NN6 7SQ (01788 822517; www.edwardsrestaurant.co.uk). Beside bridge 12. Restaurant and coffee house offering a wide-ranging menu from inexpensive snacks *L* through to a mouth-watering à la carte selection, available *all day*. Good value *Sun* lunch. Everything home-made, including the bread. Excellent wine list. *Closed Sun E and Mon (except B Hols).*

The Red Lion 52 Main Street, Crick NN6 7TX (01788 822342). Real ale dispensed in a cosy, unadulterated pub with low ceilings and coal fires. Excellent home-cooked meals served with fresh vegetables *L and E (not Sun E)*. Children *L only*. Dogs welcome. Patio seating.

The Wheatsheaf Main Street, Crick NN67TU (01788 822284). Lively, friendly local dispensing real ale. Food available *L and E and all day Sun*. Children welcome. Pool. Garden. *Open all day*.

The Royal Oak Church Street, Crick NN6 7TP (01788 822340). Attractive old village local. Real ales. Bar snacks available *Fri, Sat and Sun*. Garden. Skittles, pool and darts. *Open Mon–Fri 16.30–23.00, Sat and Sun all day*. B & B.

The Knightly Arms 49 High Street, Yelvertoft NN6 6LF (01788 822401). Popular village local serving real ale. Home-cooked food available *L and E*. Traditional *Sun* lunch. Children and dogs welcome. Garden. Dominoes and crib. *Occasional* entertainment.

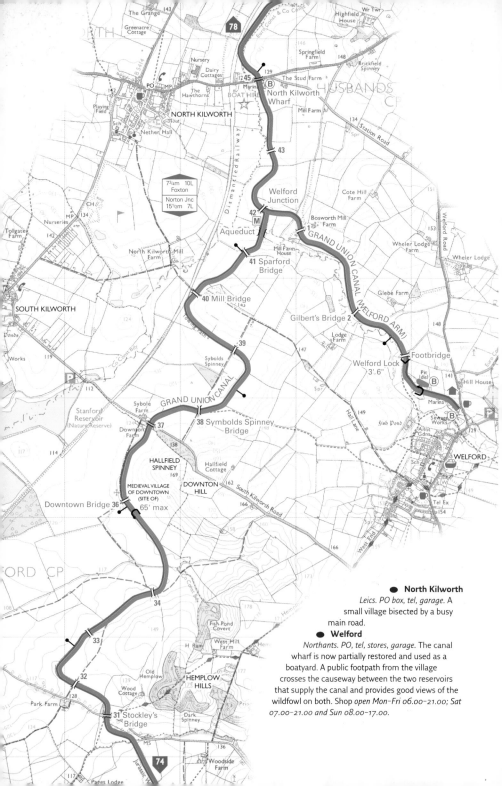

78

The Grange 143

Greenacre Cottage

B5414

Nursery

Dairy Cottages

The Hawthorns

PO MP

Nether Hall

NORTH KILWORTH

Sch

Playing Field

Highfield House

Wr Twr

Springfield Farm 148

Brickfield Spinney

146

45 129

Marina

The Stud Farm

North Kilworth Wharf

BOAT HIRE

Mill Farm

HUSBANDS CP

134 Station Road

Spr

43

CH

Nurseries

MP 134

Tollgate Farm

142

North Kilworth Mill Farm

7¾m 10L
Foxton

Norton Jnc
15½m 7L

Dismantled Railway

Welford Junction

Cote Hill Farm

151

42
M

Bosworth Mill Farm

153

Wheler Lodge Farm

Wheler Lodge

Aqueduct

Mill Farm House

GRAND UNION CANAL (WELFORD ARM)

Welford Road

41 Sparford Bridge

SOUTH KILWORTH

Ponds

Works 119

124

40 Mill Bridge 143

Gilbert's Bridge **2**

Lodge Farm

Glebe Farm

148

39

Sybolds Spinney

147

Welford Lock 3'-6"

Footbridge

Pit (dis) **B** 141

Hill House

P

112

Sybole Farm

Stanford Reservoir (Nature Reserve)

Downton Farm

37

GRAND UNION CANAL

38 Symbolds Spinney Bridge

Marina

Sewage Works

B

P

WELFORD 129

138

Hallfield Cottage

149

Hall Lane

fish pond

Allot Gdns

HALLFIELD SPINNEY 169

DOWNTON HILL

162 South Kilworth Road

Sch

WELFORD

117 114

MEDIEVAL VILLAGE OF DOWNTOWN (SITE OF)

Downtown Bridge **36**

65' max

166

Tel Ex

154

ORD CP

117

34

Fish Pond Covert

178

West Hill Farm

H Ram

166

West End

33

108

124

32

139

Old Hemplow

Wood Cottage

HEMPLOW HILLS

177

Park Farm

128

31 Stockley's Bridge

Dark Spinney

136

74

Woodside Farm

117

Pages Lodge

● **North Kilworth**
Leics. PO box, tel, garage. A
small village bisected by a busy
main road.

● **Welford**
Northants. PO, tel, stores, garage. The canal
wharf is now partially restored and used as a
boatyard. A public footpath from the village
crosses the causeway between the two reservoirs
that supply the canal and provides good views of the
wildfowl on both. Shop *open Mon-Fri 06.00-21.00; Sat
07.00-21.00 and Sun 08.00-17.00.*

Welford

Continuing north east the canal wanders on through open fields, backed by wooded hills to the east. To the west there are splendid views over the Avon valley. The river passes under the canal before the Welford Arm. Beyond the valley the spires of South and North Kilworth churches can be seen for several miles. The Welford Arm, which was completed in 1814, branches away to the south east for 1¼ miles, linking the canal with the Welford and Sulby reservoirs, and reaches its terminus in a small basin; there is one shallow lock on the arm. Otherwise it is quiet and tree-lined, following closely the path of the Avon, whose source is just east of Welford. The arm was reopened to navigation in 1969, having been derelict for some years. The main line continues, entering the wooded cutting that announces Husbands Bosworth Tunnel. There are no locks, but many of the bridges are original, fine faded red brick, echoing the seclusion of the canal.

Battle of Naseby 1645 2 miles east of Welford. Here Fairfax's New Model Army routed the Royalists under King Charles I, ensuring the end of the Civil War.

Stanford Hall Lutterworth LE17 6DH (01788 860250; www.stanfordhall.co.uk). Two miles west of bridge 31. A William and Mary brick mansion (the south elevation is in stone), built in 1697–1700, with a Georgian stable block. Furniture, paintings, costume and a replica of the experimental flying machine built by Percy Pilcher in 1898. Walled rose garden and nature trail. Teas, shop and craft centre. *Open Easter–Sep, Sun, B Hol Mon 13.30–17.30. Last admission 17.00. (Craft centre open Sun and B Hols.)* Charge.

Boatyards

Ⓑ **Welford Marina** Canal Wharf, Welford NN6 6JQ (01858 575995). ☂ ♻
🛢 D E Gas, overnight mooring, long-term mooring, boat and engine repairs, boat fitting out, wet dock, dry dock, DIY facilities, solid fuel, toilets.

Ⓑ **Kilworth Wharf Leisure** Kilworth Marina, North Kilworth LE17 6JB (01858 880484; www.kilworthmarina.co.uk). By bridge 45. ☂ ♻
🛢 D E Pump out, gas, day-hire boats, overnight mooring, long-term mooring (up to 26ft only), winter storage, slipway, wet dock, chandlery, boat sales and repairs, engine sales and repairs, boat fitting out, DIY facilities, books, maps and gifts, toilets, solid fuel. *Emergency call out.*

Pubs and Restaurants

🍺 ✗ **The Wharf Inn** Canal Wharf, Welford NN6 6JQ (01858 575075; www.wharfinn.co.uk). Warm, friendly pub over 200 years old, popular with the locals, dispensing real ale and home-made food *L and E (not Sun E)* and for takeaway. Carvery *Sun L*. Children and dogs welcome. Large, well-kept garden. Live music *first Thu of month*. Open-air theatre functions *during Aug*. B & B.

🍺 ✗ **The Elizabethan** 8 High Street, Welford NN6 6HT (01858 575311; www.theelizabethan.co.uk). Country pub and restaurant serving real ale and food *L and E*. Specially priced cocktails at *weekends*. Children and dogs welcome (dogs in bar area only). Garden. Karaoke *at weekends*. Large-screen TVs.

🍺 ✗ **The White Lion** Lutterworth Road, North Kilworth, Lutterworth LE17 6EP (01858 880260). Real ales and food available *L and E*. Children and dogs welcome. Garden and pub games.

🍺 ✗ **The Swan Inn** Lutterworth Road, North Kilworth, Leicester LE17 6EP (01858 880957). Real ales and bar snacks *L and E (not Wed L)*. Traditional *Sun* roasts. Children welcome.

Husbands Bosworth

Continuing north east, the canal enters a remote, but attractive stretch. There are no villages on the canal here, Husbands Bosworth being hidden by the tunnel. The A50 crosses over the tunnel and meets the A427 in Husbands Bosworth. The canal runs north east through fields to the top of Foxton Locks. It then falls 75ft to join the former Leicester & Northampton Union Canal. At the bottom of the locks the 5½ mile Market Harborough Arm branches off to the east.

NAVIGATIONAL NOTES

Foxton Locks are open daily as per Watford Locks, *see* page 68.

● **Husbands Bosworth**
Leics. PO, tel, stores (www.husbandsbosworth.info). Access from canal: walk up the lane from bridge 46. The shop is *open daily 05.30–17.30 (Wed and Sat 19.30).*
Husbands Bosworth Tunnel 1166yds long, the tunnel was opened in 1813.
Foxton Locks Gumley Road, Foxton, Market Harborough LE16 7RA (www.foxtonlocks.com). The Foxton staircase was opened in 1812. There are two staircases of five locks each with a passing pound in the middle. Check each flight of five is clear before you enter.
Foxton Inclined Plane Foxton, Market Harborough LE16 7RA. In 1900 an inclined plane was opened to bypass Foxton Locks. Two caissons carrying either two narrowboats or one barge moved sideways on rails up and down the plane. A steam-driven winch pulling an endless cable was used to start the caissons moving. The journey time was reduced from 70 to 12 minutes. Mechanical problems and high running costs, plus the fact that the planned widening of the Watford flight never took place, soon made the plane a white elephant. The cut leading to the bottom of the plane is still navigable, and the plane itself can still be traced, running at right angles to the east of the locks. Exploratory trail and museum *open Easter–Oct, daily 10.00–17.00; Nov–Easter, weekends 10.00–16.00 and some weekdays.* Telephone for details. Charge. Restoration is in the hands of **Foxton Inclined Plane Trust** Middle Lock, Foxton Locks, Foxton, Market Harborough LE16 7RA (0116 279 2657; www.fipt.org.uk). There is a picnic site, car park and toilets (including disabled) at bridge 60, beside the Gumley road. Charge.

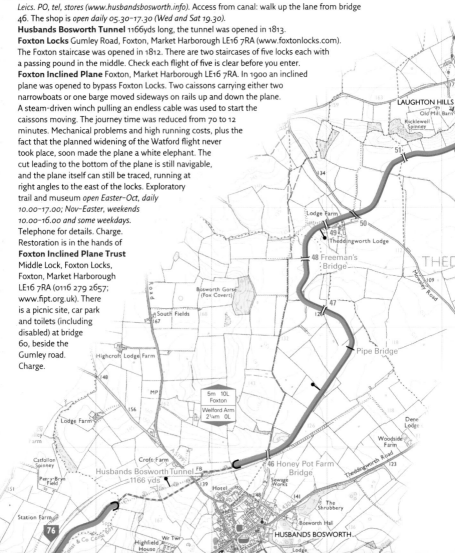

Boatyards

ⓑ **Foxton Boat Services** Bottom Lock, Foxton, Market Harborough LE16 7RA (0116 2792285; www.foxtonboats.co.uk). 🛆 🛆 ⚓ D Pump out, gas, narrowboat hire, day-craft hire, overnight mooring, long-term mooring, winter storage, slipway, crane (20 tons), boat fitting-out, chandlery, boat sales and repairs, engine sales and repairs, wet dock, DIY facilities, telephone, toilets, showers, groceries, tearoom, laundrette, books, maps and gifts. Commercial boat hire. *24 hour emergency call-out.*

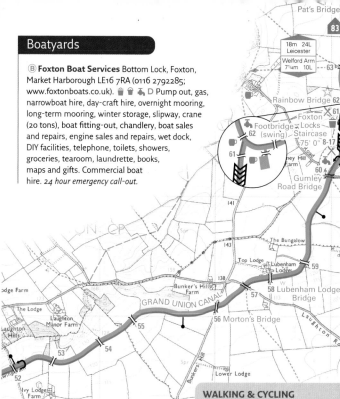

WALKING & CYCLING

Walkers and cyclists confronted with Husbands Bosworth Tunnel should take the track climbing up to the left of the tunnel mouth and follow it over the hill to the road on the outskirts of the village (A50). Cross this road and follow the track over the disused railway line, down a tree-lined glade, rejoining the waterway at the eastern tunnel portal.

Pubs and Restaurants

🍺 ✗ **The Bell Inn** Kilworth Road, Husbands Bosworth LE17 6JZ (01858 880246). Real ale and food available *L and E, daily.* Family room – children welcome. Garden. Live entertainment *Sat evening.*

🍺 **The Bell** Main Street, Gumley LE16 7RU (0116 279 2476). Friendly, old village local serving real ale and real cider. Food available *L and E (not Sun or Mon E).* Children over 5 catered for. Traditional pub games (no machines) and fires in winter. Garden.

🍺 **Bridge 61** Bottom Lock, Foxton, Market Harborough LE16 7RA (0116 279 2285).

Small, popular pub serving real ale and bar snacks. Children welcome and there is outside seating.

🍺 ✗ **The Foxton Locks Inn** Bottom Lock, Foxton, Market Harborough LE16 7RA (0116 279 1515). At the foot of the famous Foxton Locks. Pub garden overlooking the canal. Real ales and food available *L and E,* together with morning coffee's and pastries.

✗ **Top Lock Coffee Shop** Top Lock, Foxton Market Marborough LE16 7RA (0116 279657). *Open daily, 10.00–18.00.* Coffee, tea, breakfasts, various hot rolls and cream teas.

BOAT TRIPS

Vagabond Foxton Boats, Bottom Lock, Foxton, Market Harborough LE16 7RA (0116 279 2285; www.foxtonboats.co.uk). Canal trips for casual visitors *on summer Sun afternoons and B Hols* from Foxton bottom lock; available for charter by parties any other day.

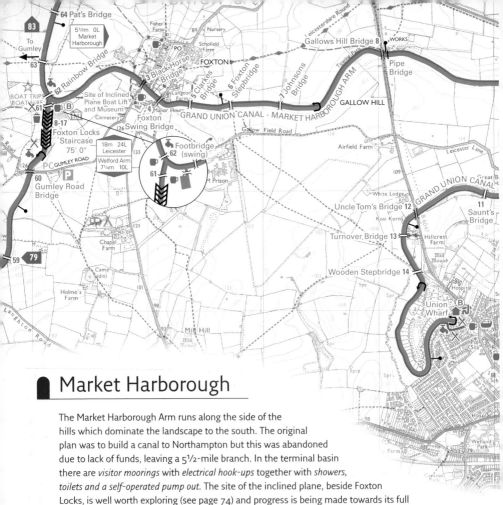

Market Harborough

The Market Harborough Arm runs along the side of the
hills which dominate the landscape to the south. The original
plan was to build a canal to Northampton but this was abandoned
due to lack of funds, leaving a 5½-mile branch. In the terminal basin
there are *visitor moorings* with *electrical hook-ups* together with *showers,
toilets and a self-operated pump out*. The site of the inclined plane, beside Foxton
Locks, is well worth exploring (see page 74) and progress is being made towards its full
restoration with a grant of £1.78m from the Heritage Lottery Fund.

● **Foxton**
Leics. PO box, tel. A village built on the side of a hill,
either side of the canal, in pretty countryside. There is
an excellent information leaflet and village trail
available from Foxton Boat Services and Market
Harborough Tourist Information Centre.

● **Market Harborough**
*Leics. PO, tel, stores, off-licence, takeaways, chemist,
fish & chips, garage, banks, station.* Established as a
market town by 1203, Market Harborough still retains
much of its rural elegance and local importance.
There is an antique and collectors market *every Sun* in
the market hall (01604 882399).
Traveline (0870 608 2 608). For details on bus
travel. *Open 07.00–21.00.*
Frank Haynes Gallery 50 Station Road, Great
Bowden, Market Harborough LE16 7HN (01858
464862; www.harborough.gov.uk). 3/4 mile north of

the station. Two galleries with paintings and pottery
from the region. Cards, etc. *Open Thu–Sun
10.00–17.00. Free.*
Harborough Leisure Centre Northampton Road,
Market Harborough LE16 9HF (01858 410115;
www.harboroughleisurecentre.com). The usual mix of
swimming pool, child-enticing water features, fitness
room, etc. Also bar, bistro and crèche.
Harborough Museum Council Offices, Adam and
Eve Street, Market Harborough LE16 7AG (01858
821085; www.harborough.gov.uk). Contains the Civic
Society's own collection and illustrates local life from
the earliest times. Relics of the Battle of Naseby, a
reconstructed bootmaker's workshop and the
Symington Collection of corsetry. *Open Jan–Dec,
Mon–Sat 10.00–16.30 and Sun 14.00– 17.00.*
Free. Disabled access via council offices so contact
staff in advance *on Sat, Sun and B Hols.*

Harborough Theatre Church Square, Market Harborough LE16 7NB (01858 463673; www.harboroughtheatre.com).

Market Harborough Canal Basin Significant as the site of the first Inland Waterways Association campaigning rally held in 1950 which, arguably, laid the foundations for a resurgence in canal interest that could easily be taken for granted by the contemporary pleasure boater. The canal basin – or Union Wharf – has been extended and the surrounding area developed with apartments, a time-share base and small business units, making it completely unrecognisable from the wharfs and timber storage sheds that used to predominate.

Parish Church of St Dionysius High Street, Market Harborough LE16 7NB (www.harborough-anglican.org.uk). Built in the 14thC by Scropes and enlarged a century later.

Old Grammar School High Street, Market Harborough LE16. Founded by Robert Smyth. It stands on wooden carved pillars, and behind the arches was held the ancient butter market. The building was used as the grammar school until 1892 and is now a meeting hall.

Tourist Information Centre Council Offices, Adam and Eve Street, Market Harborough LE16 7AG (01858 821010; www.harborough.gov.uk). *Open Mon–Fri 08.45–17.00, Sat 09.30–12.30.*

NAVIGATIONAL NOTES

A Watermate key is required to operate Foxton Swing Bridge No 4.

WALKING & CYCLING

Brampton Valley Way runs for 14 miles along an old railway track and links Market Harborough with the northern outskirts of Northampton. It makes use of two old tunnels and passes a selection of old steam locomotives at Chapel Brampton.

Pubs and Restaurants

The Black Horse Main Street, Foxton, Market Harborough LE16 7RD (01858 545250). Real ales and lovely gardens. An excellent selection of home-made food available *L and E, daily (not Mon, or Sun E)*. (Bookings advisable *E in summer, and Sun L*). Children and dogs welcome. Garden with animals for children. Jazz *Wed*. Crib, darts and skittle alley.

The Shoulder of Mutton Main Street, Foxton, Market Harborough LE16 7RB (01858 545666; www.theshoulderofmutton.co.uk). Real ales and Chinese food (including takeaway) available *L and E (not Mon in winter)* in a pub close to Foxton Locks. Children welcome. Large garden. Patio seating. B & B.

Waterfront Restaurant Union Wharf, Leicester Road, Market Harborough LE16 7UW (01858 468100). Bright, airy restaurant in a canalside warehouse serving a wide range of snacks and meals. Children welcome. *Open Tue–Fri L and E; weekends all day from 11.00.*

The Union Inn Hotel and Restaurant Leicester Road, Market Harborough LE16 7AY (01858 433277). Family inn with a relaxed atmosphere. Real ales and a wide variety of food available *L and E (not Sun E)*. Children welcome. Garden and children's play area. B & B.

The Angel Hotel High Street, Market Harborough LE16 7AF (01858 462702; www.theangelhotel.net). Hotel serving food from full à la carte restaurant menu through to bar meals, served *L and E, daily*.

Three Swans Hotel High Street, Market Harborough LE16 7NJ (01858 466644; www.bestwestern.co.uk). Real ales and a comprehensive range of bar and restaurant food *L and E, daily*. Children welcome. Courtyard seating. B & B.

The Red Cow 58–59 High Street, Market Harborough LE16 7AF (01858 463637). Real ale and food available *L*. Outside seating.

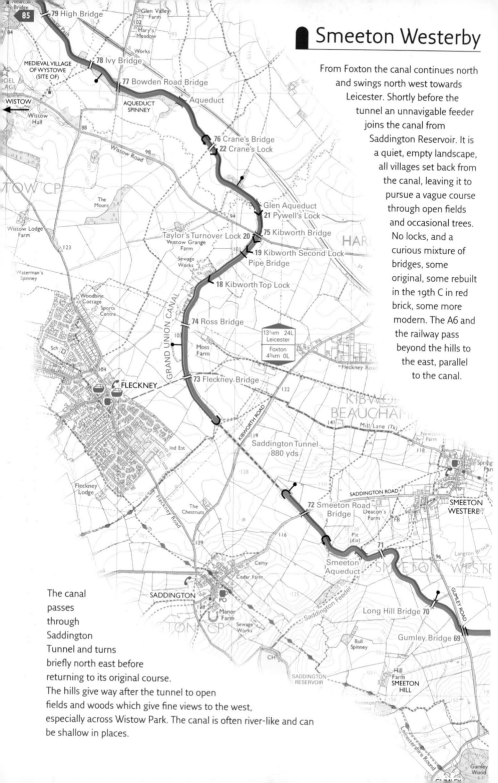

Smeeton Westerby

79 High Bridge

Glen Valley Farm

Mary's Meadow

Works

78 Ivy Bridge

MEDIEVAL VILLAGE OF WYSTOWE (SITE OF)

77 Bowden Road Bridge

Aqueduct

AQUEDUCT SPINNEY

WISTOW

Wistow Hall

76 Crane's Bridge
22 Crane's Lock

Wistow Road

The Mount

Wistow Lodge Farm

Glen Aqueduct
21 Pywell's Lock

Taylor's Turnover Lock 20
Wistow Grange Farm

75 Kibworth Bridge

HAR

19 Kibworth Second Lock
Pipe Bridge

Sewage Works

Waterman's Spinney

18 Kibworth Top Lock

Woodbine Cottage
Sports Centre

74 Ross Bridge

13¼m   24L
Leicester

Foxton
4¾m   0L

Moss Farm

FLECKNEY

Fleckney Road

73 Fleckney Bridge

GRAND UNION CANAL

Sch

Ind Est

Fleckney Lodge

The Chestnuts

KIBWO
BEAUCHAM

Mill Lane (Tk)

Newton Farm

Saddington Tunnel
880 yds

SADDINGTON ROAD

SMEETON
WESTERB

Spring Farm

KIBWORTH ROAD

72 Smeeton Road Bridge

Deacon's Farm

FB

Pit (dis)

71

Langton Brook

SMEETON WEST

Smeeton Aqueduct

SADDINGTON

PO

Manor Farm

Cedar Farm

Sewage Works

Cemy

Saddington Feeder

Long Hill Bridge 70

Gumley Bridge 69

GUMLEY ROAD

Bull Spinney

CH

SADDINGTON RESERVOIR

Hill Farm
SMEETON HILL

Gumley Wood

Leicestershire Road

From Foxton the canal continues north and swings north west towards Leicester. Shortly before the tunnel an unnavigable feeder joins the canal from Saddington Reservoir. It is a quiet, empty landscape, all villages set back from the canal, leaving it to pursue a vague course through open fields and occasional trees. No locks, and a curious mixture of bridges, some original, some rebuilt in the 19th C in red brick, some more modern. The A6 and the railway pass beyond the hills to the east, parallel to the canal.

The canal passes through Saddington Tunnel and turns briefly north east before returning to its original course. The hills give way after the tunnel to open fields and woods which give fine views to the west, especially across Wistow Park. The canal is often river-like and can be shallow in places.

Gumley

Leics. PO box, tel. ½ mile west of bridge 63. Small village scattered among trees, set on a hillside high above the canal. The Italianate tower of Gumley Hall rises above the trees, overlooking the valley.

Saddington

Leics. Tel. Small village set back from the canal, with only the church tower breaking the skyline.

Smeeton Westerby

Leics. Tel. The village undulates over the hills to the east of the canal, built along the sides of the main street.

Saddington Tunnel 880yds long, the tunnel was completed in 1797, after great difficulties owing to its being built crooked. Naturalists enthuse about the bats that nowadays live in the tunnel.

Fleckney

Leics. PO, tel, stores, library,takeaway, bakery, chemist, off-licence, garage. An industrial village just 10 minutes' walk from the canal. Shop *open Mon–Sat 08.00–21.00 & Sun 09.00–16.00.*

Wistow

Leics. For a while the canal runs through woods and parkland to the west adjoining Wistow Park. Wistow itself has a church and a Hall, the church with Norman work but mostly 18th-C, including fine monuments. The Hall is Jacobean in principle but was largely rebuilt in the 19th C. For amusement there is a maize maze.

Pubs and Restaurants

◉ ✗ **The Queens Head** Main Street, Saddington LE8 0QH (0116 240 2536). A village centre pub with attractive gardens and a cosy restaurant, set in a tasteful extension with superb views over Saddington Reservoir. Real ale. A wide range of food from a full à la carte menu to tasty snacks and an extensive range of bar meals *L and E (not Sun E)*. Children and dogs welcome. Booking advisable *especially at weekends*.

◉ **The Kings Head** Main Street, Smeeton Westerby LE8 0QJ (0116 279 2676).

Unadulterated, village local offering a friendly welcome and real ale. Inexpensive food available *L and E (not Mon L or Mon and Tue E)*. Children and dogs welcome. Small patio area. Darts, dominoes, crib.

◉ **The Old Crown** 7 High Street, Fleckney LE8 0AJ (0116 240 2223; www.theoldcrown.co.uk). West of bridge 73. Wide range of appetising snacks and nourishing main meals in this friendly, welcoming village pub. Food is available *L and E, and all day Fri and Sat.* Breakfasts served *11.00–12.00.* Real ale. Children welcome. Large garden.

Boatyards

ⓑ **Debdale Wharf Marina** Debdale Wharf, Kibworth LE8 0XA (0116 279 3034; enquiries@debdalewharf.co. uk). 🚿 🚽 🛒 D E Pump out, gas, overnight mooring, long-term mooring, winter storage, crane (30 tons), dry dock, wet dock, chandlery, boat lengthening, boat sales and repairs, engine sales and repairs, boat building and boat fitting out, DIY facilities, books and maps, solid fuel, general fabrication, laundry. *Emergency call out.*

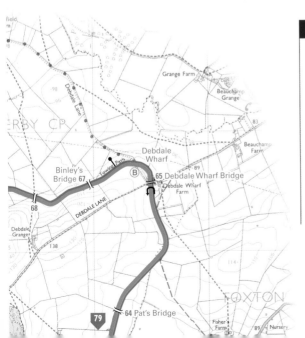

Wigston

Newton Harcourt breaks the unwritten rule of this navigation by being right beside it (other villages keep their distance). The tunnel, the bridges and the locks which begin the descent to Leicester provide plenty of canal interest although the amount of rubbish in the waterway begins to increase. The A6 and the main railway slowly encroach on the canal to the east. The navigation follows the north westerly course of the River Sence, bounded by low hills to east and west and still remote, until Kilby Bridge (*showers and toilets*) where indications of the city of Leicester begin with distant views of housing estates and factories. By Ervin's Lock at South Wigston the city seems, for a while, to take over. The locks continue the steady fall, giving the stretch its individuality. Immediately to the north west of Leicester Road Bridge (98) is the original site of Pickfords Canal Carriers, established when they transferred their activities from horse and cart to the newly burgeoning canals. A little further west, before the navigation swings north, are the disused clay pits and derelict brickyard, once owned by the Union Canal Company; they produced the materials used to construct its locks and bridges.

Boatyards

BW Kilby Bridge Yard Kilby Bridge, Welford LE18 (0115 973 4278; enquiries.sawley@ britishwaterways. co.uk). Pump out, moorings, showers.

NAVIGATIONAL NOTES

A BW Watermate key is required to operate the water saving devices between Kilby Bridge and Aylestone Mill.

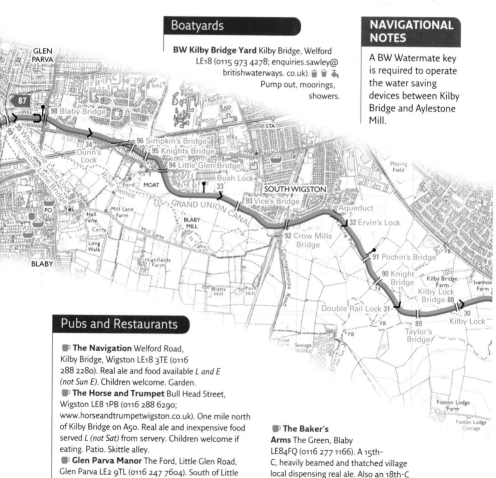

Pubs and Restaurants

🍺 **The Navigation** Welford Road, Kilby Bridge, Wigston LE18 3TE (0116 288 2280). Real ale and food available *L and E (not Sun E)*. Children welcome. Garden.

🍺 **The Horse and Trumpet** Bull Head Street, Wigston LE8 1PB (0116 288 6290; www.horseandtrumpetwigston.co.uk). One mile north of Kilby Bridge on A50. Real ale and inexpensive food served *L (not Sat)* from servery. Children welcome if eating. Patio. Skittle alley.

🍺 **Glen Parva Manor** The Ford, Little Glen Road, Glen Parva LE2 9TL (0116 247 7604). South of Little Glen Bridge (94). Real ale and food available *L and E daily*. Children welcome. Garden.

🍺 **The Baker's Arms** The Green, Blaby LE84FQ (0116 277 1166). A 15th-C, heavily beamed and thatched village local dispensing real ale. Also an 18th-C museum bakery to see. Food available *L*. Children welcome *until 20.00*. Garden. Quiz *Mon*.

Newton Harcourt

Leics. Scattered village bisected by the railway in a cutting. The Hall is 17th-C, with later rebuilding; it has a fine gateway. Newton Harcourt is a well-known Leicester beauty spot, popular on *Sun afternoons.*

Traveline (0870 608 2 608). For full details on bus travel to local (and not so local) attractions. Open *07.00–21.00 daily.*

Brocks Hill Country Park & Environment Centre Washbrook Lane, Oadby LE2 5JJ (0116 271 4514; www.brockshill.co.uk). Unique environment centre built to demonstrate wind and solar power, photovoltaics, rainwater recycling and sewerage composting. Set in 67 acres of country park with woodland, meadowland and an arboretum. Café and disabled access. Park *open all year* and Centre *open Mon–Fri 10.00–17.00; Sat, Sun and B Hols 10.00–16.00.* Free. Although a 2½ mile walk north along footpath from Clifton Bridge (85) and then via A5199 and B582, a visit to the centre makes a very worthwhile day out.

Kilby Bridge

Leics. PO, tel.

Wistow Garden Centre Wistow, nr Great Glen LE8 0QF (0116 259 2009; www.wistow.com). Take the footpath south from Ivy Bridge (78) to the church. Acclaimed model village (setting for the children's storybook *Tales from Old Wistan*), ⅛th scale, mid-Victorian period. Village railway. Also craft shop, artists' studios, teashop serving lunches, teas and coffee, garden centre and village store. *Open daily except Tue.* Donations to Rainbow, a children's hospice charity.

South Wigston

Leics. PO, tel, stores, chemist, off-licence, fish & chips, takeaways, garage, station. Wigston is now part of Leicester, but traces of its earlier independence can still be found. Much of the handsome church dates from the 14th C, especially the interior, while the cottages in Spa Lane, with their long strips of upper window, indicate an old Leicester industry, stocking making. At Wigston Parva there is a tiny Norman church and a monument to the Roman town of Veronae. Unfortunately, only housing estates and a school can be seen from the canal, but exploration is worthwhile.

Wigston Framework Knitters Museum 42/44 Bushloe End, Wigston LE18 2BA (0116 288 3396). About ½ mile north of Kilby Bridge (87). Heritage award winning 18th-C knitters house and workshop. Demonstrations. Refreshments. *Open every Sun, first Sat of month and B Hol Mon (except Xmas and New Year) 14.00–17.00.* Charge.

Blaby

Leics. PO, tel, stores, takeaways, butcher, banks, off-licence, fish & chips, chemist, garage. The church is partly 14th-C, with a fine 18th-C gallery unsuited to the Blaby of today. The shop is *open Mon–Sat 08.00–22.00 & Sun 10.00–16.00.*

WALKING & CYCLING

The navigation from Blaby into Leicester runs through a linear country park and mostly parallels the off-road cycleway along the old Great Central trackbed. It is covered in three sections by a detailed series of leaflets, entitled *Discover Leicester's Riverside Park*, and available from Tourist Information Centres in the area. Both the towpath and the cycleway offer excellent walking and cycling opportunities. Throughout the city itself there is a series of well-marked cycle routes using coloured banding.

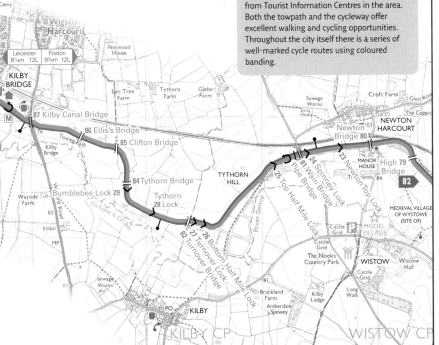

Aylestone

Following the River Sence to its junction with the Soar, the navigation makes a wide swing around Glen Parva and then flows north into Leicester along the Soar valley. After Glen Parva the buildings suddenly cease, and there follows a mile of pleasant rural waterway, lightly wooded to the east, and with the extensive water meadows of the Soar to the west. Sometimes the river and canal flow side by side separated only by the towpath; sometimes they share the same bed. Inevitably in winter this can cause flooding, *and anyone intending to navigate this stretch after heavy rainfall should check the state of the water before proceeding.* Only the pylons and the distant views of Braunston and Aylestone reveal the closeness of Leicester. Now, with the football ground in full view, the canal and the River Soar meet for the penultimate time above a huge weir; care is needed during times of flood. The canal enters Leicester along a pleasant cutting. A variety of buildings line the banks and there is a fine canalside walk under the ornamental bridges that lead straight into the town centre by West Bridge. These factors combine to make the canal entry to Leicester outstanding among large towns. The A46 and A426 run parallel to the canal, but the railway which follows it, the old Great Central line, is now closed.

NAVIGATIONAL NOTES

1   Strong Stream Warning markers are fixed below all locks on the river sections between here and the River Trent. Boaters should check the readings and observe the warnings.
2   The canal and the River Soar meet just above Freeman's Meadow Lock, where there is an enormous unprotected weir. Care is needed, especially in time of flood. KEEP WELL OVER TO THE TOWPATH SIDE.

● **Glen Parva**
Leics. Suburb of Leicester inseparable now from the main town. Curiously enough there was a Saxon cemetery in the town from which 6th-C grave ornaments have been excavated.

● **Aylestone**
Leics. PO, tel, stores, takeaways, chemist, bank, garage. A Leicester suburb coming down to the east bank of the canal. The church contains an interesting stained-glass window of 1930. To the west of the canal the Soar is crossed by an old stone packhorse bridge of eight low arches, perhaps dating from the 15th C. This area still retains the feel of a country village, at least in the area sandwiched between the main Rugby road and the navigation. Narrow streets, bordered by pretty brick cottages, isolate the walker from the bustle of what is otherwise a busy suburb of Leicester. Aylestone Hall and its surrounding gardens and recreational park is a particular haven of peace. On the west of the waterway Aylestone Meadows is now a nature reserve stretching for 1½ miles along the canal and Great Central Way (once the route of the Great Central Railway and now a cycle route and footpath). There are waymarked circular walks along a network of paths together with excellent illustrated interpretation boards. The nature reserve is operated by Leicester City Council who employ rangers who patrol the riverside on motorcycles and can provide advice and assistance. Access for shops and the Union Inn is east from Freestone Bridge (106). There is also a useful farm shop between Packhorse Bridge (105) and the railway bridge.
Traveline (0870 6082608). For full details on bus travel to local (and not so local) attractions. *Open 07.00–22.30 daily.*
Gas Museum National Gas Museum Trust, 195 Aylestone Road, Leicester LE2 7QH (0116 250 3190; www.gasmuseum.co.uk). Situated in the Victorian gatehouse of one of the city's gas works: the first museum to tell the story of the impact of gas on our lives from 19th-C lighting to a gas hairdryer and radio. *Open Tue–Thu 12.00–16.30 (closed Xmas–New Year's Day).* Free. Disabled access to ground floor.
Raw Dykes Ancient Monument Aylestone Road, Leicester (0116 252 7218; www.leicester.gov.uk). A large earthwork near to the canal and River Soar; presumed to be a Romano-British aqueduct. Viewing area *open at all times.*

TO DYE – THE DEATH

For nearly two decades the appearance of the combined River Soar and canal skirting Aylestone – and along the Mile Straight, bordering the city itself – was of an inky, opaque blackness far removed from the image of a burbling, infant stream. This off-putting and unnatural phenomenon served only to reinforce the perception that Leicester was not a city to linger in. In reality the cause was trade effluent from several dye works, established in Wigston since the year dot, passing straight through the local sewerage treatment works. New legislation, however, imposed colour conditions on discharges amounting to full colour removal: a real challenge for the Environment Agency's hard-pressed chemists.

Yet what remained was the puzzle of the problem's relatively recent origins. One plausible explanation lay in the changing nature of the fashion industry. Once, ostensibly, buyer-led (we responded to the length of a skirt or the cut of a suit) our sartorial whims became firmly orchestrated by the industry itself, colour consistently being its key device. In unison went a definite movement towards man-made fibres and their reactive dye processes; bright colours predominated in wardrobes, their turgid residues lingered in rivers.

Pubs and Restaurants

✕ **Kings Lock Tearooms** Kings Lock, Aylestone LE18 8LR (07771 505881). Cosy, welcoming tearooms in the delightful old lock keeper's cottage beside the lock serving cream teas, coffee, ices, baguettes and appetising daily specials all home-made. Outside seating. Dogs and children welcome. *Open Thu–Sat 11.00–16.00; Sun & B Hol Mon 11.00–17.00.*

🍺 **Black Horse** Narrow Lane, off Sanvey Lane, Aylestone, Leicester (0116 283 2811; www.philspub.co.uk). East of Packhorse Bridge (105); fork left up Sanvey Lane, and then first left. Real ale. Home-cooked meals *Tue–Fri L and Fri E*. Children welcome (play area). Garden. Darts, table and long alley skittles, pool, dominoes. Quiz night *Sun*, live music and occasional comedy club.

87

Leicester

For almost all of its journey through the city of Leicester, the navigation pursues a course quite separate from the river, the navigation having been rebuilt towards the end of the 19th C as part of Leicester's flood prevention scheme. For more than ½ mile south of West Bridge, the navigation, a section known locally as the Mile Straight, is like a formal avenue, tree-lined and crossed by several ornamental iron bridges, but where it curves under the old Great Central Railway it begins to follow a less public course through the nether regions of Leicester. A combination of locks, once-derelict canal basins (some now restored for moorings), tall factory buildings and a substantial stretch of parkland adds up to a stretch of urban canal that offers a greater variety of interest than exists in most other cities. At Belgrave Lock the canal joins the Soar, which proceeds to meander carelessly through the city's outskirts. The city centre is remarkably compact, and there are some gems amongst the façades jostled together along its main thoroughfares, with everything surprisingly close to the secure moorings at Castle Gardens. As is the case with all large towns, if you moor at an unprotected site make sure your boat is securely locked if you leave it unattended. Birstall provides a useful mooring and place to shop to the north of the city: tie up near the lock and walk up beside the White Horse.

NAVIGATIONAL NOTES

It is worth remembering that the River Soar may flood at any time, so boaters travelling after heavy rainfall should enquire about the navigational conditions in advance in order to avert the risk of running aground in the middle of a water meadow.

● **Leicester**
All services. A prosperous city with two universities. Fortunes were founded on the hosiery and the boot and shoe trades, but now a variety of light industries flourish in Leicester. There are a great many things to see, for this was the Roman town of Ratae and there is plenty of evidence of the Roman buildings, plus a castle that dates from 1088, with the delightful church of St Mary de Castro next to it. The travel agent Thomas Cook started business in Leicester; in 1841 he organised the first publicly advertised excursion by train. It was a great success, and Cook made the organising of such trips a regular occupation. Leicester has a particularly good selection of museums, and it is fortunate that most of these are near the Grand Union Canal which forms the western boundary of Castle Park. The city should be commended, both for the comprehensive manner in which it markets its copious wealth of attractions and for promoting its cultural diversity in such a positive fashion. The opportunities to sample Asian cuisine, produce, jewellery, cloth, faith and festivals must be second to none outside the Indian sub-continent and could, alone, fill this page. With the provision of secure visitor moorings at Castle Gardens boaters have no reason to ignore a city that has so much to offer.
Abbey Park Abbey Park Road, Leicester LE4 5AQ. All that remains of the abbey is a mansion built

from the ruins and the old stone wall surrounding the grounds. Cardinal Wolsey was buried here in 1530. The park itself, very much in the Victorian mould, has a boating lake, Chinese garden, bandstand and riverside café and is the setting for music festivals and fairs. There is a landing stage in Abbey Park Basin. *Open daily.*
Abbey Pumping Station Corporation Road, Abbey Lane, Leicester LE4 5PX (0116 299 5111; www.leicester.gov.uk/museums). Dating from 1891 this refurbished site features the Victorian steam-powered beam engines that used to pump the city's sewerage to the nearby treatment plant. Also a unique public health exhibition and the manager's house c. World War II. *Open Feb–Nov, Sat–Wed 11.00–16.30, Sun 13.00–16.30. Closed G Fri, Xmas Day and Boxing Day.* Free. Partial disabled access. Moorings.
Belgrave Hall and Gardens Church Road, Belgrave, Leicester LE4 5PE (0116 266 6590; www. www.leicester.gov.uk/museums). Three-storey Queen Anne house dating from 1709 with attractive period and botanical gardens, and 18th- and 19th-C room settings including kitchen, drawing room and nursery. *Open Mon–Sat 10.00–17.30, Sun 14.00–17.30. Closed G Fri, Xmas Day and Boxing Day.* Free. Disabled access to gardens and ground floor only. Moorings.

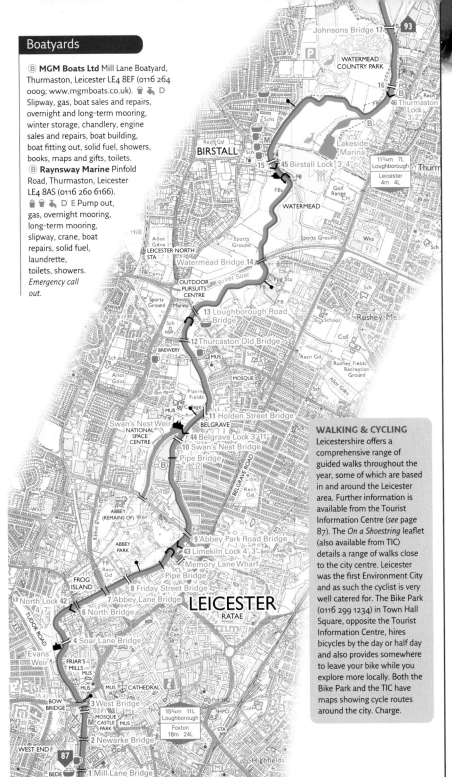

Boatyards

Ⓑ **MGM Boats Ltd** Mill Lane Boatyard, Thurmaston, Leicester LE4 8EF (0116 264 0009; www.mgmboats.co.uk). 🚾 🛒 D Slipway, gas, boat sales and repairs, overnight and long-term mooring, winter storage, chandlery, engine sales and repairs, boat building, boat fitting out, solid fuel, showers, books, maps and gifts, toilets.

Ⓑ **Raynsway Marine** Pinfold Road, Thurmaston, Leicester LE4 8AS (0116 260 6166). 🚾 🛒 🛠 D E Pump out, gas, overnight mooring, long-term mooring, slipway, crane, boat repairs, solid fuel, laundrette, toilets, showers. *Emergency call out.*

WALKING & CYCLING

Leicestershire offers a comprehensive range of guided walks throughout the year, some of which are based in and around the Leicester area. Further information is available from the Tourist Information Centre (*see* page 87). The *On a Shoestring* leaflet (also available from TIC) details a range of walks close to the city centre. Leicester was the first Environment City and as such the cyclist is very well catered for. The Bike Park (0116 299 1234) in Town Hall Square, opposite the Tourist Information Centre, hires bicycles by the day or half day and also provides somewhere to leave your bike while you explore more locally. Both the Bike Park and the TIC have maps showing cycle routes around the city. Charge.

Castle Gardens & Castle Motte (www.leicester.gov.uk). Riverside between St Nicholas Circle and The Newarke. Once a low-lying marshy area of reeds and willows, it was drained in the late 19th C as part of the city's flood alleviation scheme and initially used as allotments. The public gardens were established in 1926. The raised mound, or motte, dates from the 11th C and would originally have been surmounted by a timber fortification. Garden *open daily during daylight hours and as an access for boaters to secure moorings.*

Cathedral 21 St Martins, Leicester LE1 5DE (0116 262 5294; www.cathedral.leicester.anglican.org). Originally the parish church of St Martin's, it was extended in the 14th and 15th C, restored in the 19th C and became the cathedral in 1927. *Open daily.* Donations. Disabled toilets.

De Montfort Hall Granville Road, Leicester LE1 7RU (0116 233 3111; www.demontforthall.co.uk). Prime venue for touring opera and ballet companies and for orchestras and soloist alike.

Eco House Western Park, Hinckley Road, Leicester LE3 (0116 285 5489; www.gwll.org.uk/ecohouse). Environment-friendly show home featuring energy-efficient, sustainable living with emphasis on renewable energy, organic garden, water conservation and health. Playground, shop and refreshments. *Open all year, Wed–Fri 14.00–17.00, weekends 10.00–17.00.* Free. Buses every 10 mins from High Street – numbers 16, 63, 64, 152, 153, 157, 158.

Golden Mile An area centred on Belgrave Road, to the north of the city centre, where the focus lies on the superb range of Asian cultural delights and cuisine, reflecting Leicester's status as a truly cosmopolitan city. Excellent guide entitled *A Taste of Asia* available from Tourist Information Centre (see page 87). Free.

Guildhall Guildhall Lane, Leicester LE1 5FQ (0116 253 2569). Built by the Guild of Corpus Christi and dating from the 14th C, it contains fine oak panelling and an elaborately carved chimney-piece from 1637. It includes the Old Town Library, 19th-C police cells and a Great Hall with civic murals. *Open Feb–Nov, Sat–Wed 11.00–16.30, Sun 13.00–17.30. Closed G Fri, Xmas Day and Boxing Day.* Free. Disabled toilets.

Guru Nanak Gurdwara & Sikh Museum 9 Holy Bones, Leicester LE1 4LJ (0116 262 8606; www.thesikhmuseum.com). An impressive Sikh Temple in a transformed hosiery factory. Also spectacular models of shrines, manuscripts, paintings, coins, photographic portrayal of the part played by Sikh soldiers in both World Wars in a museum depicting the history of the Sikh nation. *Open to devotees daily. Museum open Thu 13.00–16.00. Other times by appointment.* Free.

Haymarket Theatre 1 Garrick Walk, Leicester LE1 3YQ (0870 330 3131; www.lhtheatre.co.uk). Venue for hit shows bound for the West End, with the emphasis on musicals. Also hard-hitting modern drama and the classics. **Studio Theatre** is home to more avant-garde productions. Café and bar.

Jain Centre 32 Oxford Street, Leicester LE1 5XU (0116 254 3091). A fine example of traditional Indian architecture in the western world and a place of pilgrimage for Jains. Shrines of white marble, hand-carved pillars, stained glass, mirror walls, a dome and ceilings in sandstone. *Open Mon–Sat 09.00–22.00.* Donations appreciated.

Jewry Wall Museum St Nicholas Circle, Leicester LE1 4LB (0116 225 4971; www.leicester.gov.uk/museums). Collection of the county's archaeology from early times through to the Middle Ages overlooking the Jewry Wall, a small portion of which remains. This is thought to have been part of a basilica or Roman baths dating from the 2nd C. Two Roman mosaic pavements can be seen *in situ. Open Mon–Sat 10.00–17.30, Sun 14.00–17.30. Closed G Fri, Xmas Day and Boxing Day.* Free.

Little Theatre Dover Street, Leicester LE1 6PW (0116 255 1302; www.thelittletheatre.net). Amateur dramatics, social activities and theatre workshops.

Markets Market Place, Leicester LE1 5 (0116 223 2376). The Food Hall, selling fresh meat, poultry, dairy produce and fish from all over the world, is *open Tue–Sat 06.30–18.00.* The retail market, composed of over 300 covered stalls, is *open Mon–Sat 07.00–18.00.*

New Walk Museum & Art Gallery New Walk, Leicester LE1 7EA (0116 255 4900; www.leicester.gov.uk/museums). Italian, Spanish and Flemish old masters. 18th–20th C English paintings. Also French Impressionists and German Expressionists, ceramics, silver, archives, natural history and geology. *Open Mon–Sat 10.00–17.00, Sun 11.00–17.00. Closed G Fri, Xmas Day and Boxing Day.* Free.

National Space Centre Exploration Drive, Leicester LE4 5NS (0116 261 0261; www.spacecentre.co.uk). The opportunity to explore many facets of space travel, to meet the furthest reaches of our universe face to face and to interact with both science fact and science fiction. Boosters Restaurant and Satellite Bar. Full disabled facilities. *Open Tue–Sun and B Hols 10.00–17.00; Mon 12.00–16.30 during school holidays only.* Charge. Frequent bus service (no 54) to Abbey Lane.

Newarke Houses Museum The Newarke, Leicester LE2 7BY (0116 225 4980; www.leicester.gov.uk/museums). The social history of the area from 1500 to the present day. Locally made clocks and a clockmaker's workshop. Also shows the history of the hosiery, costume and lace industries. There is a reconstructed Victorian street scene.

Phoenix Arts Centre Newarke Street, Leicester (0116 255 4854; www.phoenix.org.uk). Cinema and live performances of contemporary dance, mime, jazz and folk. Café serving a varied menu *L and E.*

Royal Infirmary Museum Knighton Street Nurses Home, Royal Infirmary, Leicester LE1 5WW (0116 254 1414). History of the Infirmary from 1771 including medical and surgical equipment. *Open Tue and Wed 12.00–14.00.* Donations appreciated.

Shires Shopping Centre High Street, Leicester LE1 4FP (0116 251 2461). All the usual big name (and not so big) stores under one high, glass-arched roof plus cafés, pizzeria and gelateria. *Open Mon, Tue, Thu and Fri 09.30–18.00, Wed 09.30–20.00, Sat 09.00–18.00, Sun and B Hols 11.00–17.00.*

St Martins Square & Loseby Lane Between Cank Street and Silver Street, Leicester (0116 253 8247). Speciality shopping centre in the heart of the city. Food, fashion, wine and flowers amongst which to browse placidly, take in some street entertainment or simply unwind. Most shops *open Mon–Sat 09.00–17.00.*

St Mary de Castro Castle Yard, Leicester LE1 5WN (0116 262 8727). Founded in 1107 with excellent examples of Norman glass, stone and wood carving. Henry VI was knighted here in 1426 and Geoffrey Chaucer was probably married here.

St Nicholas Church St Nicholas Circle, Leicester LE1 5LX. The oldest church in the city, dating back to Anglo-Saxon times, and retaining examples of Saxon construction and Roman brickwork in the tower. *Open for services.*

Wygston's House 12 Applegate, St Nicholas Circle, Leicester LE1 5LD. An attractive, timber-framed building originally constructed for Roger Wygston, a 15th-C merchant.

'Y' Theatre YMCA East Street, Leicester LE1 6EY (0116 255 6507). A mixed programme of largely local productions.

Tourist Information Centre 7-9 Every Street, Town Hall Square, Leicester LE1 6AG (0906 294 1113; www.goleicestershire.com). *Open Mon 10.00–17.30, Tue–Fri 09.00–17.30, Sat 09.00–17.00, B Hols and Sun during summer 10.00–16.00.* Leicestershire also offers a comprehensive range of guided walks throughout the year, some of which are based in the Leicester area. Contact the TIC for further details.

● **Thurmaston**
Leics. PO, tel, stores, garage. This unexciting suburb stretches along the Roman road, the old Fosse Way, now bypassed by a dual carriageway. However, the opportunity thus afforded to Thurmaston has not been exploited. Evidence of Roman habitation was discovered in 1955, when excavation of an Anglo-Saxon cemetery brought to light 95 urns dating from 50 years after Julius Caesar's invasion.

● **Birstall**
Leics. PO, tel, stores, takeaways, fish & chips, off-licence, DIY shop, library, butcher. A quiet suburb of Leicester which, together with peaceful moorings, makes it a useful place to stop for supplies. The stores are *open Mon–Sat 08.00–20.00, Sun 10.00– 16.00* and gas is available from the DIY shop.

Pubs and Restaurants

In a large city such as Leicester there is a wide range of pubs and restaurants to choose from; those listed are close to the waterway.

🍺 **The Hat & Beaver** 60 Highcross Street (off High Street), Leicester LE1 4NN (0116 262 2157). Close to the Shires shopping centre, a basic and friendly pub serving real ale and good bar snacks *L Mon–Sat.* Children welcome. Pub games. Occasional music at *weekends.*

🍺 **Voodoo Bar** 29 Market Street, Leicester LE1 6DN (0116 255 6877). Bar with a James Bond theme serving real ale and food *12.00–18.00 (not Sun).* Happy hour on cocktails *17.00–19.00.* Also a downstairs bar *open until midnight.* No children. Outside seating. Guest DJs *Thu–Sat.*

🍺 **The Salmon** 19 Butt Close Lane, Leicester LE1 4QA (0116 253 2301). Near to St Margaret's bus station, a friendly brewery pub serving real ale and food *L, daily.* Children welcome. Beer garden.

✕ ⧖ **Altoco** St Martins Square, Leicester LE1 5DF (0116 253 3977). Stylish pizza and pasta house offering good value meals. *Open Mon–Sat L 12.00–14.30 and E 18.00–22.30 (closes 23.00 Fri–Sat). Closed Sun.*

✕ ⧖ **Golden Mile** Consult *A Taste of Asia (see opposite under Golden Mile)* for a wide-ranging selection of excitingly different and authentic eating experiences. This is a detailed and comprehensive selection numbering nearly 30 establishments.

🍺 ✕ **The Mulberry Tree** White Horse Lane, off Front Street, Birstall, Leicester LE4 4EF (0116 267 1038). Large, friendly, riverside gastro-pub serving real ale and bar meals *all day*, and restaurant meals *L and E daily.* Children welcome and there is a beer garden.

🍺 **The Old Plough** Front Street, Birstall, Leicester LE4 4DP (0116 267 4836). Friendly village pub. Food served *E and Sun L.*

Mountsorrel

North of Thurmaston the canal leaves the river and heads north through an area scarred by busy gravel workings. Just beyond the boatyard, the River Wreake – once the course largely followed by The Melton Mowbray Navigation – flows in from the north east; the name of the nearby boatyard and the next lock hints at the significance of this little river. The River Soar rejoins the canal by Cossington Lock. The villages of Cossington and Rothley are one mile away from Cossington Lock, on opposite sides of the Soar. The Rothley Brook joins the canal north of the lock. At Sileby Lock is another water mill. There has been a mill here since 1608 and the present building has been restored as a private residence. From here it is a short distance to Mountsorrel. The lock here is very much a waterways showplace, and the extensive moorings and lockside pub make it a busy one.

● **Cossington**
Leics. Tel. A mile east of Cossington Lock, this is a pretty village with wide, well-kept grass verges and plenty of trees.

● **Sileby**
Leics. PO, tel, stores, takeaways, fish & chips, garage, chemist, off-licence, bank, station. Once a thriving community based around hosiery manufacture, this large village is much swollen by dormitory housing for neighbouring Leicester and Loughborough. Shop open 06.00–23.00.

● **Mountsorrel**
Leics. PO, tel, stores, takeaway, off-licence, library, butcher, fish & chips, garage. It is but a few yards from the lock here to the centre of the village with its long main street. Shop open Mon–Sat 05.30– 17.30 (Wed & Sat 19.30) & Sun 05.30–12.30.

● **Barrow-Upon-Soar**
Leics. PO, tel, stores, takeaways, off-licence, chemist, butcher, bakery, fish & chips, station. Busy village running up from the canal useful for supplies. Shop open Mon–Sat 08.00–19.00 & Sun 09.00–15.00.
Traveline (0870 608 2 608). Open 07.00–21.00. For full details on bus travel to local (and not so local) attractions.

The Melton Mowbray Navigation & the Oakham Canal
This waterway was opened in 1797 as a broadlocked river navigation from the canal north of Syston to Melton Mowbray, 15 miles away to the east. Beyond Melton the Oakham Canal, constructed in 1802, extended the navigation as far as Oakham, in Rutland. When the railways were built the two waterways could not compete and the Oakham Canal was closed as early as 1841. More than a century later, some lengths still hold water; in other places the former canal bed is only a faint depression. The Melton Mowbray Navigation was closed to traffic in 1877.

Stonehurst Family Farm and Museum
Loughborough Road, Mountsorrel LE12 7AR (01509 413216; www.stonehurstfarm.co.uk). A chance to see a working farm, a museum of memorabilia and old cars, and for children to cuddle and stroke small animals. Teashop serving light lunches and cream teas. Farm shop selling fresh produce, home-made bread and preserves. *Open daily 09.30–17.00.* Charge. Shop and tearoom *open all year.* Disabled visitors telephone for assistance.

Boatyards

ⓑ **L.R. Harris & Son** Old Junction Boatyard, Meadow Lane, Syston LE7 1NR (0116 269 2135; www.lrharris.co.uk). 🚽 🚿 🔥 Gas, overnight mooring, chandlery and extensive spares, slipway, winter storage, boat sales and repairs, boat building and fit outs, inboard and outboard engines sales and repairs, welding specialists.

ⓑ **Sileby Mill Boatyard** Mill Lane, Sileby, Loughborough LE12 7NF (01509 813583; www.surftech.co.uk/canal/sileby). 🚽 🚿 🔥 D E Pump out, gas, narrowboat hire, day-craft hire, overnight mooring, long-term mooring, winter storage, slipway, boat sales and repairs, engineering, welding and structural repairs, wooden boat repair specialists, chandlery, engine sales and repairs, solid fuel, books, maps and gifts, ice creams, toilets, showers.

ⓑ **Meadow Farm Marina** Huston Close, Barrow upon Soar, Loughborough LE12 8NB (01509 812215/816035) 🚽 🚿 🔥 D Pump out, gas, free visitor moorings, long-term mooring (20–6oft boats), slipway, crane, boat sales, toilets, showers. Private club for moorers. Disabled facilities.

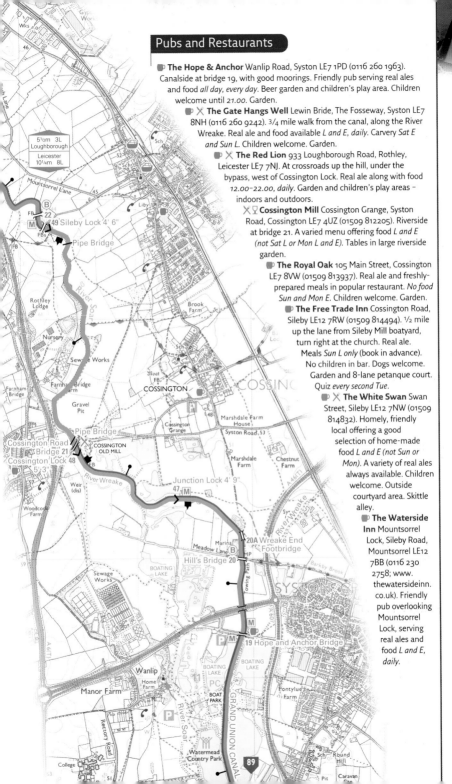

Pubs and Restaurants

The Hope & Anchor Wanlip Road, Syston LE7 1PD (0116 260 1963). Canalside at bridge 19, with good moorings. Friendly pub serving real ales and food *all day, every day*. Beer garden and children's play area. Children welcome until *21.00*. Garden.

The Gate Hangs Well Lewin Bride, The Fosseway, Syston LE7 8NH (0116 260 9242). 3/4 mile walk from the canal, along the River Wreake. Real ale and food available *L and E, daily*. Carvery *Sat E and Sun L*. Children welcome. Garden.

The Red Lion 933 Loughborough Road, Rothley, Leicester LE7 7NJ. At crossroads up the hill, under the bypass, west of Cossington Lock. Real ale along with food *12.00–22.00, daily*. Garden and children's play areas – indoors and outdoors.

Cossington Mill Cossington Grange, Syston Road, Cossington LE7 4UZ (01509 812205). Riverside at bridge 21. A varied menu offering food *L and E (not Sat L or Mon L and E)*. Tables in large riverside garden.

The Royal Oak 105 Main Street, Cossington LE7 8VW (01509 813937). Real ale and freshly-prepared meals in popular restaurant. *No food Sun and Mon E*. Children welcome. Garden.

The Free Trade Inn Cossington Road, Sileby LE12 7RW (01509 814494). 1/2 mile up the lane from Sileby Mill boatyard, turn right at the church. Real ale. Meals *Sun L only* (book in advance). No children in bar. Dogs welcome. Garden and 8-lane petanque court. Quiz *every second Tue*.

The White Swan Swan Street, Sileby LE12 7NW (01509 814832). Homely, friendly local offering a good selection of home-made food *L and E (not Sun or Mon)*. A variety of real ales always available. Children welcome. Outside courtyard area. Skittle alley.

The Waterside Inn Mountsorrel Lock, Sileby Road, Mountsorrel LE12 7BB (0116 230 2758; www.thewatersideinn.co.uk). Friendly pub overlooking Mountsorrel Lock, serving real ales and food *L and E, daily*.

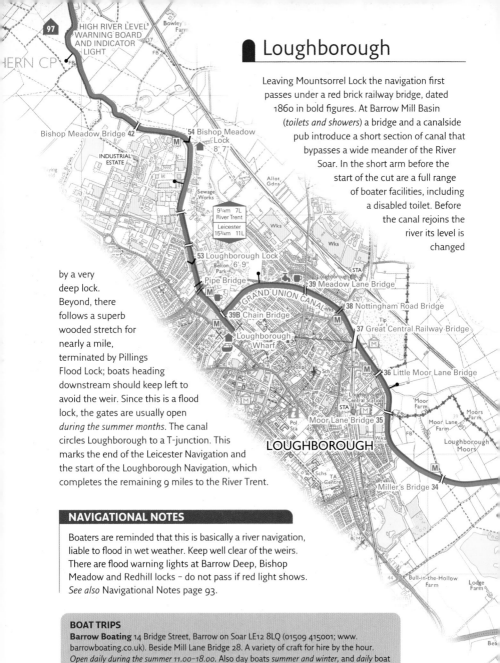

Loughborough

Leaving Mountsorrel Lock the navigation first passes under a red brick railway bridge, dated 1860 in bold figures. At Barrow Mill Basin (*toilets and showers*) a bridge and a canalside pub introduce a short section of canal that bypasses a wide meander of the River Soar. In the short arm before the start of the cut are a full range of boater facilities, including a disabled toilet. Before the canal rejoins the river its level is changed by a very deep lock. Beyond, there follows a superb wooded stretch for nearly a mile, terminated by Pillings Flood Lock; boats heading downstream should keep left to avoid the weir. Since this is a flood lock, the gates are usually open *during the summer months*. The canal circles Loughborough to a T-junction. This marks the end of the Leicester Navigation and the start of the Loughborough Navigation, which completes the remaining 9 miles to the River Trent.

NAVIGATIONAL NOTES

Boaters are reminded that this is basically a river navigation, liable to flood in wet weather. Keep well clear of the weirs. There are flood warning lights at Barrow Deep, Bishop Meadow and Redhill locks – do not pass if red light shows. *See also Navigational Notes page 93.*

BOAT TRIPS

Barrow Boating 14 Bridge Street, Barrow on Soar LE12 8LQ (01509 415001; www.barrowboating.co.uk). Beside Mill Lane Bridge 28. A variety of craft for hire by the hour. *Open daily during the summer 11.00–18.00.* Also day boats *summer and winter*, and *daily boat trips during the summer*, leaving Barrow on Soar *at 18.30 and returning 21.00.* Charter trips.

● **Loughborough**
Leics. All services (including launderette). A busy industrial town. There is a bric-a-brac market held in the Queens Hall, Granby Street *every Fri.*

Bell Foundry Museum Freehold Street, Nottingham Road, Loughborough LE11 1AR (01509 212241; www.taylorbells.co.uk). South of bridge 38. Gift shop. *Open Tue-Sat 10.00–12.30 and 13.30–16.30. Tour of works first Sun of month 14.00 (advanced bookings only). Charge.*

Carillon & War Memorial Queens Park, Loughborough LE11 3DU (01509 263370; www.loughboroughcarillon.com). *Open daily Good Fri–Sep 14.00–18.00. Carillon recitals Sun and B Hols 15.30, and Thu 13.00.* Charge.

Charnwood Museum Queen's Park, Granby Street, Loughborough LE11 3DU (01509 233754; www.leics.gov.uk). Find out how different groups of people have contributed to life in Charnwood over the past 4000 years; discover more about the area's natural world; how the land has nurtured its inhabitants and how they, in turn, have earned a living. Gift shop and café with outdoor patio. *Open Mon–Sat 10.00–16.30, Sun 13.00–17.00.* Free.

Great Central Railway Great Central Road, Loughborough LE11 1RW (01509 230726; www.gcrailway.co.uk). South west of bridge 36. 8 miles of preserved main line taking you back to the days of express steam haulage. *Open weekends and B Hols throughout the year and daily Jun–Sep.* Charge. Telephone for details of special events.

Tourist Information Centre Town Hall, Market Place, Loughborough (01509 218113; www.leicestershire.gov.uk).

Pubs and Restaurants

The Navigation Mill Lane, Barrow on Soar LE12 8LQ (01509 412842). Traditional, canalside country pub, with a copper-topped bar made from old pennies and halfpennies, dispensing real ales and home-cooked food *L, daily*. Well-behaved children and dogs welcome.

The Soar Bridge Inn Bridge Street, Barrow on Soar LE12 8PN (01509 412686). Near Barrow Deep Lock. Real ale and food available *L and E, daily (not Mon–Sat L in winter)*. Children welcome and there is a bouncy castle. Garden.

✗ **The Riverside** Bridge Street, Barrow on Soar LE12 8PN (01509 412260). Riverside, below Barrow Deep Lock. A selection of real ales and food served *L and E, daily*. Children and dogs welcome. Large lawn and children's play area.

The Boat Meadow Lane, Loughborough LE11 1JY (01509 214578). Real ale and food served *L and E, daily*. Children welcome *before 21.00*. Canalside seating. Quiz *Sun. Shops, takeaway, station and PO nearby*.

The Swan in the Rushes 21 The Rushes, Loughborough LE11 5BE (01509 217014). A genuine, real ale pub with a friendly atmosphere serving home-made food prepared from fresh ingredients *L and E (not Sun E)*. Draught cider. Children and dogs welcome. Outside seating. Skittle alley. B & B.

The Three Nuns 30 Churchgate, Loughborough LE11 1UD (01509 611989). Warm, friendly traditional pub serving a range of real ales and home-made food *L and E Mon–Thu*. Breakfast available *Sat 09.00–11.00*. Children welcome. Outside seating.

The Albion Inn Canal Bank, Loughborough LE11 1QA (01509 213952). ¼ mile north of Loughborough Wharf. Traditional, unspoilt canalside pub serving real ale and home-made food *L and E daily*. Well-behaved children and dogs welcome. Canalside seating and pub games.

Boatyards

Ⓑ ✗ **Pilling's Lock Marina** Flesh Hovel Lane, Quorn LE12 8FE (01509 620 990; www.pillingslock.com). Overnight and long term mooring. Pump out, diesel, slipway, chandlery, DIY facilities, boat servicing and maintenance. Facilities building includes showers, toilets and launderette with bar/restaurant.

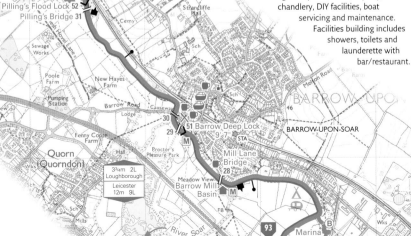

Kegworth

The Loughborough Navigation has the same physical characteristics as the Leicester Navigation. It continues the fall towards the Trent with a similar pattern of meandering river reaches and the occasional canal cut, with locks bypassing the weirs. Normanton on Soar is visible some way away because of its prominent church steeple; on approaching, one finds the church is only a matter of yards from the river bank. However the inhabitants of Normanton guard their waterfront jealously, making it extremely difficult to get ashore. Below Normanton is the settlement of Zouch which has a certain weary and less conventional charm, together with easier access. At Devil's Elbow boats heading downstream should keep right to stay in the main navigation channel. At the point where the A6 and the Soar almost touch there is a riverside pub and a boatyard. North of the pub a willow-lined reach leads to a stone mansion with spreading lawns where the channel divides. To the left (nearer Kegworth) is a maze of shallow and weedy backwaters, weirs and a water mill; boats should keep to the right for Kegworth Deep Lock where a lock has been constructed beside the old as part of a flood prevention scheme. After another sharp swing to the north the channel divides again, and northbound boats should once more bear right for Kegworth Shallow Lock: a flood lock usually left open *during the summer months*.

- **Whatton House**
Visible from the river near the Devil's Elbow, this mansion was built about 1802, damaged by fire and restored in 1876. Its fine 25-acre gardens are *open summer, Sun 14.00–18.00*. Charge. For further details telephone 01509 842268.

- **Normanton on Soar**
Notts. PO box, tel. A quiet and carefully preserved village with wide grass verges and some discreetly pretty buildings. The cruciform church has a central tower and spire, rare in so small a church. On the east wall of the nave there are some excellent stone carvings; the centre one is an elaborate coat of arms with a quizzical lion in the middle. The plain glass windows make the church enjoyably light. A ferry here once again links Nottinghamshire to Leicestershire.

- **Kegworth**
Leics. PO, tel, stores, chemist, fish & chips, chemist, off-licence, butchers, takeaways, garage. Kegworth has an attractive situation up on a wooded hill that is crowned by the church spire, but although it is close to the river, access is easy only from Kegworth Shallow Lock. The shop is *open Mon–Sat 07.00–22.00 & Sun 08.00–22.00*.

- **Kegworth Museum** 52 High Street, Kegworth DE74 2DA (01509 670137; www.kegworthmuseum.org.uk). Award-winning displays include Victorian parlour, local school, saddlers, knitting industry, Royal British Legion war memorabilia and local transport history. *Open Easter–Sep, Sun, Wed and B Hol Mon 14.00–17.00*. Small charge.

- **Kingston on Soar**
Notts. Tel. Situated east of the railway embankment, this is a small quiet estate village which looks much as it must have done 100 years ago. The church, still very much the focus of the village, is a pretty building dating from 1900.

Boatyards

- Ⓑ **East Midlands Boat Services** London Road, Kegworth DE74 2EY (01509 672385; www.eastmidboatserv.co.uk). 🛢 🔧 D Pump out, gas, overnight mooring, long-term mooring, slipway, winter storage, boat sales and repairs, engine sales and repairs, chandlery, DIY facilities. *Emergency call out.*

- Ⓑ **Bridgefields Boatyard** Bridgefields, Kegworth DE74 2FW (01509 672084). 🔧 Long-term mooring, boat repairs, engine repairs and sales, boat fitting out. Incorporating Riverview Narrowboats – boat building.

- Ⓑ **Kegworth Marine** Kingston Lane, Kegworth DE74 2FS (01509 672300). 🔧 D Day-hire craft, gas, long-term mooring, covered slipway, boat and engine repairs, DIY facilities, wet dock (60ft).

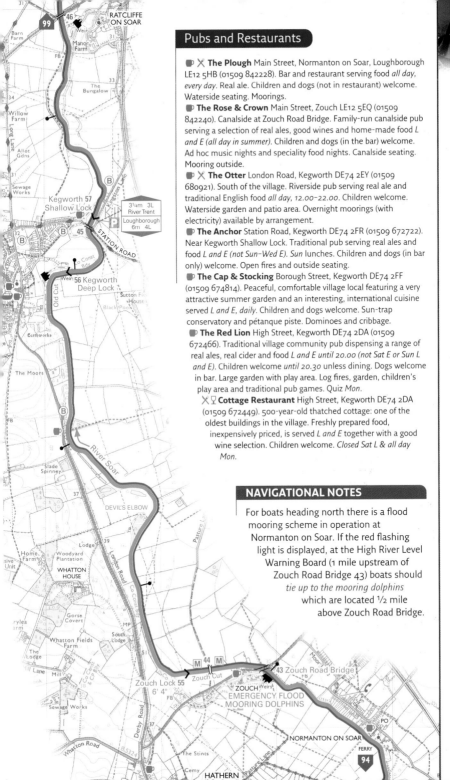

Pubs and Restaurants

🍺 ✕ **The Plough** Main Street, Normanton on Soar, Loughborough LE12 5HB (01509 842228). Bar and restaurant serving food *all day, every day*. Real ale. Children and dogs (not in restaurant) welcome. Waterside seating. Moorings.

🍺 **The Rose & Crown** Main Street, Zouch LE12 5EQ (01509 842240). Canalside at Zouch Road Bridge. Family-run canalside pub serving a selection of real ales, good wines and home-made food *L and E (all day in summer)*. Children and dogs (in the bar) welcome. Ad hoc music nights and speciality food nights. Canalside seating. Mooring outside.

🍺 ✕ **The Otter** London Road, Kegworth DE74 2EY (01509 680921). South of the village. Riverside pub serving real ale and traditional English food *all day, 12.00–22.00*. Children welcome. Waterside garden and patio area. Overnight moorings (with electricity) available by arrangement.

🍺 **The Anchor** Station Road, Kegworth DE74 2FR (01509 672722). Near Kegworth Shallow Lock. Traditional pub serving real ales and food *L and E (not Sun–Wed E)*. *Sun* lunches. Children and dogs (in bar only) welcome. Open fires and outside seating.

🍺 **The Cap & Stocking** Borough Street, Kegworth DE74 2FF (01509 674814). Peaceful, comfortable village local featuring a very attractive summer garden and an interesting, international cuisine served *L and E, daily*. Children and dogs welcome. Sun-trap conservatory and pétanque piste. Dominoes and cribbage.

🍺 **The Red Lion** High Street, Kegworth DE74 2DA (01509 672466). Traditional village community pub dispensing a range of real ales, real cider and food *L and E until 20.00 (not Sat E or Sun L and E)*. Children welcome *until 20.30* unless dining. Dogs welcome in bar. Large garden with play area. Log fires, garden, children's play area and traditional pub games. Quiz *Mon*.

✕ 🍷 **Cottage Restaurant** High Street, Kegworth DE74 2DA (01509 672449). 500-year-old thatched cottage: one of the oldest buildings in the village. Freshly prepared food, inexpensively priced, is served *L and E* together with a good wine selection. Children welcome. *Closed Sat L & all day Mon*.

NAVIGATIONAL NOTES

For boats heading north there is a flood mooring scheme in operation at Normanton on Soar. If the red flashing light is displayed, at the High River Level Warning Board (1 mile upstream of Zouch Road Bridge 43) boats should *tie up to the mooring dolphins* which are located ½ mile above Zouch Road Bridge.

Ratcliffe on Soar

From Kegworth Shallow Lock to the Trent the navigation is somewhat more isolated, but two notable landmarks are the spire of Ratcliffe on Soar church and the eight cooling towers and vast chimney of the Ratcliffe Power Station that totally dominate the landscape for miles around. The navigation skirts round the west side of Red Hill. The last lock here has a well-painted bridge on which are shown the flood levels for 1955 and 1960, explaining the necessity for the flood prevention works. A few hundred yards below Red Hill Lock the Soar flows into the River Trent and loses its identity in this much bigger waterway.

NAVIGATIONAL NOTES

1 Boats negotiating the junction of the rivers Soar and Trent should keep well away from Thrumpton Weir, which is just east (downstream) of the big iron railway bridge. Navigators are reminded that the main line of the Trent Navigation is the Cranfleet Cut. This begins 200yds upstream of the mouth of the Soar, right by the large, wooden building which houses one of the many sailing clubs on the Trent. The entrance to the Erewash Canal is also here, marked by a lock and a cluster of buildings. **If the warning light at Redhill Lock shows red – do not pass**.

2 The sanitary station at Sawley Locks should only be accessed from the backwater moorings on the river below the Lock.

● **Ratcliffe on Soar**
Notts. Tel. A tiny village with a spired church dating from the 13th C. The interior of the nave is pleasantly uncluttered and rather spartan. There is no stained glass to darken it, and the whitewashed walls accentuate the bold and ancient arches. In the chancel, on the other hand, there is a profusion of stone effigies and wall memorials, many of them to the Sacheverell family.

● **Trent Lock**
A busy and unusual boating centre at the southern terminus of the Erewash Canal (*see page 61*). There are two boatyards, two pubs and a delightful tearoom here.

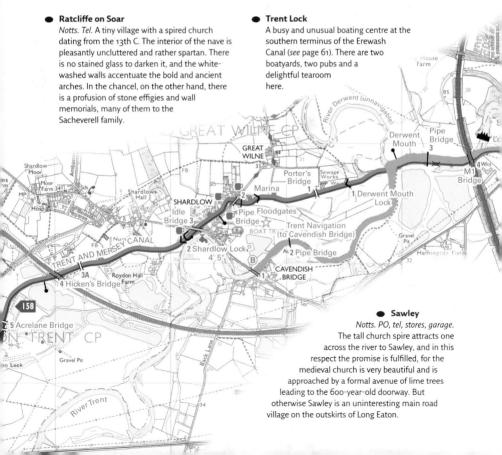

● **Sawley**
Notts. PO, tel, stores, garage.
The tall church spire attracts one across the river to Sawley, and in this respect the promise is fulfilled, for the medieval church is very beautiful and is approached by a formal avenue of lime trees leading to the 600-year-old doorway. But otherwise Sawley is an uninteresting main road village on the outskirts of Long Eaton.

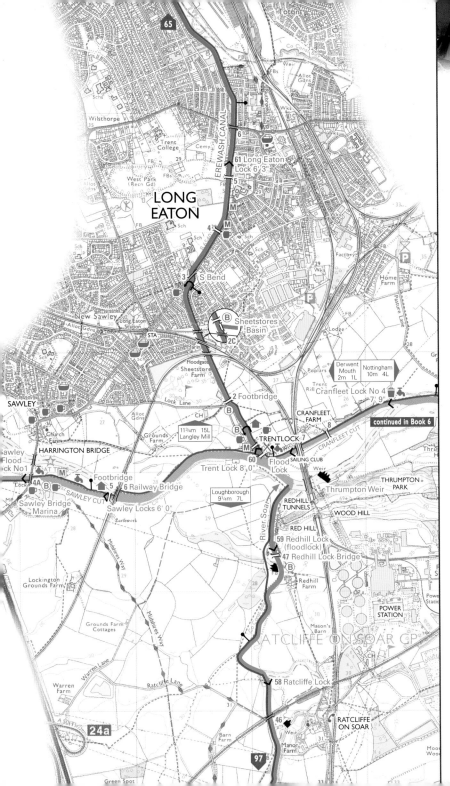

65

EREWASH CANAL

Wilsthorpe

Trent College

West Park (Recn Gd)

LONG EATON

6

61 Long Eaton Lock 6' 3"

5

M

M

4

3 S Bend

New Sawley

Long Eaton Station

STA

B Sheetstores Basin

2C

Floodgate Sheetstores Farm

Lock Lane

2 Footbridge

SAWLEY

Church Farm

Grounds Farm

B

11¾m 15L
Langley Mill

CH

B

M

60

5 6 Railway Bridge

Footbridge

Sawley Bridge Marina

Lock 4A

B

M

SAWLEY CUT

Sawley Locks 6' 0"

HARRINGTON BRIDGE

Sawley Flood Lock No1

Trent Lock 8' 0"

TRENTLOCK 7

Flood Lock

SAILING CLUB

CRANFLEET FARM

Cranfleet Lock No 4
7' 9"

CRANFLEET CUT

8

Derwent Mouth
2m 1L

Nottingham
10m 4L

Poplars

Home Farm

P

Lodge

Trent Rifl

continued in Book 6

Loughborough
9¼m 7L

Weir

Thrumpton Weir

THRUMPTON PARK

REDHILL TUNNELS

WOOD HILL

RED HILL

Redhill Farm

59 Redhill Lock (floodlock)

47 Redhill Lock Bridge

B

POWER STATION

RATCLIFFE ON SOAR GP

River Soar

Lockington Grounds Farm

Midshires Way

Grounds Farm Cottages

Warren Lane

Warren Farm

Ratcliffe Lane

58 Ratcliffe Lock

Mason's Barn

Manor Farm

Barn Farm

46

Weir

RATCLIFFE ON SOAR

24a

A 50(T)

97

Green Spot

● **Sawley Cut**

In addition to a large marina and a well-patronised BW mooring site, the Derby Motor Boat Club have a base on the Sawley Cut. All kinds of boats are represented here: canal boats, river boats and even seagoing vessels. It is certainly no place to be passing through on a *summer Sunday late-afternoon*, for there will be scores of craft queuing up to pass through the locks after spending the weekend downstream. There are windlasses for sale at Sawley Lock, as well as the more conventional facilities.

Boatyards

Ⓑ ✕ **Redhill Marine Ltd** Redhill Marina, Radcliffe on Soar, Nottingham NG11 0EB (01509 672770; www.redhill-marina.co.uk). 🛈 🛠 Gas, overnight and long-term mooring, winter storage, crane, slipway, hoist, boat sales and repairs, engine sales and repairs, boat refurbishment, chandlery, DIY facilities, toilets, general store, café.

Ⓑ ✕ **Sawley Marina** Sawley, Long Eaton NG10 3AE (01159 734278; www.bwml.co.uk). 🛈 🛈 P D Gas, overnight and long-term mooring, winter storage, slipway, crane, boat and engine sales, engine repairs, telephone, chandlery, solid fuel, toilets, showers, restaurant, laundrette, groceries.

Ⓑ **Mills Dockyard** Trent Lock, Lock Lane, Long Eaton NG10 2FY (01159 732595). Overnight and long-term mooring, winter storage, engine repairs, dry dock, wooden boat restoration and repairs, general boat maintenance, fitting out and repairs, houseboat construction.

Pubs and Restaurants

🍽 ✕ **Chandlery Restaurant** Sawley Marina, Long Eaton NG10 3AE (0115 946 0300). Part of the marina complex this café/restaurant serves food *L (not Mon)*, specialising in large portions at low prices. Children and dogs welcome.

🍽 **Plank & Leggit** Tamworth Road, Sawley, Long Eaton NG103AE (0115 972 1515). A new pub 200yds south of Sawley Cut, behind the marina, serving real ale. A wide ranging, inexpensive menu, majoring on healthy eating, is available *all day* as are inexpensive children's and special menus (wide V choice). Indoor and outdoor children's play areas, outside seating and summer barbecues. Dogs welcome on outdoor patio area.

🍽 ✕ **Harrington Arms** Tamworth Road, Sawley Long Eaton NG10 3AU (0115 973 2614). North of the flood lock. 400-year-old, heavily beamed pub, ¼ mile from Sawley Marina, serving an extensive (and ever-changing) international à la carte menu with food *available all day*. Excellent real ale selection. No children or dogs. Large garden and heated patio area. Real fires.

🍽 **Nag's Head** Old Wilne Road, Sawley, Long Eaton (0115 973 2983). Village local serving real ale and sandwiches *L (not Sun)*. No children or dogs. Darts and skittles. *Monthly* quiz.

🍽 ✕ **White Lion** Sawley, Long Eaton NG10 3AT (0115 973 3961). North of the flood lock. Skittles, darts, pool and real ale. Children welcome. Garden. Karaoke *Sat*.

🍽 **Navigation Inn** Trent Lock, Long Eaton NG10 2FY (0115 973 2984). Large, popular, family pub with a garden and play area. Real ales and a wide range of reasonably priced food available *L and E, daily*. Moorings.

🍽 **Steamboat Inn** Trent Lock, Long Eaton NG10 2FY. (0115 972 6300). On the Erewash Canal. Built by the canal company in 1791, when it was called the Erewash Navigation Inn, it is now an upmarket canalside pub and restaurant. Real ale available. Food served *all day* from bar and à la carte restaurant. Children welcome *until 20.00*. Live music *Thu* and *regular* quiz nights.

GRAND UNION CANAL – MAIN LINE

MAXIMUM DIMENSIONS

Norton Junction to Camp Hill
Top Lock (Birmingham)
Length: 72'
Beam: 7'
Headroom: 7' 6"
Craft up to 12' 6" beam are permitted between Norton Junction and Camp Hill but all craft of this size must seek advice before proceeding. Permission must be obtained from BW (01908 302500; enquiries.southeast@britishwaterways.co.uk) for passage through the tunnels.

Camp Hill to Aston Junction and Salford Junction
Length: 70'
Beam: 7'
Headroom: 6' 6"

MILEAGE

NORTON JUNCTION to:
Braunston Turn: 4¼ miles
Napton Junction: 9¼ miles
Kingswood Junction: 31 miles
Bordesley Junction: 45¼ miles
Salford Junction: 48 miles
Locks: 68

MANAGERS

Norton Junction to Napton: 01908 302500
enquiries.southeast@britishwaterways.co.uk
Napton to Salford Junction: 01827 252000
enquiries.westmidlands@britishwaterways.co.uk

The whole length of the Grand Union Canal is unique among English canals in being composed of at least eight separate canals, linking London with Birmingham, Leicester and Nottingham. Up to the 1920s all these canals were owned and operated by quite separate companies: five between London and Birmingham alone.

The original – and still the most important – part of the system was the Grand Junction Canal, constructed at the turn of the 18th C to provide a short cut between Braunston on the Oxford Canal and Brentford, west of London on the Thames. Previously, all London-bound traffic from the Midlands had to follow the Fazeley, Coventry and Oxford canals down to Oxford, there to tranship into lighters to make the 100-mile trip down river to Brentford and London. The new Grand Junction Canal cut this distance by fully 60 miles, and with its 14ft-wide locks and numerous branches to important towns rapidly became busy and profitable. The building of wide locks to take 70-ton barges was a brave attempt to persuade neighbouring canal companies – the Oxford, Coventry and the distant Trent & Mersey – to widen their navigations and establish a 70-ton barge standard throughout the waterways of the Midlands. Unfortunately, the other companies were deterred by the cost of widening, and to this day those same canals can only pass boats 7ft wide.

The mere proposal of the building of the Grand Junction Canal was enough to generate and justify plans for other canals linked to it. Before the Grand Junction itself was completed, independent canals were built linking it in a direct line to Warwick and Birmingham, and a little later a connection was established from the Grand Junction to Market Harborough and Leicester, and thence via the canalised River Soar to the Trent.

These canals made up the spine of southern England's transport system until the advent of the railways. When the Regent's Canal Company acquired the Grand Junction and others, the whole system was integrated as the Grand Union Canal Company in 1929. In 1932 the new company, aided by the Government, launched a massive programme of modernisation: widening the 52 locks from Braunston to Birmingham. But when the grant was all spent, the task was unfinished and broad beam boats never became common on the Grand Union Canal.

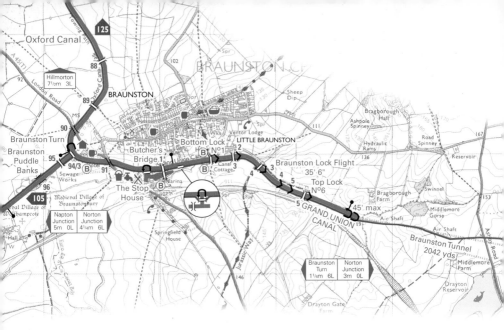

Braunston

From Norton Junction to Braunston the canal runs westward through hills and wooded country, then into a wooded cutting which leads to Braunston Tunnel. There is a good track over the top of the hill, which passes the brick tops of the ventilation shafts. A cutting follows the tunnel, and then the landscape opens out although the hills stay present on either side. Long rows of moored craft flank the canal, but there is usually plenty of space to moor, and a fine selection of old buildings at Braunston. Note especially the iron side-bridge and the 18th C dry dock. The arm in fact was part of the old route of the Oxford Canal before it was shortened by building a large embankment (Braunston Puddle Banks) across the Leam Valley to Braunston Turn. The entrance to this arm was thus the original Braunston Junction. The delightful building alongside, known as the Stop House, was originally the Toll Office between the Oxford Canal and the Grand Junction Canal.

Boatyards

The Boat Shop Bottom Lock, Dark Lane, Braunston NN11 7HJ (01788 891310; www.boatshopbraunston.co.uk). Started on board a boat moored at Braunston Turn, this is now a shop selling a comprehensive range of chandlery, gifts and provisions, including fresh-baked bread. *Open mid Mar–mid Oct 08.00–20.00; rest of the year 08.00–18.00.*

Ⓑ **Braunston Boats** Bottom Lock, Braunston NN11 7HJ (01788 891079). D Gas, boatbuilding, fitting-out.

Ⓑ **Wharf House Narrowboats** Braunston Boat Haven, Botton Lock, Dark Lane, Braunston N11 7HJ (01788 899041; www.wharfhouse.co.uk). Boat building, fitting out and refits, electrics, chandlery, books, maps and gifts.

Ⓑ **Union Canal Carriers** Canalside at Braunston Pump House, Dark Lane NN11 7HU (01788 890784; www.unioncanalcarriers.co.uk). 🔧 D Pump out, gas,

narrowboat hire, day-boat hire, dry dock, engine sales, boat and engine repairs.

Ⓑ **Braunston Marina** The Wharf, Braunston NN11 7JH (01788 891373; www.braunstonmarina. co.uk). Through the fine bridge dated 1834 and into an historic canal wharf. 🚿 🚻 🔧 D E Pump out, gas, overnight and long-term mooring, dry and wet dock, chandlery, boat building sales and repairs, engine repairs, limited chandlery, toilets, showers, public telephone, gift shop selling books and maps, laundrette, coal, DIY facilities. There are also boatbuilders, fitters, fender makers and furnishers at the marina.

Ⓑ **Midland Chandlers** London Road, Braunston NN11 7HB (01788 891401; www.midlandchandlers. co.uk) In operation for almost 30 years. A wide range of chandlery.

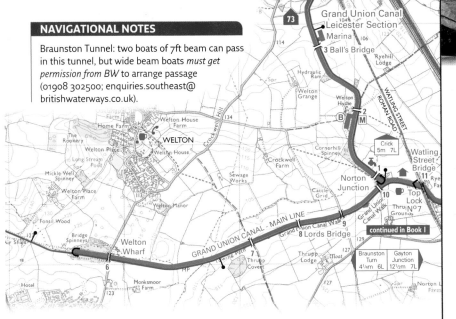

NAVIGATIONAL NOTES

Braunston Tunnel: two boats of 7ft beam can pass in this tunnel, but wide beam boats *must get permission from BW* to arrange passage (01908 302500; enquiries.southeast@ britishwaterways.co.uk).

continued in Book 1

WALKING & CYCLING
A footpath south west of bridge 91 crosses the sites of the medieval villages of Braunstonbury and Wolfhampcote.

- **Welton**
  Northants. Tel. The village climbs up the side of a steep hill, which makes it compact and attractive, especially around the church.
- **Braunston Tunnel**
  Opened in 1796 to bore through the Northamptonshire heights, the tunnel is 2042yds long. Its construction was hindered by quicksands, and a mistake in direction whilst building has given it a slight S bend.
- **Braunston**
  Northants. PO, tel, stores, butcher, fish & chips. Set up on a hill to the north of the canal. The village is really a long main street a little separate from the canal, with houses of all periods. A well-known canal centre, it is no less significant today than when the Oxford and Grand Junction canals were first connected here.

Pubs and Restaurants

The White Horse Inn High Street, Welton NN11 2JP (01327 702820). 3/4 mile from the canal at bridge 6. A 400-year-old public house serving real ale. A wide range of bar and restaurant food is served *all day, every day*. Large garden. Children welcome.

The Wheatsheaf The Green, Braunston NN11 7HW (01788 890748) A locals' pub with a warm atmosphere incorporating a Chinese and Thai takeaway. Real ale. Meals, including traditional *Sun* lunch, are served *L and E*. Children welcome *until 21.00*. Garden with a barbecue. Live music *Fri and Sat.*

The Old Plough 82 High Street, Braunston NN11 7HS (01788 890000). A fine village pub dating from 1672, with open fires and serving real ale. Good food *L and E daily (no Tue L)*, with *Sun* roasts. Children are welcome, and there is a garden. Quiz every other *Sun*.

The Millhouse Hotel London Road, Braunston NN11 7HB (01788 890450). Once the Rose & Castle, it is now a welcoming hotel and restaurant, serving real ale. Grills, *Sun* roasts, carvery meals *L and E*. Children's room and fine canalside garden with swings. Overnight mooring for patrons. Live jazz *Sun*. B & B.

The Gongoozler's Rest Narrowboat café moored outside the Stop House NN11 7JQ (07730 125849). Breakfasts, sandwiches, omelettes and a variety of good fare. *Open Wed-Sun and B Hols, 09.00-18.00 (16.00 winter).*

Napton Junction

The canal now passes through open countryside with a backdrop of hills, seeming very quiet and empty following all of the waterway activity around Braunston. The land is agricultural, with just a few houses in sight. There are initially no locks, no villages and the bridges are well spaced, making this a very pleasant rural stretch of canal running south west towards Napton Junction, on a length once used by both the Grand Junction Company and the Oxford Canal Company. As the Oxford Canal actually *owned* this stretch, they charged excessive toll rates in an attempt to get even with their rival, whose more direct route between London and the Midlands had attracted most of the traffic. At Napton Junction the Oxford Canal heads off to the south while the Grand Union Canal strikes off north towards Birmingham. The empty landscape rolls on towards Stockton, broken only by Calcutt Locks. The windmill on top of Napton Hill can be seen from Napton Junction.

Boatyards

Ⓑ **Wigrams Turn Marina** Shuckburgh Road, Napton, Southam CV47 8NL (01926 817175; www.black-prince.com).

Ⓑ **Napton Narrowboats** Napton Marina, Stockton, Southam (01926 813644; www.napton-marina.co.uk). 🚿 🛏 �úD Pump out, gas, narrowboat hire, overnight & long-term mooring, boatbuilding, boat & engine repairs, toilets, chandlery, gifts.

Ⓑ **Calcutt Boats** Calcutt Top Lock, Stockton, Southam (01926 813757; www.calcuttboats.com). 🚿 🛏 �úD Pump out, gas, narrowboat hire, day-boat hire, overnight mooring, long-term mooring, slipway, crane, dry dock, boat and engine sales and repairs, boatbuilding, chandlery, toilets, solid fuel, breakdown service.

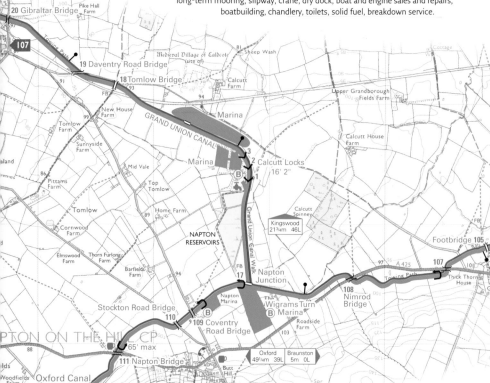

Pubs and Restaurants

🍺 ✕ **The Bridge at Napton** Southam Road CV47 8NQ (01926 812466). A haunted canalside pub at bridge 111 on the Oxford Canal. Real ale. Excellent bar and restaurant food served *L and E, daily*. Range of choice from steaks to fish to spicy pasta. Children welcome. Pleasant garden with a children's playground, and often entertainment during *summer months*. Well-behaved dogs welcome.

🍺 **Old Olive Bush** Flecknoe CV23 8AT (01788 891134). A cosy village pub serving home-cooked meals (booking preferred) *E Tue–Sun*, and bar snacks *L Sat and Sun*. Children welcome, and there is a garden. *Closed L Mon–Fri in winter*.

● **Lower Shuckburgh**
Warwicks. PO box. A tiny village along the main road. The church, built in 1864, is attractive in a Victorian way, with great use of contrasting brickwork inside.

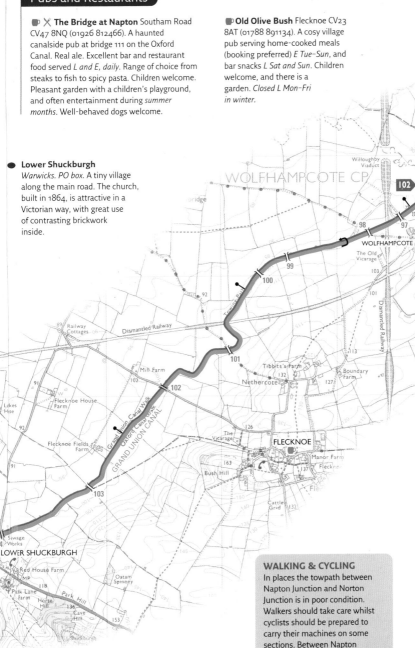

WALKING & CYCLING
In places the towpath between Napton Junction and Norton Junction is in poor condition. Walkers should take care whilst cyclists should be prepared to carry their machines on some sections. Between Napton Junction and Banbury there are again similar isolated problem areas.

Stockton

Continuing west, the canal passes to the north of Stockton and descends Stockton Locks, where you will notice the remains of the old narrow locks beside the newer wide ones. Around here there is a change in landscape, with the hills coming much closer to the canal, broken by old quarries and thick woods along the south bank. The quarries produced blue lias, a local stone, and cement which was used in the construction of the Thames Embankment. Huge fossils have been found in the blue lias clay, which is the lowest layer from the Jurassic period. This section contrasts greatly with the open landscape that precedes and follows it. The canal passes Long Itchington, a village with a large number of pubs, including two on the canal, all the while flanked by open arable land backed on both sides by hills. This pleasant emptiness is broken only by further locks continuing the fall to Warwick. Of particular interest are the top two locks at Bascote, just beyond the pretty toll house, which form a staircase. Then the canal is once again in quiet, wooded, countryside.

- **Stockton**
Warwicks PO, tel, stores, Chinese and Indian takeaways.
Stockton is a largely Victorian village in an area which has been dominated by the cement works to the west. St Michael's church is built of blue lias, quarried near Stockton Locks, although the tower is of red sandstone.
- **Long Itchington**
Warwicks. PO, tel, stores, garage. A large housing estate flanks the busy A423; the village proper lies a

short walk to the north west, and is very attractive. Apart from several pubs there are houses of the 17th and 18th C, and impressive poplars around the village pond. St Wulfstan, who later became Bishop of Worcester, was born here in 1012.
Holy Trinity A largely 13th C church whose tall spire was blown down in a gale in 1762, and replaced with a stump. Parts of the south aisle date from the 12th C, although the 13th C windows are perhaps the building's best feature.

Boatyards

ⓑ **Stockton Top Marina** Stockton, Rugby Road CV47 8HN (01926 492968; www.kateboats.co.uk). By bridge 21. 🛉 🛠 D Pump out, gas, long-term mooring, slipway, toilets.

ⓑ **Warwickshire Fly Boat Company** Stop Lock Cottage, Stockton (01926 812093; www.wfbco.co.uk). By the Kayes Arm. 🛉 🛉 🛠 D Pump out, gas, long-term mooring, dry dock, boat sales, engine repairs, chandlery, telephone, toilets, showers, solid fuel, laundrette, books and maps. Tea room.

ⓑ **Stockton Dry Dock Company** Stop Lock Cottage, Stockton (01926 814441, www.sddpearce.supanet.com). Boatbuilding and repairs. Dry dock.

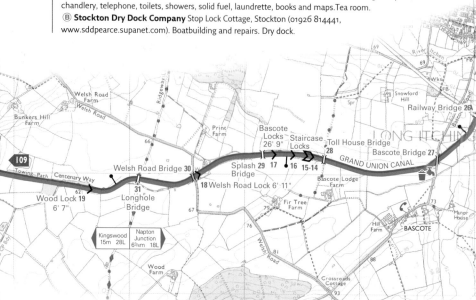

Pubs and Restaurants

🍺 ✕ **The Crown** 8 High Street, Stockton CV47 8JZ (01926 812255). A cosy, traditional village pub where bar meals are served in large portions *L and E*. Real ales. Children welcome. Outside seating and boules court. *Open all day.*

🍺 **The Boat Inn** Birdingbury Wharf, Rugby Road CV23 8HQ (01926 812349). Canalside at bridge 21. A pleasant old pub with a fine map, painted by Dusty Miller, around the top of the bar. Real ale. Grills and bar meals *L and E*. Children welcome, canalside garden with play area. Blues and jazz bands *Sat eves*. Annual beer and blues festival *June/July*. B & B.

🍺 **The Blue Lias Inn** Stockton Road, Stockton CV47 8LD (01926 812249; www.bluelias.com). Canalside at bridge 23. A well-kept and attractive pub, with a pleasant canalside garden. Be prepared for the uneven interior brickwork, which may look straighter when you have enjoyed one of the real ales they regularly keep. Bar meals *L and E*. Live music outside *Sat eves in summer*. Children are welcome, but they must remain seated. Moorings.

🍺 **The Two Boats Inn** Southam Road, Long Itchington CV47 9QZ (01926 812640). Canalside at bridge 25. A good selection of real ale is available in this fine pub, built in 1743. At one time there was a forge and stables here for the boat horses. Bar meals and grills *L and E*. Children welcome. Garden. Live music *Sat*.

🍺 **The Cuttle Inn** Southam Road, Long Itchington CV47 9QZ (01926 812314). Canalside at bridge 25. Traditional locals' pub with outside seating and children's play area. Live bands at *weekends*. Moorings. B & B.

🍺 **The Duck on the Pond** The Green, Long Itchington CV47 9QJ (01926 815876). Specialising in food, this pub overlooks the village green and pond. Queen Elizabeth I once stayed in the black and white timbered building opposite. Real ale, and a wide range of meals are served *L and E*. Children welcome *L*, and there is sometimes jazz *during the summer*. Garden.

🍺 ✕ **The Buck & Bell** The Green, Long Itchington CV47 9QZ (01926 811177). Real ale. Bar Meals *L and E*.

🍺 ✕ **The Harvester** Church Road, Long Itchington CV47 9PG (01926 812698). Small, family-run village local serving real ale. Bar and restaurant meals, *L and E*. Children welcome.

🍺 **The Green Man** Church Road, Long Itchington CV47 9PW (01926 812208). Just past the church, this is a fine traditional community pub with a very low ceiling in the corridor. Real ale and bar snacks. Family room and garden.

WALKING & CYCLING
The Warwickshire Feldon Cycleway crosses the canal at bridge 18 and National Cycle Route 41 makes use of the towpath between bridge 21 and the disused railway bridge east of bridge 27. It re-joins at bridge 34, making its way into Leamington and offers an attractive alternative route.

Royal Leamington Spa

The waterway makes its descent through the quiet Fosse Locks and continues west through attractive and isolated country to pass to the north of Radford Semele, where there is a fine wooded cutting. Emerging from the cutting, the canal joins a busy road for a short while, then carves a fairly discreet course through Leamington. Midway through the town the canal enters a deep cutting that hides it from the adjacent main road and railway. Leaving Leamington the canal swings north west under a main road and crosses the railway and the River Avon on aqueducts, to immediately enter the outskirts of Warwick. There are good *moorings*, *shops* and two *Indian takeaways* by bridge 40.

Pubs and Restaurants

The Stags Head Welsh Road, Offchurch CV33 9AQ (01926 425801). A thatched 15th C pub, serving real ale and food *L and E*. Children welcome *until 19.30*. Garden with swings.

The White Lion Southam Road, Kingshurst, Radford Semele CV31 1TE (01926 425770). Real ale, and meals served *all day, every day*. Children welcome in the restaurant *until 21.00*.

The Fusilier Sydenham Drive, Leamington Spa CV31 1NJ (01926 336048). Children welcome. Lawn at the back. Karaoke *Sat*, quiz and disco *Sun*. Fish & chips next door, and shops nearby.

The Lock, Dock & Barrell 7 Brunswick Street, Leamington Spa CV31 2DS (01926 430333). Canalside by bridge 40. Old-fashioned locals' pub serving quality food *L and E* (not *Tue*). Outside seating with decking area. Moorings.

✕ ♀ **The Grand Union** 66 Clemens Street, Leamington Spa CV31 2DN (01926 421323; www.thegrandunion.co.uk). At bridge 40, overlooking the canal. Home-made English food. One evening sitting, restaurant *opens 19.30 for dinner at 20.00, Mon–Sat*. Also Sunday brunch at *12.00 Sun only*. Reservations only. Children welcome, garden.

The Tiller Pin Queensway, Leamington Spa CV31 3JZ (01926 435139). Real ale. Food is available *L and E Mon–Fri*, and all day until 21.00 at *weekends*. Children welcome. Large garden.

✕ The Moorings Myton Road, Leamington Spa CV31 3NY (01926 425043; mooringsbar@yahoo.co.uk; www.mooringsbarleamingtonspa.co.uk). By bridge 43. Real ale. Meals available *L and E, daily*. Email lunch ordering service. Children welcome *until 21.00*. Quiz night alternate *Wed*. Mooring.

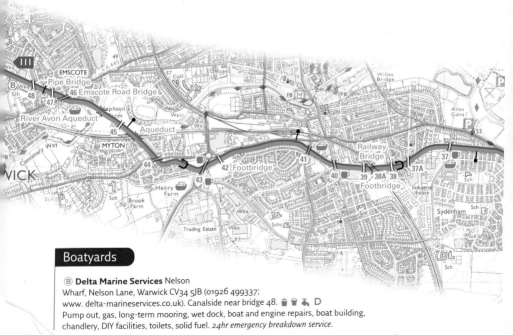

Boatyards

ⓑ **Delta Marine Services** Nelson Wharf, Nelson Lane, Warwick CV34 5JB (01926 499337; www. delta-marineservices.co.uk). Canalside near bridge 48. 🚽 🛢 🔧 D Pump out, gas, long-term mooring, wet dock, boat and engine repairs, boat building, chandlery, DIY facilities, toilets, solid fuel. *24hr emergency breakdown service*.

- **Offchurch** *Warwicks. Tel.* A scattered residential village reflecting the proximity of Leamington. It takes its name from Offa, the Saxon King of Mercia, reputedly buried near here. The church, with its tall grey stone tower, contains some Norman work. To the west lies Offchurch Bury, whose park runs almost to the canal. Originally this was a 17th C house, but it has since been entirely rebuilt. The façade is now early 19th C Gothic.
- **Radford Semele**
Warwicks. PO, tel, stores. A main road suburb of Leamington, Radford Semele takes no notice of the canal that runs below the village, alongside the River Leam and what was once the railway line to Rugby. Among the bungalows are some fine large houses, including Radford Hall, a reconstructed Jacobean building. The Victorian church of St Nicholas, recently completely gutted by fire and now rebuilt, is set curiously by itself, seeming to be in the middle of a field.
- **Royal Leamington Spa**
Warwicks. All services. During the 19th C the population of Leamington increased rapidly, due to the late 18th- and 19th C fashion for spas generally. As a result the town is largely Regency with later Victorian additions resulting in a most pleasingly spacious layout. Several hotels and churches were designed by J. Cundall, a local architect of some note who also built the brick and stone town hall. The long rows of villas, elegant houses in their own grounds spreading out from the centre, all express the Victorian love of exotic styles – Gothic, Classical, Jacobean, Renaissance, French and Greek are all mixed here with bold abandon. Since the Victorian era, however, much industrialisation has taken place.
Assembly Rooms, Art Gallery & Museum Royal Pump Rooms, The Parade CV32 4AA (01926 742700; www.warwickdc.gov.uk/royalpumprooms).

British, Dutch and Flemish paintings of the 16th and 17th C. Also a collection of modern art, pottery and porcelain through the ages and a specialist series of 18th C English drinking glasses. Victorian costumes and objects. Tea room. *Open Tue, Wed, Fri 10.30– 17.00, Sat, Thu 13.30–20.00, Sun 11.00–16.00. Closed Mon.* Free.
All Saints' Church Bath Street CV33 9HA Begun in 1843 to the design of J. C. Jackson, who was greatly influenced by the then vicar, Dr John Craig. It is of Gothic style, apparently not always correct in detail. The north transept has a rose window patterned on Rouen Cathedral; the west window is by Kempe. The scale of the building is impressive, being fully 172ft long and 80ft high.
Jephson Gardens Alongside Newbold Terrace, north of bridge 40, CV32 4AB. Beautiful ornamental gardens named after Dr Jephson (1798– 1878), the local practitioner who was largely responsible for the spa's high medical reputation.
Tourist Information Centre Royal Pump Rooms, The Parade CV32 4AB (01926 742762).

BOAT TRIPS
Prince Regent II is a 50-seater wide-beam Edwardian luxury cruising restaurant, which departs from Radford Bottom Lock, Offchurch Lane, CV31 1TX *evenings and Sun lunchtimes.* Good food and wine, and entertainment can be arranged. Booking for a meal is essential. Telephone 01789 261558/07974 176389. Their office address is: The Edwardian Dining Company, Wisteria House, 76 Hawthorn Way, Shipston-on-Stour, Warwicks CV36 4FD. Also available for private charter.

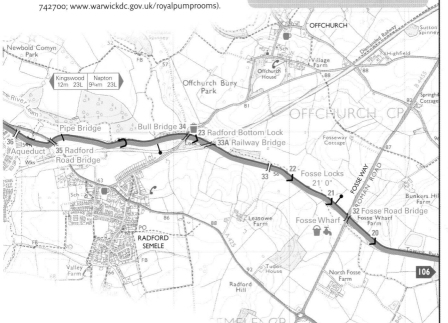

Warwick

The canal passes around the north side of central Warwick, so if you wish to visit the town centre, it is best to approach from bridge 49 (walking to the south for a little over half a mile), or from the Saltisford Canal Centre (*see* below). After climbing the two Cape Locks, the canal swings south to Budbrooke Junction, where the old Warwick and Napton Canal joined the Warwick and Birmingham Canal. A short section of the arm to the east of the junction has been restored, and has a *winding hole*, *moorings* and other *facilities*. To the west of the junction, beyond a large road bridge, is the first of the 21 locks of the Hatton flight, with distinctive paddle gear and gates stretching up the hill ahead, a daunting sight for even the most resilient boatman. Consolation is offered by the fine view of the spires of Warwick as you climb the flight. A fine pair of traditional working boats are often moored in front of an old British Waterways van by the old Hatton Yard. The Hatton Locks Café (01926 409432) is between locks 45 and 46. On reaching the top, the canal turns to the north west, passing the wooded hills that conceal Hatton village and Hatton Park. It then enters the wooded cutting that leads to Shrewley Tunnel.

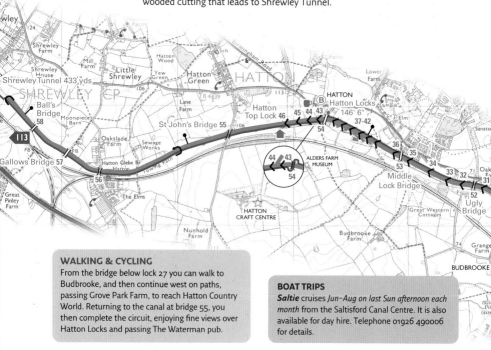

WALKING & CYCLING
From the bridge below lock 27 you can walk to Budbrooke, and then continue west on paths, passing Grove Park Farm, to reach Hatton Country World. Returning to the canal at bridge 55, you then complete the circuit, enjoying fine views over Hatton Locks and passing The Waterman pub.

BOAT TRIPS
Saltie cruises *Jun–Aug* on last Sun afternoon each month from the Saltisford Canal Centre. It is also available for day hire. Telephone 01926 490006 for details.

Boatyards

Ⓑ **Saltisford Canal Centre** Budbrooke Road CV34 5RJ (01926 490006; www.saltisfordcanal.co.uk). 🚽 🎁 🪣 Pump out, day-hire craft, overnight and long-term mooring, winter storage, telephone nearby, toilets, gifts. Gardens and picnic areas. Snacks available. An excellent place in its own right, with good access to Warwick.

Ⓑ **Kate Boats Warwick** The Boatyard, Nelson Lane CV34 5JB (01926 492968; www.kateboats.co.uk). 🚽 🎁 🪣 D Pump out, gas, narrowboat hire, overnight

& long-term mooring, boat & engine repairs, boatbuilding, chandlery, toilets, books.
Get Knotted Lower Cape CV34 5DP (01926 410588). Next door to the Cape of Good Hope pub. Rope fender-making specialist, plus general ropework and an expanding chandlery.

Ⓑ **Stephen Goldsbrough Boats** Hatton CV47 2XD (01295 770934; www.sgboats.com). Dry dock on the Hatton flight, boat painting and repairs, boat building, engine repairs, DIY facilities.

Warwick

Warwicks. All services. Virtually destroyed by fire in 1694 the town rose again, with Queen Anne styles now mixed with the medieval buildings which survived the blaze.

Warwick Castle Castle Hill CV34 4QU (telephone 0870 442 2000 for information line). Built on the site of a motte and bailey constructed by William the Conqueror in 1068, the present exterior is a famous example of a 14th C fortification, with the tall Caesar's Tower rising to a height of 147ft. The castle grounds were laid out by Capability Brown. *Open daily 10.00–18.00. Closed Xmas.* Charge. Programme of events *throughout the year.*

Collegiate Church of St Mary's Church Street, CV34 4AB Of Norman origin (01926 403940; www.stmaryswarwick.org.uk). The most striking feature of the rebuilt church is its pseudo-Gothic tower, built 1698–1704. Climb to the top to enjoy the view (*May–Sep, 10.00–16.00 weather permitting*). Church *open summer 10.00–18.00; winter 10.00–16.30.* Free (charge for tower).

Warwick County Museum Market Place CV34 4SA (01926 412500/412501; www.warwickshire.gov.uk/museum). Housed in the Market Hall. Includes the Sheldon tapestry map of Warwickshire, which dates from 1588. *Open May–Sep, Tue–Sat and B Hols 10.00–17.00, Sun 11.30–17.00.* Free.

Lord Leycester Hospital High Street CV34 4BH (01926 491422). A superbly preserved group of 14th C timber-framed buildings. Chapel of St James, Great Hall and galleried courtyard. The Museum of the Queen's Own Hussars is also here. *Open Tue–Sun and B Hol Mon 10.00–17.00 (16.00 winter).* The restored gardens are *open during the summer.* Charge.

Tourist Information Centre The Court House, Jury Street CV34 4EW (01926 492212; www.warwick-uk.co.uk). Guided walks are arranged from here *during the summer.*

Hatton

Warwicks. A heavily wooded village.

Hatton Country World George's Farm, Hatton CV35 8XA (01926 843411; www.hattonworld.com). South of bridge 55. Rare breeds, craft workshops and a children's play area. Arts and crafts shops. *Open daily 10.00–17.00 (closed Xmas).* Entrance to the craft village is free, but a charge is made for the Farm Park. Restaurant.

Shrewley

Warwicks. PO, stores. Best approached from the north western end of the Shrewley Tunnel, through an exciting, but slippery, towpath tunnel.

Shrewley Tunnel 433yds long, the tunnel was opened in 1799 with the completion of the Warwick and Birmingham Canal. *This tunnel allows two 7ft boats to pass: keep to the right.*

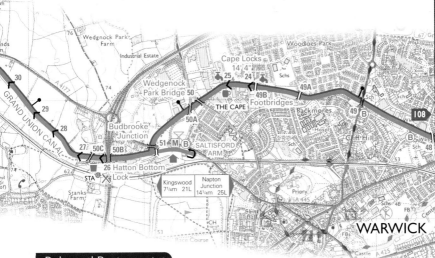

Pubs and Restaurants

✗ **The Station Café** Warwick Parkway Station CV35 8RH Independent and friendly establishment offering reliable refreshment before the ascent – or after the descent – of Hatton Locks. Children and dogs welcome.

🍺 **The Cape of Good Hope** Cape Locks, 66 Lower Cape CV34 5DP (01926 498138; www. capeofgoodhope.co.uk). A canalside pub where good food, especially fish, is served *L and E daily.*

Real ales. Children welcome, lockside seating. Live music *Fri.*

🍺 ✗ **The Waterman** Birmingham Road (A4177), Hatton CV35 7JJ (01926 492427). Excellent and extensive bar menu available *all day, every day (not Sun E)* in this country pub which has fine views over the Hatton flight. Real ale. Children welcome. Large garden.

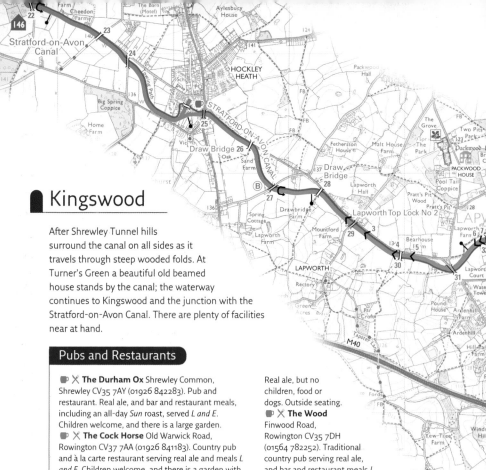

Kingswood

After Shrewley Tunnel hills surround the canal on all sides as it travels through steep wooded folds. At Turner's Green a beautiful old beamed house stands by the canal; the waterway continues to Kingswood and the junction with the Stratford-on-Avon Canal. There are plenty of facilities near at hand.

Pubs and Restaurants

🍺 ✕ **The Durham Ox** Shrewley Common, Shrewley CV35 7AY (01926 842283). Pub and restaurant. Real ale, and bar and restaurant meals, including an all-day *Sun* roast, served *L and E*. Children welcome, and there is a large garden.

🍺 ✕ **The Cock Horse** Old Warwick Road, Rowington CV37 7AA (01926 841183). Country pub and à la carte restaurant serving real ale and meals *L and E*. Children welcome, and there is a garden with a children's play area. Folk and jazz club, *mid-summer* charity ball, and beer and jazz festival.

🍺 **The Case is Altered** Case Lane, just off Five Ways, Haseley Knob CV35 7JD (01926 484206). A brisk 45-minute walk from bridge 62, but worth it to find this quiet old-fashioned ale house. Pass Rowington Hall, then north east past South Lawn.

Real ale, but no children, food or dogs. Outside seating.

🍺 ✕ **The Wood** Finwood Road, Rowington CV35 7DH (01564 782252). Traditional country pub serving real ale, and bar and restaurant meals *L and E*. Children welcome, and garden by the canal.

🍺 **The Navigation** Old Warwick Road, canalside at Kingswood B94 6JU (01564 783337). Real ale and real draught cider. Bar meals *L and E*. Children welcome. Moorings.

> ### WALKING & CYCLING
> By walking west from the Tom o'the Wood pub and crossing Dick's Lane Bridge on the Stratford-on-Avon Canal, you can follow paths past Ardenhill Farm to bring you to bridge 31 on the Lapworth Flight. It is then an excellent and fascinating walk back, passing the locks and returning to the Grand Union via Kingswood Junction.

● **Rowington**
Warwicks. Near the canal the 13th C church retains some furnishings and a fine peal of bells.

● **Kingswood**
Warwicks. Garage, station. The village is scattered over a wide area from the Grand Union Canal to the Stratford-on-Avon Canal. The centre is a mile to the west, around the ambitious 15th C church.

Packwood House *NT* Lapworth, Solihull B94 6AT (01564 782024; www.nationaltrust.org.uk). 2 miles west of bridge 66. Much-restored timber-framed Tudor house. Cromwell's general, Henry Ireton, slept here before the Battle of Edgehill in 1642. Gardens with notable topiary; lakeside walk. Park *open all year*. House *open Feb–Oct, Wed–Sun and B Hols 11.00–17.00*. Charge.

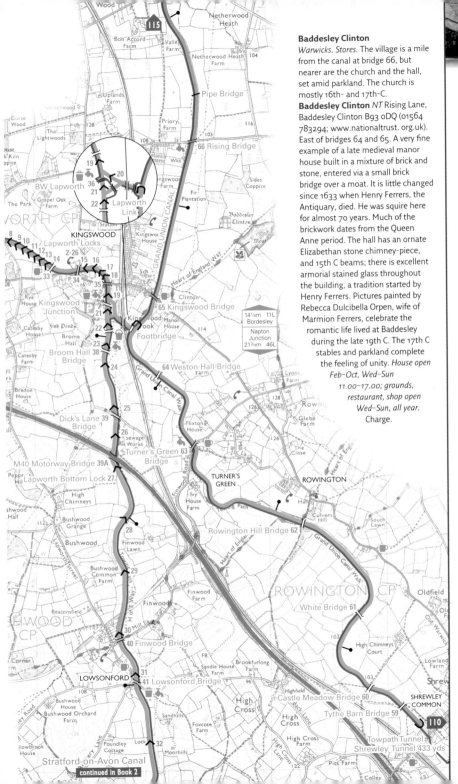

Baddesley Clinton

Warwicks. Stores. The village is a mile from the canal at bridge 66, but nearer are the church and the hall, set amid parkland. The church is mostly 16th- and 17th-C.

Baddesley Clinton *NT* Rising Lane, Baddesley Clinton B93 0DQ (01564 783294; www.nationaltrust. org.uk). East of bridges 64 and 65. A very fine example of a late medieval manor house built in a mixture of brick and stone, entered via a small brick bridge over a moat. It is little changed since 1633 when Henry Ferrers, the Antiquary, died. He was squire here for almost 70 years. Much of the brickwork dates from the Queen Anne period. The hall has an ornate Elizabethan stone chimney-piece, and 15th C beams; there is excellent armorial stained glass throughout the building, a tradition started by Henry Ferrers. Pictures painted by Rebecca Dulcibella Orpen, wife of Marmion Ferrers, celebrate the romantic life lived at Baddesley during the late 19th C. The 17th C stables and parkland complete the feeling of unity. *House open Feb–Oct, Wed–Sun 11.00–17.00; grounds, restaurant, shop open Wed–Sun, all year. Charge.*

14¼am	11L
Bordesley	
Napton Junction	
21¾am	46L

continued in Book 2

Knowle

The canal now continues its northerly route, passing through countryside which is surprisingly peaceful. Knowle Locks introduce more hilly countryside again, and this green and pleasant land continues right through to Solihull, concealing the nearness of Birmingham. The flight of five wide locks at Knowle used to be six narrow ones, until the 1930 improvements; the remains of the old locks can still be seen alongside the new, together with the side ponds (originally built to save water). The locks are comparatively deep, and are very well maintained and pleasantly situated. They are also the northernmost wide locks for many miles now, since all the Birmingham canals have narrow locks. Knowle is set back from the canal, but warrants a visit, especially to see the church. Continuing north west through wooded country, the canal passes under the M42 motorway and crosses the River Blythe on a small aqueduct. The waterway is quite shallow between Knowle and Bordesley Junction.

● **Knowle**
W. Midlands. All services. Despite its proximity to Birmingham, Knowle still survives as a village, albeit rather self-consciously. A number of old buildings thankfully remain, some dating from the Middle Ages and including such gems as Chester House (now the library), which illustrate the advances in timber-frame construction from the 13th to the 15th C. Have a look at the splendid knot garden around the back. Half-a-mile north of the village is Grimshaw Hall, a gabled 16th C house noted for its decorative brickwork. There are good views of it from the canal.
Church of St John the Baptist, St Lawrence and St Anne Knowle B93 oLN. This remarkable church was built as a result of the efforts of Walter Cook, a

wealthy man who founded a chapel here in 1396, and completed the present church in 1402. Prior to its building the parishioners of Knowle had to make a 6-mile round trip each Sunday to the church at Hampton-in-Arden. This involved crossing the River Blythe, an innocuous brook today, but in medieval times 'a greate and daungerous water' which 'noyther man nor beaste can passe wt. owte daunger of peryshing'. The church is built in the Perpendicular style, with a great deal of intricate stonework. There is much of interest to be seen inside, including the roof timbers, the original font and a medieval dug-out chest. Behind the church is the 3-acre 'Children's Field', given to the National Trust by the Reverend T. Downing 'to be used for games'.

WE ARE THE OVALTINE-EES . . .

Dr George Wander founded the company which was to manufacture Ovaltine in Switzerland in 1864. Finding a ready market in England, the company established a factory at Kings Langley, beside what is now the Grand Union Canal. In 1925 they decided to build their own fleet of narrowboats to bring coal to this factory from Warwickshire. Their boats were always immaculately maintained, with the words 'Drink delicious Ovaltine for Health' emblazoned in orange and yellow on a very dark blue background. The last boat arrived at Kings Langley on 17 April 1959.

Pubs and Restaurants

◖ **The Black Boy** Warwick Road B93 oEB, at bridge 69 (01564 772655). Traditional family-owned pub, built in 1793, sporting a canalside garden with children's play area. Real ale and excellent bar meals with a wide choice of main courses served *L and E*. Children welcome *until 20.00.*Heated canalside patio for chilly evenings.
◖ ✕ **The Wilsons Arms** Warwick Road, Knowle B93 9AH (01564 772559). Toby Carvery pub which

dates from the 16th C. The older part still retains much of its character. Real ale, and fresh food and carvery served *L and E until 22.00.* Children welcome. Outside seating.
◖**The Heron's Nest** Warwick Road, B93 oEE (01564 771177). Canalside at bridge 70. Attractive country pub serving real ale, and traditional seasonal food *L and E.* Children welcome. Garden with a heated terrace.

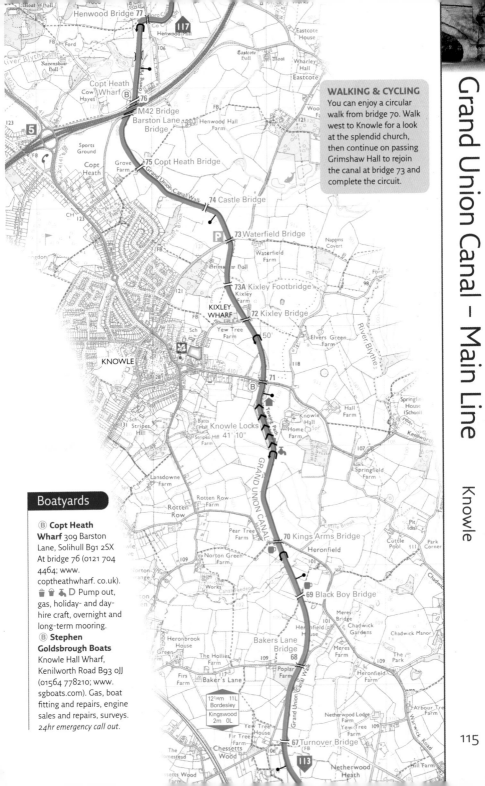

Henwood Bridge 77

117

Henwood Hill

Eastcote House

Eastcote Hall

Moat

Wharley Hall Eastcote

Copt Heath Cow Wharf
Hayes

76

M42 Bridge
Barston Lane Bridge

Henwood Hall Farm

WALKING & CYCLING
You can enjoy a circular walk from bridge 70. Walk west to Knowle for a look at the splendid church, then continue on passing Grimshaw Hall to rejoin the canal at bridge 73 and complete the circuit.

5

Sports Ground

Copt Heath

Grove Farm

75 Copt Heath Bridge

Grand Union Canal Walk

74 Castle Bridge

P 73 Waterfield Bridge

Nappins Covert

Waterfield Farm

Ford

Grimshaw Hall

73A Kixley Footbridge

Kixley Farm

KIXLEY WHARF

72 Kixley Bridge

Elvers Green Farm

River Blythe

Yew Tree Farm

50'

KNOWLE

118

71

B

Knowle Hall

Hall Farm

Springle House (School)

Towing Path

Knowle Locks 41' 10"

Home Farm

Kenilworth

Batts Hall
Stripes Hill

Stripes Hill

107

Springfield Farm

GRAND UNION CANAL

Lansdowne Farm

Rotten Row Farm

Rotten Row

Pit (dis)

Park Corner

Cuttle Pool

Pear Tree Farm

Little Brook

70 Kings Arms Bridge

Heronfield

Boatyards

B Copt Heath Wharf 309 Barston Lane, Solihull B91 2SX At bridge 76 (0121 704 4464; www. coptheathwharf. co.uk). 🛏 🚿 🚻 D Pump out, gas, holiday- and day-hire craft, overnight and long-term mooring.

B Stephen Goldsbrough Boats Knowle Hall Wharf, Kenilworth Road B93 0JJ (01564 778210; www. sgboats.com). Gas, boat fitting and repairs, engine sales and repairs, surveys. *24hr emergency call out.*

Norton Green Farm

Grand Union Canal Walk

69 Black Boy Bridge

Meres Bridge

Chadwick Gardens

Chadwick Manor

Heronbrook House

Heronfield House

Meres Farm

The Park

The Hollies Farm

Bakers Lane Bridge 68

Poplar Farm

Heronfield Farm

Firs Farm

Baker's Lane

12¼m 11L
Bordesley
Kingswood
2m 0L

Yew Tree House

Fir Tree Farm

Chessetts Wood

Netherwood Lodge Farm

Yew Tree Farm

Arbour Tree Farm

Warwick Road

67 Turnover Bridge

113

Netherwood Heath

Hill Farm

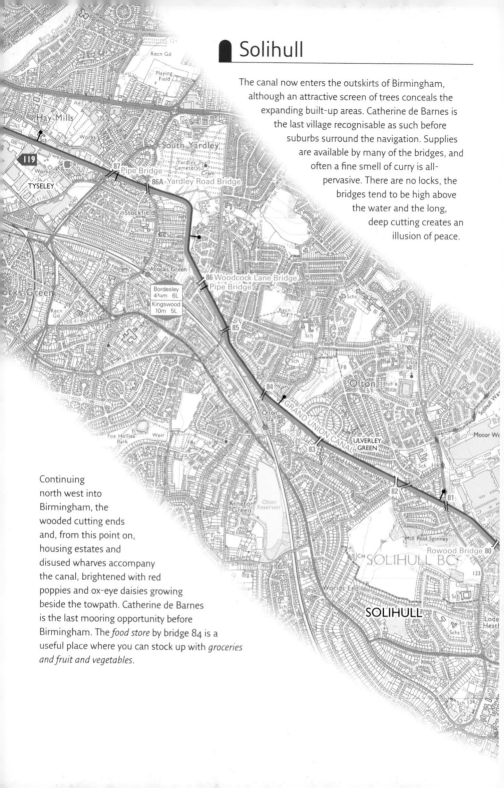

◗ Solihull

The canal now enters the outskirts of Birmingham,
although an attractive screen of trees conceals the
expanding built-up areas. Catherine de Barnes is
the last village recognisable as such before
suburbs surround the navigation. Supplies
are available by many of the bridges, and
often a fine smell of curry is all-
pervasive. There are no locks, the
bridges tend to be high above
the water and the long,
deep cutting creates an
illusion of peace.

Continuing
north west into
Birmingham, the
wooded cutting ends
and, from this point on,
housing estates and
disused wharves accompany
the canal, brightened with red
poppies and ox-eye daisies growing
beside the towpath. Catherine de Barnes
is the last mooring opportunity before
Birmingham. The *food store* by bridge 84 is a
useful place where you can stock up with *groceries
and fruit and vegetables*.

- **Catherine de Barnes**
  W. Midlands. PO, stores. A small village with new housing, which takes its name from the 12th C Lord 'Ketelberne'. The houses and flats known as Catherine's Court were once a 'fever hospital', built in 1907. The village is a convenient supply centre, with easy access from the canal, before the bulk of Birmingham begins to make its presence felt.
- **Elmdon Heath**
  W. Midlands. PO, stores, takeaways. A suburb of Solihull useful for supplies.
- **Solihull**
  W. Midlands. PO, tel, stores, garage, cinema, station.

A modern commuter development, with fine public buildings. What used to be the town centre, dominated by the tall spire of the parish church, is now a shopping area.

St Alphege Church Church Hill Road B91 3RQ. Built of red sandstone, it is almost all late 13th C and early 14th-C. The lofty interior contains work of all periods, including a Jacobean pulpit, a 17th C communion rail, 19th C stained glass and a few notable monuments.

Tourist Information Centre Central Library, Homer Road B91 3RG (0121 704 6130; www.solihull.gov.uk).

Pubs and Restaurants

The Boat Inn 222 Hampton Lane, Catherine de Barnes B91 2TJ (0121 705 0474). A well-kept and friendly pub, offering real ale, together with bar meals *all day, every day*. Children welcome, garden.

Longfellows English Restaurant 255 Hampton Lane, Catherine de Barnes (0121 705 0547; www.long-fellows.co.uk). Cosy and intimate family-run restaurant serving fresh food, including game and seafood, *L Tue–Fri 12.00 until last orders 13.30; E Mon–Sat from 18.00*. Theme nights. Seating outside in landscaped garden.

The Barge Stop Tyseley (0121 628 2339). Between bridges 87 and 88. Restaurant and bar with B & B for truckers. Café *open Mon-Fri 06.00-21.30, and Sat morning*. Canalside seats.

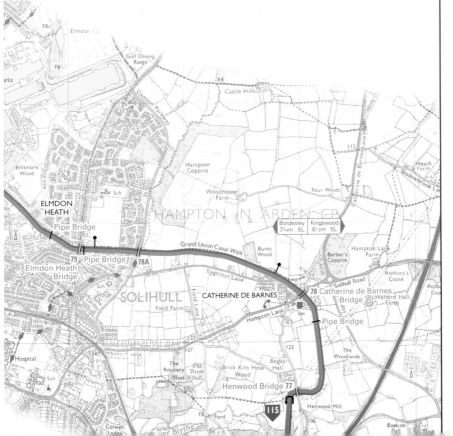

Birmingham

The canal curves past the large Energy from Waste plant and the Ackers Trust Basin before reaching Camp Hill Locks. These, and all the succeeding locks, are narrow. After passing through subterranean vaults formed by the criss-crossing of railway viaducts, Bordesley Junction is reached. Ahead, beyond the junction, the canal continues towards the Birmingham Canal Main Line, joining the Birmingham & Fazeley Canal at Aston Junction, passing a very fine collection of old wharf buildings on the way. Heading north from Bordesley Junction, the Grand Union is accompanied by pleasantly transformed surroundings to join the Birmingham & Fazeley Canal at Salford Junction.

Salford Junction 1¾m 11L
Farmer's Bridge 1½m 13L
Aldersley Junction via Birmingham Level 15m 24L
King's Norton 5½m 0L

NAVIGATIONAL NOTES

Moor only at recognised sites in the city, such as Gas Street, Cambrian Wharf or boatyards (by arrangement). Contact the local Waterway Unit for advice if you are in doubt.

Pubs and Restaurants

🍺 **The Marlborough** Anderton Road, Sparkbrook B11 1ND (0121 772 2459). West of bridge 90. A large red-brick pile, marked with a prominent clock-tower. Children welcome.

continued in Book 2

110

Tame Valley Canal
Salford Bridge
Salford Junction

Birmingham & Fazeley Canal
Bromford Bridge No 1
Bromford Bridge No 2

Works

Erdington Hall
Bridge
River Tame

41

Boro Const Bdy

M6

Site of
Nechells' Shallow Lock

Rushall
Junction
5m 13L

Fazeley
Junction
11¾m 14L

Cuckoo
Wharf

Aston
Bottom
Lock

24

Holborn Hill
Bridge

STA

Cuckoo
Bridge

Star
City

New
Troutpool
Bridge

NECHELLS

Pipe Bridges

23

22

Industrial Estate

Rocky Lane Bridge
Pipe Bridge

GRAND UNION CANAL

109

Washwo

47

108AA

108A

108

Industrial
Estate

NECHELLS GREEN

Sch

Duddeston

River Rea

107

63
106
62
61

Vauxhall
Garrison Locks
34' 5"

Adderley
Park

Adderley
Park Sta

Pipe Bridge

60

105

105

60

Recn
Footbridge

59

102A
101

104
103

Sch

99
98 100

102

57

BORDESLEY
Bordesley
Junction

94

St Andrews

Salford
Junction
2¾m 5L

Boro

55

Pipe Bridge

93 Camp Hill Locks
41' 8"

54

52

53

52

SMALL HEATH

Aston
Junction
1¼m 6L

91 Small Heath Bridge

Kingswood
14¾m 11L

Small Heath Park

SPARKBROOK

GRAND UNION CANAL

90 Anderton Road Bridge

Golden Hillock 89
Road Bridge

Grand Uni Can

Railway
Bridge 88E

Ackers Trust
Basin

Pipe
Bridge

88A

Hay Mills

88 Kings Road Bridge

Works

116

SKIING

Gt Heath

TYSELEY

Tyseley
TYSELEY
STA

● **Birmingham**
W. Midlands. All services. It
is strange to think that the
medieval town which centred
around a parish church and moated
manor originally stood on the site of the
present Smithfield market. Industrial and
commercial development continued with
such speed during the 19th C that Birmingham
began to be considered as the trade centre of the
Midlands.

Tourist Information Centre The Rotunda, 150 New
Street, Birmingham B2 4PA (0121 202 5099; www.
beinbirmingham.com). *Open 09.30-17.30 Mon-Sat.*
Tyseley Locomotive Works & Visitor Centre 670
Warwick Road, Tyseley (0121 708 4960; www.
vintagetrains.co.uk). A short walk south west of bridge 88.
Located on the site of a former Great Western Railway
steam shed, the museum covers 7 acres and houses both
static and working exhibits. There are steam locomotives to
see, from the mighty *Clun Castle* to the tiny *Henry*, an
industrial tank engine. One locomotive is usually in steam
each weekend throughout the year. Other things to see include
a Royal Mail van, a 1908 royal saloon car, a fully operational
turntable plus lots of steam railway paraphernalia. The
museum also rebuilds locomotives for themselves and for
other preserved steam railways, and these are on view.
Courses are run on how to drive a steam engine, but booking
is essential. Birmingham to Stratford steam train service on
summer Suns. Restaurant and shop. *Open Sat, Sun and B Hols
10.00-16.00 (closed Christmas period) – telephone to check
before travelling.* Charge.

StarCity Cuckoo Road Link, just off M6, junction 6 (0871
230 0013). One of the country's largest leisure
destinations. Multiplex cinema, bowling, casino,
Mexican, Spanish and traditional English restaurants.
Health and fitness facility. 30m mini snow slope,
30ft high rock climbing wall, rope assault
course, interactive Chamber of Horrors and
a snow play area for younger children.
Skate park. Moorings.

Crick (see page 74)

Husbands Bosworth (see page 78)

OXFORD CANAL

MAXIMUM DIMENSIONS
Length: 70'
Beam: 7'
Headroom: 7'

MILEAGE
BRAUNSTON TURN to:
Hillmorton Bottom Lock: 7½
Rugby Wharf Arm: 10¼
Stretton Stop: 15¾

HAWKESBURY JUNCTION
(*Coventry Canal*): 22¾ miles
Locks: 4

MANAGER
01908 30255
enquiries.southeast@britishwaterways.co.uk
Stone Bridge (9) to Hawkesbury:
01827 288071
enquiries.westmidlands@britishwaterways.co.uk

The Oxford Canal was one of the earliest and, for many years, one of the most important canals in southern England. It was authorised in 1769, when the Coventry Canal was in the offing, and was intended to fetch coal southwards from the Warwickshire coalfield to Banbury and Oxford, at the same time giving access to the River Thames. James Brindley was appointed engineer: he built a winding contour canal 91 miles long which soon began to look thoroughly outdated and inefficient for the carriage of goods. Brindley died in 1772, and was replaced by Samuel Simcock: he completed the line from Longford, where a junction was made with the Coventry Canal, to Banbury, in 1778. After a long pause, the canal was finally brought into Oxford in 1790, and thereafter through-traffic flowed constantly along this important new trade route.

In 1780, however, the Grand Junction Canal opened (excepting the tunnel at Blisworth) from London to Braunston, and the Warwick & Napton and Warwick & Birmingham Canals completed the new short route from London to Birmingham. This had the natural – and intended – effect of drawing traffic off the Oxford Canal, especially south of Napton Junction, but the Oxford Company protected itself very effectively against this powerful opposition by charging outrageously high rates for their 5½-mile stretch between Braunston and Napton, which had become part of the new London–Birmingham through route. Thus the Oxford Canal maintained its revenue and very high dividends for many years to come.

By the late 1820s, however, the Oxford Canal had become conspicuously out of date with its extravagant winding course and, under the threat of various schemes for big new canals which, if built, would render the Oxford Canal almost redundant, the company decided to modernise the northern part of their navigation. Tremendous engineering works were executed which completely changed the face of the canal north of Braunston. Aqueducts, massive embankments and deep cuttings were built, carrying the canal in great sweeps through the countryside and cutting almost 14 miles off the original 36 miles between Braunston Junction and the Coventry Canal. Much of the old main line suddenly became a series of loops and branches leading nowhere, now crossed by elegant new towpath bridges inscribed Horseley Ironworks 1828.

This very expensive programme was well worthwhile. Although toll rates, and thus revenue, began to fall because of keen competition from the railways, dividends were kept at a high level for years – indeed a respectable profit was still shown right through to the 20th C.

Braunston and Willoughby

North of Braunston the Oxford Canal soon leaves behind the excitement and interest of the village to run through wide open country, backed by bare hills to the east. It is an ancient landscape, and by bridge 87 medieval ridge and furrow field patterns are in evidence. These were created as villagers cleared forested land, and each ploughed strips throwing soil towards the centre. Gradually a collection of strips, all running parallel to each other, made up a furlong or cultura. This was then enclosed by a low bank and an access track (usually difficult to identify today) was created. Fields, consisting of dozens of furlongs, were then sometimes fenced. Skirting round Barby Hill, the canal swings north east towards Hillmorton and Rugby. The M45 makes a noisy crossing after Barby Hill.

Boatyards

All the following are on the *Grand Union Canal* at Braunston.

The Boat Shop Bottom Lock, Dark Lane, Braunston NN11 7HJ (01788 891310; www.boatshopbraunston.co.uk). Started on board a boat moored at Braunston Turn, this is now a shop selling a comprehensive range of chandlery, gifts and provisions, including fresh-baked bread. *Open mid Mar-mid Oct 08.00–20.00; rest of the year 08.00–18.00.*

Ⓑ **Braunston Boats** Bottom Lock, Braunston NN11 7HJ (01788 891079). D Gas, boatbuilding, fitting-out.

Ⓑ **Wharf House Narrowboats** Braunston Boat Haven, Botton Lock, Dark Lane, Braunston N11 7HJ (01788 899041; www.wharfhouse.co.uk). Boat building, fitting out and refits, electrics, chandlery, books, maps and gifts.

Ⓑ **Union Canal Carriers** Canalside at Braunston Pump House, Dark Lane NN11 7HU (01788 890784; www.unioncanalcarriers.co.uk). 🛠 D Pump out, gas, narrowboat hire, day-boat hire, dry dock, engine sales, boat and engine repairs.

Ⓑ **Braunston Marina** The Wharf, Braunston NN11 7JH (01788 891373; www.braunstonmarina.co.uk). Through the fine bridge dated 1834 and into an historic canal wharf. 🚿 🚻 🛠 D E Pump out, gas, overnight and long-term mooring, dry and wet dock, chandlery, boat building sales and repairs, engine repairs, limited chandlery, toilets, showers, public telephone, gift shop selling books and maps, laundrette, coal, DIY facilities. There are also boatbuilders, fitters, fender makers and furnishers at the marina.

Midland Chandlers London Road, Braunston NN11 7HB (01788 891401; www.midlandchandlers.co.uk) In operation for almost 30 years. A wide range of chandlery.

WALKING & CYCLING
The towpath is passable for walkers, but very bumpy in places for cyclists.

Pubs and Restaurants

🍽 ✕ **The Rose Inn** Main Street, Willoughby CV23 8BH (01788 891464). Attractively maintained thatched village pub, offering real ale. Bar, restaurant and carvery meals *L and E (not Sun or Mon E)*. Outside seating with children's play area. Regular entertainment with theme nights.

🍽 ✕ **The Mill House Hotel** London Road, Braunston NN11 7HB (01788 890450; www.millhouseinns.co.uk). Once the Rose & Castle, it is now a welcoming hotel and restaurant, serving real ale. Grills, *Sun* roasts, carvery meals *L and E*. Children's room and fine canalside garden with swings. Overnight mooring for patrons. Live jazz *Sun*. B & B.

🍽 **The Wheatsheaf** The Green, Braunston NN1 17HW (01788 890748; www.the-wheatsheaf-braunston.co.uk) A locals' pub with a warm atmosphere offering traditional home cooked food. Real ale and beer gardens. Meals, including traditional *Sun* lunch, are served *L and E*. Children welcome *until 19.30*. Pool table, skittles, darts. Garden with a barbecue. Live music every other *Sat*. Big screen sports available.

🍽 ✕ **The Old Plough** 82 High Street, Braunston NN11 7HS (01788 890000). A fine village pub dating from 1672, with open fires and serving real ale. Good food *L and E daily (no Tue L)*, with *Sun* roasts. Children are welcome, and there is a garden. Quiz every other *Sun*.

Onley Fields

Whitehall Farm

94

77 BARBY STRAIGHT 127

103

M45 Motorway Bridge

Danetre Farm

78 Barby Wood Bridge

Works

Ash Tree Farm

142

79

106

126

Home Farm

BARBY CP

Motte

80 Wise's Bridge BARBY HILL

BARBY PO

young Offender nstitution

153

161

163

Hillfie Bar

81

nley Fields Farm

82 Rowdyke Bridge

83

● **Braunston**

Northants. PO, stores, butcher, fish & chips. Set up on a hill to the north of the canal, so that the tall spire of Braunston church dominates the valley for miles around. The village is really a long main street a little separate from the canal, with houses of all periods that give the feeling of a spacious market town. A very well-known canal centre, it is no less significant today than when the Oxford and Grand Junction canals were first connected here.

● **Willoughby**

Warwicks. A mellow red-brick village to which new buildings have been unobtrusively added. The small church is dominated by a fine 18th C rectory.

Willoughby Lodge

84

Longdown Lane

Will

Navigation Farm

127

Sheep Pen

85 Navigation Bridge
Willoughby Wharf

89

OXFORD CANAL 87

WILLOUGHBY CP

Vicarage

M5

WILLOUGHBY

Bath Farm

Glebe Barn

A 45(T)

88

102

BRAUNSTON CP

London Road

Hawkesbury
22¾m 4L
Napton
5m 0L

92

M5

BRAUNSTON

Sheep Dip

111

89

loughby use

Braunston Turn 95

94/3

Braunston Puddle Banks

96

Willoughby Viaduct

Sewage Works

90

Butcher's Bridge

Bottom Lock

N91

Braunston
Turn
1¼m 6L

Norton
Junction
3m 0L

LITTLE BRAUNSTON

Canal Cottages

2

Braunston
Lock Flight
35' 6"

102

MPCOTE CP

105

Medieval Village of Braunstonbury

The Stop House

GRAND UNION CANAL

Marina

3

4

5

6

Top Lock N°6

125

98 97

Medieval Village of Wolfhampcote

Springfield

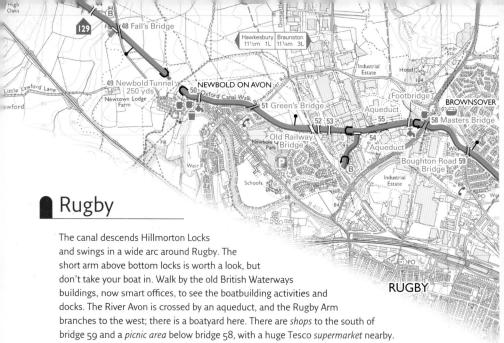

Rugby

The canal descends Hillmorton Locks and swings in a wide arc around Rugby. The short arm above bottom locks is worth a look, but don't take your boat in. Walk by the old British Waterways buildings, now smart offices, to see the boatbuilding activities and docks. The River Avon is crossed by an aqueduct, and the Rugby Arm branches to the west; there is a boatyard here. There are *shops* to the south of bridge 59 and a *picnic area* below bridge 58, with a huge Tesco *supermarket* nearby. The towpath along this stretch is in excellent condition. Moorings at Newbold Tunnel make a pleasant stop, with a choice of pubs close by.

Boatyards

ⓑ **Grantham Bridge Boat Services** The Locks, Hillmorton CV21 4PP (01788 578661/07812 039110; www.canalbreaks.com). 👕 👕 🛒 D Wet dock and dry dock, pump out, gas, boat hire, boatbuilding, boat and engine repairs, DIY facilities, books and maps, solid fuel. *24hr emergency breakdown call out.*

ⓑ **Clifton Cruisers** Clifton Wharf, Vicarage Hill, Clifton on Dunsmore CV23 0DG (01788 543570; www.cliftoncruisers.co.uk). 👕 👕 🛒 D Pump out, gas, narrowboat hire, overnight mooring, long-term mooring, winter storage, engine sales, boat

and engine repairs, boatbuilding, chandlery, gifts, RYA recognised training.

ⓑ **Willow Wren Hire Cruisers** Rugby Wharf, off Consul Road, Rugby CV21 1PB (01788 562183/569153; www.willowwren.co.uk). 👕 🛒 D Pump out, gas, narrowboat hire, overnight and long-term mooring, boat sales and repairs, engine repairs, toilets and showers, books and maps, café, DIY facilities.

ⓑ **T. F. Yates** Falls Bridge Works, Cathiron Lane, Newbold-on-Avon (01788 569140). East of bridge 44. 👕 🛒 D Pump out, gas, crane, engine sales, boat and engine repairs, boatbuilding, solid fuel.

● **Hillmorton**
Warwicks. PO, stores, garage, takeaways, but all a fair distance from the canal.

● **Rugby**
Warwicks. PO, stores, garage, station, theatre, cinema, leisure centre. There is a pedestrianised shopping centre, a leisure centre and an open market with a town crier. Look out for the tiny shop in Chapel Street, which has stood for over 500 years and is reputedly the oldest building in the town.

Rugby Art Gallery and Museum Little Elborow Street, Rugby CV21 3BZ (01788 533201;

www.rugby.gov.uk). Contemporary visual art and crafts; museum includes Roman artifacts and social history gallery. *Open Tue and Thu, 10.00-20.00; Wed and Fri, 10.00-17.00; Sat 10.00-16.00.*

Webb Ellis Rugby Football Museum 5–6 St Matthews Street, Rugby CV21 3BY (01788 533217; www.rugby.gov.uk).The museum is housed opposite Rugby School in the original building where James Gilbert, boot-maker, made the first rugby footballs in 1842. *Open Mon-Sat, 9.00-17.00.*

Tourist Information Centre Located in the foyer of the Art Gallery and Museum (01788 533217; www.rugby.gov.uk).

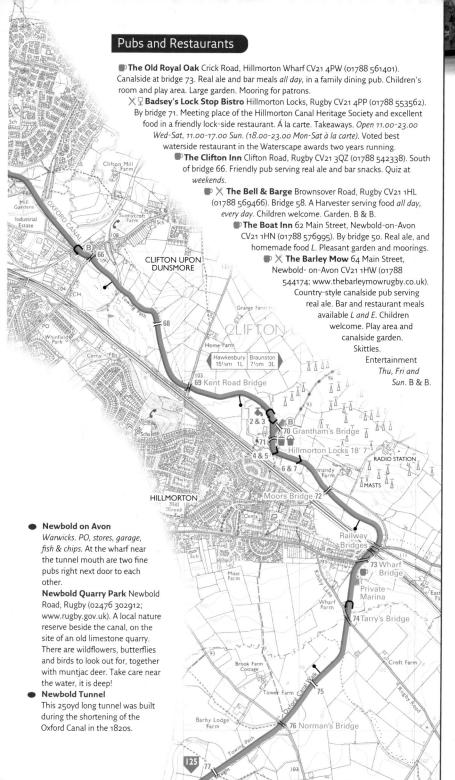

Pubs and Restaurants

🍺 **The Old Royal Oak** Crick Road, Hillmorton Wharf CV21 4PW (01788 561401). Canalside at bridge 73. Real ale and bar meals *all day*, in a family dining pub. Children's room and play area. Large garden. Mooring for patrons.

✕ 🍷 **Badsey's Lock Stop Bistro** Hillmorton Locks, Rugby CV21 4PP (01788 553562). By bridge 71. Meeting place of the Hillmorton Canal Heritage Society and excellent food in a friendly lock-side restaurant. Á la carte. Takeaways. *Open 11.00-23.00 Wed-Sat, 11.00-17.00 Sun. (18.00-23.00 Mon-Sat à la carte).* Voted best waterside restaurant in the Waterscape awards two years running.

🍺 **The Clifton Inn** Clifton Road, Rugby CV21 3QZ (01788 542338). South of bridge 66. Friendly pub serving real ale and bar snacks. Quiz at *weekends*.

🍺 ✕ **The Bell & Barge** Brownsover Road, Rugby CV21 1HL (01788 569466). Bridge 58. A Harvester serving food *all day*, *every day*. Children welcome. Garden. B & B.

🍺 **The Boat Inn** 62 Main Street, Newbold-on-Avon CV21 1HN (01788 576995). By bridge 50. Real ale, and homemade food *L*. Pleasant garden and moorings.

🍺 ✕ **The Barley Mow** 64 Main Street, Newbold- on-Avon CV21 1HW (01788 544174; www.thebarleymowrugby.co.uk). Country-style canalside pub serving real ale. Bar and restaurant meals available *L and E*. Children welcome. Play area and canalside garden. Skittles. Entertainment *Thu, Fri and Sun*. B & B.

Newbold on Avon
Warwicks. PO, stores, garage, fish & chips. At the wharf near the tunnel mouth are two fine pubs right next door to each other.

Newbold Quarry Park Newbold Road, Rugby (02476 302912; www.rugby.gov.uk). A local nature reserve beside the canal, on the site of an old limestone quarry. There are wildflowers, butterflies and birds to look out for, together with muntjac deer. Take care near the water, it is deep!

Newbold Tunnel
This 250yd long tunnel was built during the shortening of the Oxford Canal in the 1820s.

127

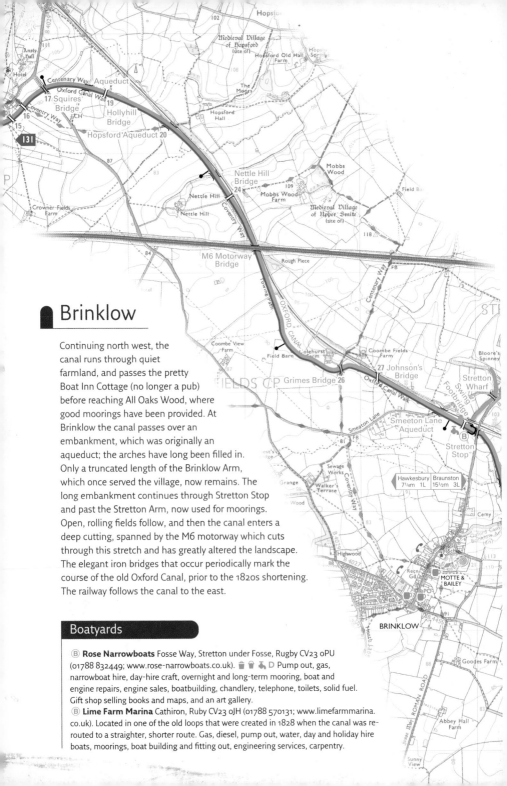

Brinklow

Continuing north west, the canal runs through quiet farmland, and passes the pretty Boat Inn Cottage (no longer a pub) before reaching All Oaks Wood, where good moorings have been provided. At Brinklow the canal passes over an embankment, which was originally an aqueduct; the arches have long been filled in. Only a truncated length of the Brinklow Arm, which once served the village, now remains. The long embankment continues through Stretton Stop and past the Stretton Arm, now used for moorings. Open, rolling fields follow, and then the canal enters a deep cutting, spanned by the M6 motorway which cuts through this stretch and has greatly altered the landscape. The elegant iron bridges that occur periodically mark the course of the old Oxford Canal, prior to the 1820s shortening. The railway follows the canal to the east.

Hawkesbury	Braunston
7¼m 1L	15½m 3L

Boatyards

Ⓑ **Rose Narrowboats** Fosse Way, Stretton under Fosse, Rugby CV23 0PU (01788 832449; www.rose-narrowboats.co.uk). 🛉 🛉 🛁 D Pump out, gas, narrowboat hire, day-hire craft, overnight and long-term mooring, boat and engine repairs, engine sales, boatbuilding, chandlery, telephone, toilets, solid fuel. Gift shop selling books and maps, and an art gallery.

Ⓑ **Lime Farm Marina** Cathiron, Ruby CV23 0JH (01788 570131; www.limefarmmarina. co.uk). Located in one of the old loops that were created in 1828 when the canal was re-routed to a straighter, shorter route. Gas, diesel, pump out, water, day and holiday hire boats, moorings, boat building and fitting out, engineering services, carpentry.

Harborough Magna

Warwicks. PO box, stores. Quiet red-brick village one mile to the north of the canal from bridges 43 or 48. The 13th–14th C church has a Victorian west tower and many Victorian additions, including an interesting stained-glass window depicting Christ rising, with two angels, against a dark blue background.

Brinklow

Warwicks. PO, tel, stores, fish & chips. A spacious pre-industrial village built along a wide main street. The church of St John Baptist is of late Perpendicular style, and has some interesting 15th C stained glass depicting birds, including a peacock. Its sloping floor climbs 12ft from west to east. Alongside is the substantial mound of a motte and bailey castle, built to defend the Fosse Way.

Pubs and Restaurants

The White Lion Broad Street, Brinklow CV23 0LN (01788 832579; www.thewhitelion-inn.co.uk). Traditional coaching inn with an old-fashioned bar, serving real ale and food *L Mon–Sat.* Children welcome. Delightful garden with a play area. Skittles, pool and darts. Camping. B & B.

The Bulls Head Coventry Road, Brinklow CV23 0NE (01788 832355; mrgriff@supanet.com). A smartly furnished family pub. Good food served *L and E.* Children welcome, indoor and outdoor play areas. Garden. B & B.

The Raven Broad Street, Brinklow CV23 0LN (01788 832655). Friendly family pub at the top of the village, where real ale is served. Bar meals *L and E (not Sun E)* Children welcome, garden.

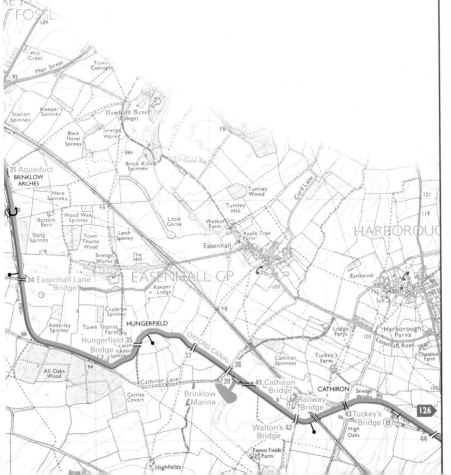

Hawkesbury Junction

The open landscape continues beyond Ansty, although the motorway is never far away. Soon the first signs of Coventry appear, with views of pylons and housing estates. The new Wyken Colliery Arm leaves to the west: it was built to replace the old one eaten up by the motorway which comes alongside the canal at this point: it is now used by the Coventry Cruising Club. Sharp bends then lead to the stop lock before Hawkesbury Junction, the end of the Oxford Canal where it joins the Coventry Canal. This last stretch of the Oxford Canal is characterised by the 1820s shortenings: straight cuttings and embankments date from this period, while the cast iron bridges mark the old route.

Pubs and Restaurants

The Rose & Castle Main Road, Ansty CV9 9HA (02476 612822). Friendly and welcoming canalside pub serving real ale and an extensive range of good food available *L and E*. Children welcome, play area and canalside garden. Moorings and 🚰

The Elephant & Castle 445 Aldermans Green Road CV2 1NL (02476 364606). Canalside, by Tusses Bridge (4). There is a good choice of real ale in this extended friendly local community pub. Huge garden with a children's play area. Pool and Darts. Moorings. Quiz *Tue*.

The Old Crown Aldermans Green Road CV2 1NP (02476 365894). South of Tusses Bridge (4). Welcoming and cosy pub with carved woodwork, beams, brasses and snug settees, serving real ale. Children welcome, garden with play area. Disco *Sat*.

✕ The Greyhound Longford CV6 6DF (02476 363046). A fascinating pub beside Hawkesbury Junction, decorated with canal memorabilia, warmed by log fires in *winter*. An imaginative selection of food, especially pies and salads, served in the bar or restaurant *L and E*, and a choice of real ale is available. Canalside garden. Moorings.

The Boat Inn Black Horse Road, Longford CV6 6DL (02476 361438). A fine friendly pub with unspoilt rooms and a cosy lounge, just a 3-minute walk north west of the junction. Real ale. Children welcome. Garden for the *summer* and a real fire for the *winter*. Quiz *Mon*.

BEDWORTH

EXHALL

LONGFORD

ALDERMAN'S GREEN

Bell Green

Coventry Canal

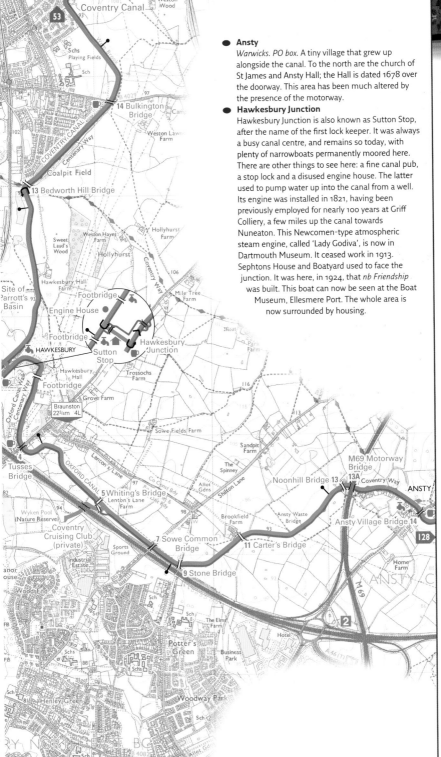

Ansty

Warwicks. PO box. A tiny village that grew up alongside the canal. To the north are the church of St James and Ansty Hall; the Hall is dated 1678 over the doorway. This area has been much altered by the presence of the motorway.

Hawkesbury Junction

Hawkesbury Junction is also known as Sutton Stop, after the name of the first lock keeper. It was always a busy canal centre, and remains so today, with plenty of narrowboats permanently moored here. There are other things to see here: a fine canal pub, a stop lock and a disused engine house. The latter used to pump water up into the canal from a well. Its engine was installed in 1821, having been previously employed for nearly 100 years at Griff Colliery, a few miles up the canal towards Nuneaton. This Newcomen-type atmospheric steam engine, called 'Lady Godiva', is now in Dartmouth Museum. It ceased work in 1913. Sephtons House and Boatyard used to face the junction. It was here, in 1924, that *nb Friendship* was built. This boat can now be seen at the Boat Museum, Ellesmere Port. The whole area is now surrounded by housing.

Brindley's Sow Aqueduct (see page 141)

STAFFORDSHIRE & WORCESTERSHIRE CANAL: NORTH

MAXIMUM DIMENSIONS

Length: 72'
Beam: 7'
Headroom: 6' 0"

MANAGER

0121 200 7400
enquiries.westmidlands@britishwaterways.co.uk

MILEAGE

AUTHERLEY JUNCTION to:
GREAT HAYWOOD JUNCTION: 20½ miles

Locks: 12

Construction of this navigation was begun immediately after that of the Trent & Mersey, to effect the joining of the rivers Trent, Mersey and Severn. Engineered by James Brindley, the Staffordshire & Worcestershire was opened throughout in 1772, at a cost of rather over £100,000. It stretched 46 miles from Great Haywood on the Trent & Mersey to the River Severn, which it joined at Stourport. The canal was an immediate success. It was well placed to bring goods from the Potteries down to Gloucester, Bristol and the West Country; while the Birmingham Canal, which joined it half-way along at Aldersley Junction, fed manufactured goods northwards from the Black Country to the Potteries via Great Haywood. In 1815 the Worcester & Birmingham Canal opened, offering a more direct but heavily locked canal link between Birmingham and the Severn. The Staffordshire & Worcestershire answered this threat by gradually extending the opening times of the locks until, by 1830, they were open 24 hours a day. When the Birmingham & Liverpool Junction Canal was opened from Autherley to Nantwich in 1835, traffic bound for Merseyside from Birmingham naturally began to use this more direct, modern canal. The Staffordshire & Worcestershire lost a great deal of traffic over its length as most of the boats now passed along only the ½-mile stretch of the Staffordshire & Worcestershire Canal between Autherley and Aldersley Junctions. The company levied absurdly high tolls for this tiny length. The B & LJ Company therefore co-operated with the Birmingham Canal Company in 1836 to promote in Parliament a Bill for the Tettenhall & Autherley Canal and Aqueduct. This project was to be a canal flyover, going from the Birmingham Canal right over the profiteering Staffordshire & Worcestershire and locking down into the Birmingham & Liverpool Junction Canal. The Staffordshire & Worcestershire company had to give way, and reduced its tolls to an acceptable level.

In spite of this set back, the Staffordshire & Worcestershire maintained a good profit, and high dividends were paid throughout the rest of the 19th C. From the 1860s onwards, railway competition began to bite, and the company's profits began to slip. Several modernisation schemes came to nothing, and the canal's trade declined. Now the canal is used almost exclusively by pleasure craft. It is covered in full in *Guide 2* of this series.

Autherley Junction

Autherley Junction is marked by a big white bridge on the towpath side. The stop lock just beyond marks the entrance to the Shropshire Union: there is a useful boatyard just to the north of it. Leaving Autherley, the Staffordshire & Worcestershire passes new housing before running through a very narrow cutting in rock, once known as 'Pendeford Rockin', after a local farm: there is only room for boats to pass in the designated places, so a good look out should be kept for oncoming craft. After passing the motorway the navigation leaves behind the suburbs of Wolverhampton and enters pleasant farmland. The bridges need care: although the bridgeholes are reasonably wide, the actual arches are rather low.

● **Autherley Junction**
A busy canal junction with a full range of boating facilities close by.

● **Coven**
Staffs. PO, tel, stores, garage, fish & chips. The only true village on this section, Coven lies beyond a dual carriageway north west of Cross Green Bridge. There is a large number of shops, including a laundrette.

Pubs and Restaurants

🍺 ✕ **Fox & Anchor Inn** Brewood Road, Cross Green, Wolverhampton WV10 7PW (01902 790786). Canalside by Cross Green Bridge. Large and friendly pub with roof-top terrace. Real ale, and meals available *all day*. Menu is traditional English, along with steaks and *Sun* roast. Children's menu, garden and good moorings.

WALKING & CYCLING
The towpath is generally in good condition for both walkers and cyclists.

Boatyards

ⓑ **Napton Narrowboats** Autherley Junction, Oxley Moor Road, Wolverhampton WV9 5HW (01926 813644). 🚿 🚽 ⛽ D E Pump out, gas, narrowboat hire, overnight mooring, long term mooring, winter storage, slipway, chandlery, provisions, books and maps, boat building, DIY facilities, boat repairs, solid fuel, gifts, showers. *Emergency call out.*

ⓑ **Oxley Marine** The Wharf, Oxley Moor Road, Wolverhampton WV10 6TZ (01902 789522; www.oxleymarine.co.uk). 🚿 D Pump out, gas, overnight and long-term mooring, winter storage, slipway, boat and engine sales and repairs, DIY facilities, *emergency call out.* Licensed bar *each evening*, snacks.

BOAT TRIPS
City of Wolverhampton Passenger Boat Services, The Wharf, Oxley Moor Road, Wolverhampton WV10 6TZ. *Nb Stafford* Carrying up to 42 passengers, with a bar and food. Public trips on *most Sun Apr–Sep*, plus private charter. For details telephone 01902 789522.

BIRD LIFE
The *Long-Tailed Tit* is a charming resident of woods, heaths and hedgerows. Feeding flocks of these birds resemble animated feather dusters. Their plumage can look black and white, but at close range there is a pinkish wash to the underparts and pinkish buff on the backs. The long-tailed tit has a tiny, stubby bill, a long tail, and an almost spherical body.

9 Chillington Bridge

Shropshire Union Canal
Par see Book 4

137

8 Park Bridge

Grange Farm

94

COVEN

Slade Heath Bridge 72

06 57 Slade Heath Railway Bridges

7 Hunting Bridge

CROSS GREEN
71 Cross Green Bridge

Cross Green Farm

River Penk

Lawn Farm Lane

Lawn Lane

FB

Coven Lawn

70 Brinsford Bridge

Brinsford

Brinsford Farm

6 Lower Hattons Bridge

The Old Hattons

The Middle Hattons

Lower Pendeford Farm

River Penk

Ash Coppice

Coven Lane

COVEN HEATH
69 Coven Heath Bridge
Pipe Bridge

Sewage Works

2

5 Upper Hattons Bridge

Island Pool

Middle Lane

Monarch's Way

Clewley Coppice

M54 Motorway

Works

Cricket Ground

P

PC

Caravan Park

Shooting Pit

Works

Pendeford Mill Nature Reserve

Monarch's Way

Forster Bridge 68

Fordhouses

4 Pendeford Bridge

Works

Upper Pendeford Farm

Marsh Lane Bridge 67

BILBROOK CP

3A

Turnover Bridge 3

Pendeford

Bathurst Bridge 2

Autherley Junction

66 Blaydon Road Bridge

21m 12L
Great Haywood

Aldersley Junction
½m 0L

40¾m 29L
Hurleston

Autherley Stop Lock

B

1 Junction Bridge

WOLVERHAMPTON

B

OXLEY

65 Oxley Moor Bridge

Pipe Bridge

Aqueducts

Railway Bridges

Elston Hall

Low Hill

Blakeley Green

Pipe Bridge

Aldersley Junction

Aldersley Bridge 64

ALDERSLEY

Birmingham Main Line

36

Staffs and Worcs
see Book 2

21

20

Dunstall Park Bridge

Claregate

Gailey Wharf

The considerable age of this canal is shown by its extremely twisting course, revealed after passing the railway bridge. There are few real centres of population along this stretch, which comprises largely former heathland. The canal widens just before bridge 74, where Brindley incorporated part of a medieval moat into the canal. Hatherton Junction marks the entrance of the former Hatherton Branch of the Staffordshire & Worcestershire Canal into the main line. This branch used to connect with the Birmingham Canal Navigations. It is closed above the derelict second lock, although the channel remains as a feeder for the Staffordshire & Worcestershire Canal. There is a campaign for its restoration. There is a marina at the junction. A little further along, a chemical works is encountered, astride the canal in what used to be woodlands. This was once called the 'Black Works', as lamp black was produced here. Gailey Wharf is about a mile further north: it is a small canal settlement that includes a boatyard and a large, round, toll keeper's watch-tower, containing a useful canal shop. The picturesque Wharf Cottage opposite has been restored as a bijou residence. The canal itself disappears under Watling Street and then rapidly through five locks towards Penkridge. These locks are very attractive, and some are accompanied by little brick bridges. The M6 motorway, and the traffic noise, comes alongside for ½ mile, screening the reservoirs which feed the canal.

Pillaton Old Hall Penkridge, ST19 5RZ (01785 712200). South east of bridge 85. Only the gate house and stone-built chapel remain of this late 15th-C brick mansion built by the Littleton family, although there are still traces of the hall and courtyard. The chapel contains a 13th-C wooden carving of a saint. Visiting is by appointment only: telephone 01785 712200. The modest charge is donated to charity.

Gailey and Calf Heath reservoirs ½ mile east of Gailey Wharf, either side of the M6. These are feeder reservoirs for the canal, though rarely drawn on. The public has access to them as nature reserves to study the wide variety of natural life, especially the long-established heronry which is thriving on an island in Gailey Lower Reservoir. In Gailey Upper, fishing is available to the public from the riparian owner. Permits for entry can be obtained from www.westmidlandbirdclub.com.

Boatyards

ⓑ **Otherton Boat Haven** Otherton, Otherton, Penkridge ST19 5NX (01785 712515; mobile 07966 184182; www.othertonboathaven.co.uk). 🛥 🚽 ⚓ D Pump out, gas, overnight and long-term mooring, boat and engine sales and repairs, toilets, coal, laundry facilities.
ⓑ **J D Boat Services** The Wharf, Gailey, Stafford ST19 5PR (01902 791811; www.jdboats.co.uk). D Pump out, gas, boat and engine repairs, engine sales, boat building, breakdown service. Gifts and provisions, chandlery and maps opposite in the Roundhouse.
ⓑ **Viking Afloat** At J D Boat Services (01905 610660; www.viking-afloat.com). Narrowboat hire.

Pubs and Restaurants

✗ ♀ **Misty's Bar & Restaurant** King's Road, Calf Heath, near Wolverhampton WV10 7DU (01902 790570). Restaurant serving excellent and reasonably priced home-cooked food L and E. Children welcome. Garden.
🍺 **Cross Keys** Filance Lane, Penkridge ST19 5HJ (01785 712826). Canalside, at Filance Bridge (84). Once a lonely canal pub, now it is modernised and surrounded by housing estates. Family orientated, it serves real ale and food L and E. Garden, with summer barbecues. 🌳 There is a useful Spar shop 100yds north, on the estate.

BOAT TRIPS
Hatherton Belle 45-seater trip boat with a bar. Details from Misty's Bar and Restaurant.

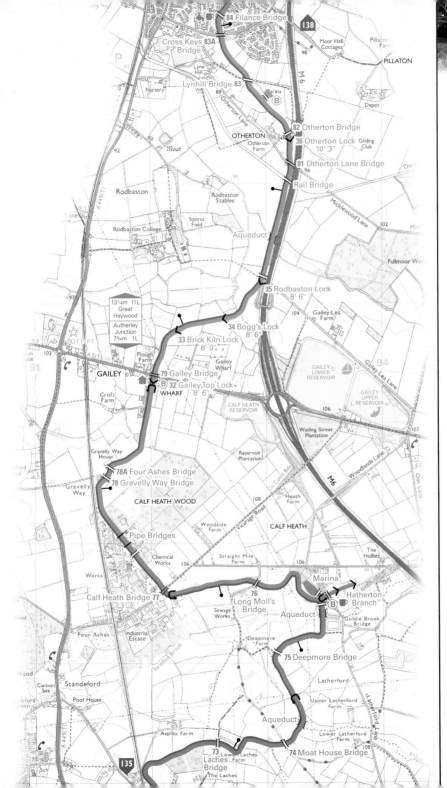

Penkridge

The navigation now passes through Penkridge and is soon approached by the little River Penk: the two water courses share the valley for the next few miles. The Cross Keys at Filance Bridge (*see* page 128) was once an isolated canal pub – now it is surrounded by housing, which spreads along the canal in each direction. Apart from the noise of the motorway this is a pleasant valley: there are plenty of trees, a handful of locks and the large Teddesley Park alongside the canal. At Acton Trussell the M6 roars off to the north west and once again peace returns to the waterway. Teddesley Park Bridge was at one time quite ornamental, and became known as 'Fancy Bridge'. It is less so now. At Shutt Hill an iron post at the bottom of the lock is the only reminder of a small wharf which once existed here. The post was used to turn the boats into the dock.

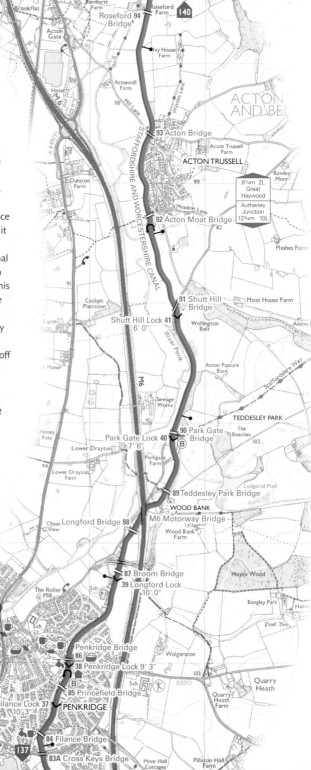

Penkridge

Staffs. PO, tel, stores, garage, bank, station, butchers, takeaway and chemist. Above Penkridge Lock is a good place to tie up in this relatively old village. It is bisected by a trunk road, but luckily most of the village lies to the east of it. The church of St Michael is tall and sombre, and is well-kept. A harmonious mixture of styles, the earliest part dates from the 11th C, but the whole was restored in 1881. There is a fine Dutch 18th-C wrought iron screen brought from Cape Town, and the tower is believed to date from c.1500. There are fine monuments of the Littletons of Pillaton Hall (*see* page 124), dating from 1558 and later.

Teddesley Park On the east bank of the canal. The Hall, once the family seat of the Littletons, was used during World War II as a prisoner-of-war camp, but has since been demolished. Its extensive wooded estate still remains.

Acton Trussell

Staffs. Tel, stores. A village overwhelmed by modern housing: much the best way to see it is from the canal. The church stands to the south, overlooking the navigation. The west tower dates from the 13th C, topped by a spire built in 1562.

Boatyards

Ⓑ **Teddesley Boat Company** Park Gate Lock, Teddesley Road, Penkridge ST19 5RH (01785 714692; www.narrowboats.co.uk). D Pump out, gas, narrowboat hire, overnight and long-term mooring, winter storage, crane, boat and engine sales and repairs, boat building, telephone, books and maps. For chandlery telephone 01785 712437.

Ⓑ **Tom's Moorings** Cannock Road, Penkridge ST19 5DT (01543 414808). Above Penkridge Lock. 🪝 Pump out, gas, overnight and long-term mooring.

PLANT LIFE
The *Bluebell* is a familiar bulbous perennial, often carpeting whole woodland floors if the situation suits its requirements. The leaves are narrow and all basal. Bell-shaped flowers in one-sided spikes appear April–June.

Pubs and Restaurants

🍺 **The Boat** Cannock Road, Penkridge ST19 5DT (01785 714178). Canalside, by Penkridge Lock. Mellow and friendly red-brick pub dating from 1779, with plenty of brass and other bits and pieces in the homely bars. Real ale. Food is available *L and E, all day*. Children welcome, garden.

🍺 **Star** Market Place, Penkridge ST19 5DJ (01785 712513). Fine old pub serving real ale and bar meals *12.00–17.00 in summer, reduced hours in winter*. Children welcome. Outside seating.

🍺 **White Hart** Stone Cross, Penkridge ST19 5AS (01785 712242). This historic former coaching inn, visited by Mary, Queen of Scots, and Elizabeth I, has an impressive frontage, timber framed with three gables. It serves real ale, and meals *L and E*. Outside seating.

🍺 **Railway** Clay Street, Penkridge ST19 5AF (01785 712685). Real ale is available in this listed and historic main road pub, along with meals *L and E*. Children welcome and there is a wonderful garden.

🍺 **Littleton Arms** St Michael's Square, Penkridge ST19 5AL (01785 716300; www.thelittletonarms.com). Hotel, bar and restaurant. Real ale and excellent food L and E. Outside seating. Children welcome. B & B.

🍺 **Flames** Mill Street, Penkridge ST19 5AY (01785 712955). Contemporary eastern cuisine.

WALKING & CYCLING
The Staffordshire Way crosses the canal between bridges 89 and 90. This 90-mile path stretches from Mow Cop in the north (near the Macclesfield Canal) to Kinver Edge in the south, using the Caldon Canal towpath on the way. It connects with the Gritstone Trail, the Hereford & Worcester Way and the Heart of England Way. A guide book is available from local Tourist Information Centres.

Tixall

Continuing north along the shallow Penk valley, the canal soon reaches Radford Bridge, the nearest point to Stafford. It is about 1½ miles to the centre of town: there is a frequent bus service. A canal branch used to connect with the town via Baswich Lock and the River Sow. If you look carefully west of bridge 101 you can just about deduce where the connection was made – some remains of brickwork are the clue. A mile further north the canal bends around to the south east and follows the pretty valley of the River Sow, and at Milford crosses the river via an aqueduct – an early structure by James Brindley, carried heavily on low brick arches. Tixall Lock offers some interesting views in all directions: the castellated entrance to Shugborough Railway Tunnel at the foot of the thick woods of Cannock Chase and the distant outline of the remarkable Tixall Gatehouse. The canal now completes its journey to the Trent & Mersey Canal at Great Haywood. It is a length of waterway quite unlike any other. Proceeding along this very charming valley, the navigation enters Tixall Wide – an amazing and delightful stretch of water more resembling a lake than a canal, said to have been built in order not to compromise the view from Tixall House (alas, no more), and navigable to the edges. The Wide is noted for its kingfisher population. Woods across the valley conceal Shugborough Hall. The River Trent is met, on its way south from Stoke-on-Trent, and is crossed on an aqueduct. There is a wharf, and fresh produce can be purchased at the farm north of bridge 74 on the Trent & Mersey, which is entered through an elegantly arched bridge. The bridge is the subject of a very famous photograph taken by the canal historian Eric de Maré.

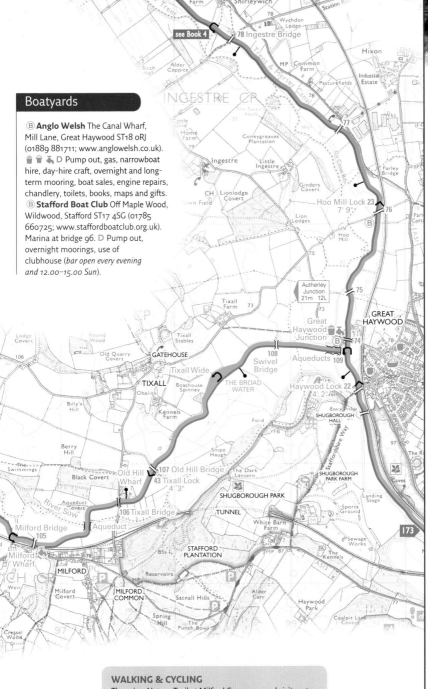

Boatyards

(B) **Anglo Welsh** The Canal Wharf, Mill Lane, Great Haywood ST18 0RJ (01889 881711; www.anglowelsh.co.uk). 🛏 🛒 ♿ D Pump out, gas, narrowboat hire, day-hire craft, overnight and long-term mooring, boat sales, engine repairs, chandlery, toilets, books, maps and gifts.
(B) **Stafford Boat Club** Off Maple Wood, Wildwood, Stafford ST17 4SG (01785 660725; www.staffordboatclub.org.uk). Marina at bridge 96. D Pump out, overnight moorings, use of clubhouse (*bar open every evening and 12.00–15.00 Sun*).

WALKING & CYCLING
There is a Nature Trail at Milford Common, and visitors to Shugborough Hall can enjoy excellent walks in the park.

Stafford

Staffs. All services. This town is well worth visiting, since there is a remarkable wealth of fine old buildings. These include a handsome City Hall complex of ornamental Italianate buildings, c.1880. The robust-looking gaol is nearby; and the church of St Mary stands in very pleasing and spacious grounds. There are some pretty back alleys: Church Lane contains a splendid-looking eating house, and at the bottom of the lane a fruiterer's shop is in a thatched cottage built in 1610.

The Shire Hall Gallery Market Square, Stafford ST16 2LD (01785 278345; www.staffordshire.gov.uk). A stimulating variety of work by local artists, craftsmen, printmakers, jewellers, photographers and others. *Open Mon–Sat 09.30–17.00, Sun 13.00–16.00.* Free.

Tourist Information Centre Market Street, Stafford ST16 2LD (01785 619619; www.visitstafford.org).

● **The Stafford Branch**
Just west of bridge 101 there was once a lock taking a branch off the Staffordshire & Worcestershire to Stafford. One mile long, it was unusual in that it was not a canal but the canalised course of the River Sow.

● **Milford**
Staffs. PO, tel, stores, garage. Best reached from Tixall Bridge (106). Milford Hall is hidden by trees.

● **Tixall**
Staffs. Tel, stores. Just to the east are the stables and the gatehouse of the long-vanished Tixall Hall. This massive square Elizabethan building dates from 1598 and is fully four storeys high. It stands alone in a field and is considered to be one of the most ambitious gatehouses in the country. The gatehouse is now available for holiday lets: telephone the Landmark Trust (01628 825925) for details.

● **Great Haywood**
Staffs. PO, tel, stores. Centre of the Great Haywood and Shugborough Conservation Area, the village is attractive in parts, but it is closely connected in many ways to Shugborough Park, to which it is physically linked by the very old Essex Bridge, where the crystal clear waters of the River Sow join the Trent on its way down from Stoke.

Shugborough Hall *NT.* Milford, near Stafford ST17 0XB (01889 881388; www.shugborough.org.uk). Walk south along the road from bridge 106 to the A513 at Milford Common. The main entrance is on your left. The present house dates from 1693, but was substantially altered by James Stuart around 1760 and by Samuel Wyatt around the turn of the 18th C. The Trust has leased the whole to Staffordshire County Council who now manage it. The house has been restored at great expense. There are some magnificent rooms and treasures inside.

Museum of Staffordshire Life This excellent establishment, Staffordshire's County Museum, is housed in the old stables adjacent to Shugborough Hall (*see above*). Open since 1966, it is superbly laid out and contains all sorts of exhibits concerned with old country life in Staffordshire.

Shugborough Park There are some remarkable sights in the large park that encircles the Hall. Thomas Anson, who inherited the estate in 1720, enlisted in 1744 the help of his famous brother, Admiral George Anson, to beautify and improve the house and the park. In 1762 he commissioned James Stuart, a neo-Grecian architect, to embellish the grounds. 'Athenian' Stuart set to with a will, and the spectacular results of his work can be seen scattered round the park.

The Park Farm Within Shugborough Park. Designed by Samuel Wyatt, it contains an agricultural museum, a working mill and a rare breeds centre. Traditional country skills such as bread-making, butter-churning and cheese-making are demonstrated. *Open Apr–Oct daily 11.00–17.00.* Charge. Parties must book. Tea rooms, shop.

Pubs and Restaurants

🍺 **Radford Bank Inn** Radford Bank, Stafford ST17 4PG (01785 242825o). Canalside at bridge 98. Food is served *all day, every day until 21.00*, along with real ale. Children are welcome, *until 21.00 and in the restaurant*, and there is a garden.

🍺 **The Clifford Arms** Main Road, Great Haywood ST18 0SR (01889 881321). There has apparently been a pub on this site for hundreds of years. At one time it was a coaching inn. Now it is a friendly village local with an open fire, serving real ale and bar and restaurant meals *L and E*. Small garden with yews. Moorings.

✕ 🍷 **Lockhouse Restaurant** Trent Lane, Great Haywood ST18 0ST (01889 881294). Friendly and handy for Anglo-Welsh visitors. Morning and afternoon tea, coffee and cakes, hot and cold carvery *L daily* and home-cooked English food . Real ale is available for the thirsty. Canalside garden, and just a couple of minutes' walk from the village.

STRATFORD-ON-AVON CANAL

MAXIMUM DIMENSIONS

King's Norton to Kingswood
Length: 70'
Beam: 7'
Headroom: 7' 3"
Kingswood to Stratford
Length: 70'
Beam: 6' 10"
Headroom: 6'

MILEAGE

KING'S NORTON JUNCTION to:
Hockley Heath: 9¾ miles

LAPWORTH, junction with Grand Union
Canal: 12½ miles
Preston Bagot: 16¼ miles
Wootton Wawen Basin: 18½ miles
Wilmcote: 22 miles

STRATFORD-ON-AVON, junction with River Avon:
25½ miles

Locks: 54

MANAGER

01827 252000
enquiries.westmidlands@britishwaterways.co.uk

The opening of the Oxford Canal in 1790 and of the Coventry Canal throughout shortly afterwards opened up a continuous waterway from London to the rapidly developing industrial area based on Birmingham. It also gave access, via the Trent & Mersey Canal, to the expanding pottery industry based around Stoke-on-Trent, to the Mersey, and to the East Midlands coalfield. When the Warwick & Birmingham and Warwick & Napton Canals were projected to pass within 8 miles of Stratford-on-Avon, the business interests of that town realised that the prosperity being generated by these new trade arteries would pass them by unless Stratford acquired direct access to the network. And so on 28 March 1793 an Act of Parliament was passed for the construction of the Stratford-on-Avon Canal, to start at King's Norton on the Worcester & Birmingham Canal.

Progress was rapid at first, but almost the total estimated cost of the complete canal was spent on cutting the 9¾ lock-free miles to Hockley Heath within the first three years. It then took another four years, more negotiations, a revision of the route and another Act of Parliament to get things going again. By 1803 the canal was open from King's Norton Junction to its junction with the Warwick & Birmingham Canal (now part of the Grand Union main line) near Lapworth. Cutting recommenced in 1812, the route being revised yet again in 1815 to include the present junction with the River Avon at Stratford.

In its most prosperous period, the canal's annual traffic exceeded 180,000 tons. By 1835 the canal was suffering from railway competition. This grew so rapidly that in 1845 the Canal Company decided to sell out to the Great Western Railway. In 1890 the tonnage carried was still a quarter of what it had been 50 years before, but the fall in ton-miles was much greater. This pattern of decline continued in the 20th C, and by the 1950s only an occasional working boat used the northern section; the southern section (Lapworth to Stratford) was badly silted, some locks were unusable and some of the short pounds below Wilmcote were dry.

In 1955 a Board of Survey had recommended sweeping canal closures, including the southern section of the Stratford Canal, but public protest was such that a Committee of Enquiry was set up in 1958, and this prompted the start of a massive campaign to save the canal. The campaign was successful: the decision not to abandon it was announced by the Ministry on 22 May 1959. On 16 October of the same year the National Trust announced that it had agreed a lease from the British Transport Commission under which the Trust would assume responsibility for restoring and maintaining the southern section.

The reopening ceremony was performed by Queen Elizabeth the Queen Mother on 11 July 1964, after more than four years of hard work by prison labourers, canal enthusiasts, Army units and a handful of National Trust staff. On 1 April 1988 control of the southern section of the Stratford-on-Avon Canal was passed to the British Waterways Board.

King's Norton

The west end of this delightful canal is at King's Norton, just outside Birmingham. The first five miles of the navigation pass entirely through the residential outskirts of Birmingham, forming a quiet, winding ribbon of green all the way through to the countryside. In conjunction with the northern section of the Worcester & Birmingham Canal, this is a far more scenically interesting route between Lapworth and Birmingham than via the Grand Union Canal. Leaving the Worcester & Birmingham Canal (*see page 151*) at King's Norton Junction, the Stratford-on-Avon Canal proceeds straight to the well-known King's Norton Stop Lock. In the days of the private canal companies, stop locks were common at junctions, as one canal sought to protect its water supply from any newcomer; but King's Norton Stop Lock is unusual in having two wooden guillotine gates mounted in iron frames, balanced by chains and counterweights. The machinery is not now used, and boats pass under the two gates without stopping. The next bridge is a small swing bridge (usually left open), followed by Brandwood Tunnel. Further east is a beautiful tree-lined cutting, then a bridge with a pub beside it (*petrol and telephone nearby*) and the remains of an old arm just beyond it. Passing over a small aqueduct, the canal reaches a steel lift bridge, which is raised and lowered electrically (see note below). Then beyond a railway bridge the canal begins to shed all traces of the suburbs, maintaining its twisting course in wooded cuttings through quiet countryside. The bridges over the navigation are mostly the generous brick-arched bridges typical of the canal between King's Norton and Lapworth Locks (in contrast to the much smaller bridges further south, and built when there were plans for a broad canal), but few roads of any significance come near the canal. At bridge 16 the canal emerges from a long cutting and is joined by a feeder from the nearby Earlswood Reservoir. Boats are moored along this, since it is the base of the Earlswood Motor Yacht Club. There are no villages along this rural stretch of canal.

NAVIGATIONAL NOTES

You will need a BW key to operate Shirley Drawbridge, 8. A single button completes the operation, and a line of piles guides you through.

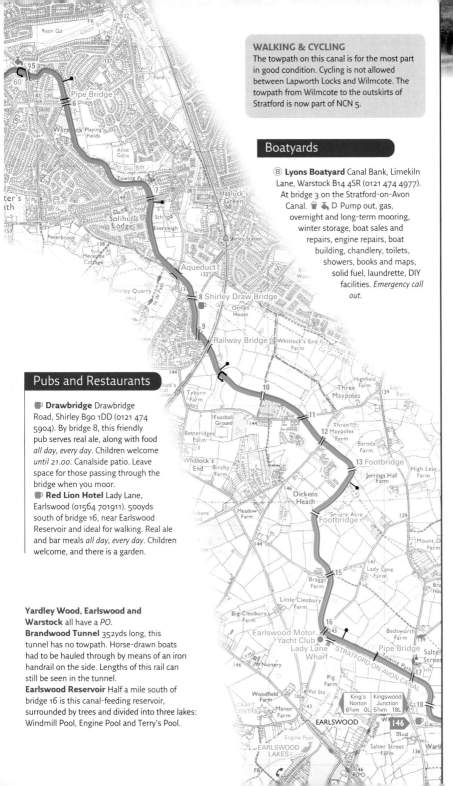

WALKING & CYCLING

The towpath on this canal is for the most part in good condition. Cycling is not allowed between Lapworth Locks and Wilmcote. The towpath from Wilmcote to the outskirts of Stratford is now part of NCN 5.

Boatyards

Ⓑ **Lyons Boatyard** Canal Bank, Limekiln Lane, Warstock B14 4SR (0121 474 4977). At bridge 3 on the Stratford-on-Avon Canal. 🚽 🛒 D Pump out, gas, overnight and long-term mooring, winter storage, boat sales and repairs, engine repairs, boat building, chandlery, toilets, showers, books and maps, solid fuel, laundrette, DIY facilities. *Emergency call out.*

Pubs and Restaurants

🍺 **Drawbridge** Drawbridge Road, Shirley B90 1DD (0121 474 5904). By bridge 8, this friendly pub serves real ale, along with food *all day, every day.* Children welcome *until 21.00.* Canalside patio. Leave space for those passing through the bridge when you moor.

🍺 **Red Lion Hotel** Lady Lane, Earlswood (01564 701911). 500yds south of bridge 16, near Earlswood Reservoir and ideal for walking. Real ale and bar meals *all day, every day.* Children welcome, and there is a garden.

Yardley Wood, Earlswood and Warstock all have a *PO.*

Brandwood Tunnel 352yds long, this tunnel has no towpath. Horse-drawn boats had to be hauled through by means of an iron handrail on the side. Lengths of this rail can still be seen in the tunnel.

Earlswood Reservoir Half a mile south of bridge 16 is this canal-feeding reservoir, surrounded by trees and divided into three lakes: Windmill Pool, Engine Pool and Terry's Pool.

145

Lapworth Locks

The canal continues on its south easterly course, passing through quiet countryside interrupted only by the incessant roar of the M42 motorway, crossing overhead. There is a good bakery and shop north of bridge 20. There are no locks, and the bridges – especially those in the cuttings – are still the big brick arches built when a broad canal was planned. At Hockley Heath (bridge 25) there is a tiny arm that once served a coal wharf. Nearby the Wharf Inn overlooks the canal, and there is a useful petrol station here. East of here things change dramatically, for the first of the locks down to Kingswood Junction is reached. The top lock is numbered 2, as the old stop lock at King's Norton is number 1. The surroundings of the top lock are indeed pleasant: a white house enclosed by walls and hemmed in by trees stands beside the lock, while a cottage with a delightful garden faces the towpath just below. To the south west can be seen the spire of Lapworth church. After the first four locks, there is a ½-mile breathing space: then the Lapworth flight begins in earnest, with each of the next nine locks spaced only a few yards from its neighbour.

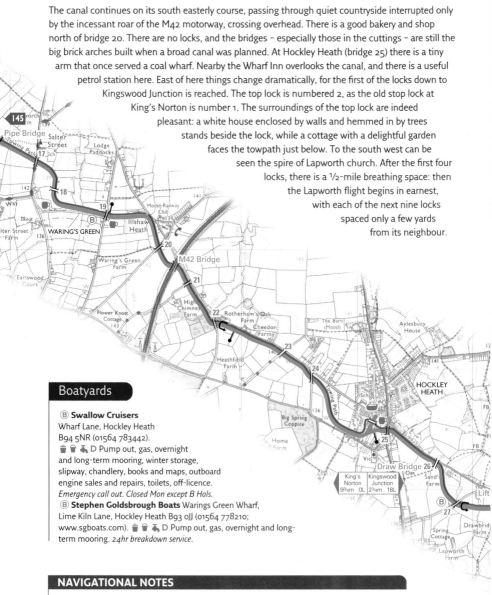

Boatyards

ⓑ **Swallow Cruisers**
Wharf Lane, Hockley Heath
B94 5NR (01564 783442).
🚿 🛢 ⚓ D Pump out, gas, overnight
and long-term mooring, winter storage,
slipway, chandlery, books and maps, outboard
engine sales and repairs, toilets, off-licence.
Emergency call out. Closed Mon except B Hols.
ⓑ **Stephen Goldsbrough Boats** Warings Green Wharf,
Lime Kiln Lane, Hockley Heath B93 0JJ (01564 778210;
www.sgboats.com). 🚿 🛢 ⚓ D Pump out, gas, overnight and long-
term mooring. *24hr breakdown service.*

NAVIGATIONAL NOTES

1 *Please go slowly* to minimise your wash.
2 Bridges 26 and 28 operate hydraulically, using a lock windlass.
3 Due to rebuilding, the chamber of lock 15 on the Lapworth flight is now over 2ft shorter than the other locks. Those in full-length boats should take extra care when descending.

There is a useful canal shop by lock 14. The short intervening pounds have been enlarged to provide a bigger working reservoir of water, so that one side of each lock is virtually an isthmus. The locks have double bottom gates so are not heavy going, and are interspersed with the old cast iron split bridges that are such a charming feature of the Stratford-on-Avon Canal. These bridges are built in two halves, separated by a one inch gap so that the towing line between a horse and a boat could be dropped through the gap without having to disconnect the horse. There are shops south of bridge 34. Below lock 19 is Kingswood Junction: boats heading for Stratford should keep right here. A short branch to the left leads under the railway line to the Grand Union Canal, or you can use the Lapworth Link after lock 22 if you are heading north to the GU, avoiding unnecessary lockage.

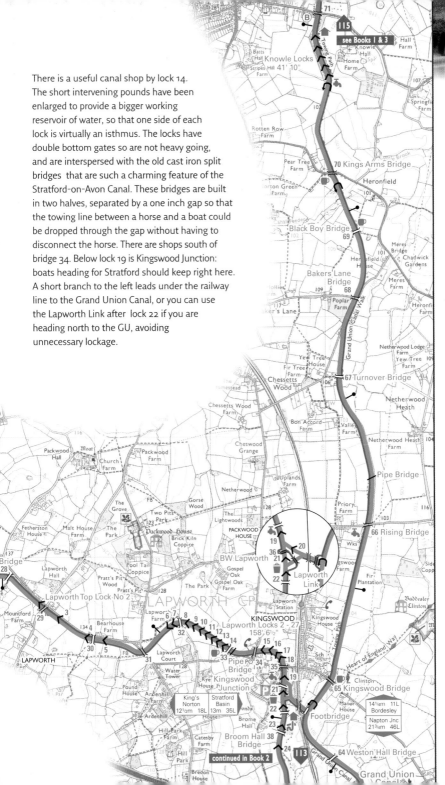

- **Hockley Heath**

Warwicks. PO, tel, stores, garage. A featureless place, but the several shops are conveniently close to the canal bridge, and the pub is pleasant.

- **Lapworth**

Warwicks. PO, tel, stores, garage, station. Indivisible from Kingswood, this is more a residential area than a village. Two canals pass through Lapworth: the heavily locked Stratford-on-Avon Canal and, to the east, the main line of the Grand Union Canal. These two waterways, and the short spur that connects them, are easily the most interesting aspect of Lapworth. The canalside buildings are attractive and there are two small reservoirs at the junction. The mostly 15th-C church is quite separate from the village and is 1½ miles west of

the junction; it contains an interesting monument by Eric Gill, 1928.

Packwood House Lapworth, Solihull B94 6AT (01564 783294). *NT.* 2 miles west of bridge 66. Timber-framed Tudor house, dating from the late 16th C and enlarged in the 17th C, where Cromwell's general, Henry Ireton, slept before the Battle of Edgehill in 1642. Owned by the Featherstones until 1869, it was eventually purchased by Alfred Ash, who repaired the house and reinstated the gardens. Collection of tapestry, needlework and furniture. Park with formal grounds and 17th-C yew garden possibly laid out to represent the Sermon on the Mount, the trees taking the place of Jesus and his followers. *House open Mar–Oct, Wed–Sun 12.00– 16.30.* Charge. Events are staged *during the summer.*

Pubs and Restaurants

🍺 **The Bull's Head** Lime Kiln Lane, Earlswood B94 6BU (01564 702335; www.bullshead94.co.uk). ¼ mile south of bridge 17. A pleasant, low-ceilinged country pub with a high bar, in converted cottages, serving traditional and continental food *L and E Mon–Sat, and Sun 12.00–18.00.* Real ale. Garden with a water pump, and there is a resident ghost – a 17th-C limekiln worker who appears during *Jul and Aug.* Dominoes are played. Live music.

🍺 **The Blue Bell Cider House** Warings Green Road, Hockley Heath B94 6BP (01564 702328). Canalside, at bridge 19. A pretty, traditional cider house serving real draught cider and a couple of guest real ales. It is a drinkers pub, but bar meals and snacks are available *L and E* with a children's menu. Garden with playground. Good mooring jetty for patrons.

✕ ♀ **Kam-Shun** 2362 Stratford Road, Hockley Heath B94 6QT (01564 782782). Highly recommended Cantonese food *E Tue–Sun.* Children welcome.

🍺 ✕ **The Wharf Tavern** Stratford Road, Hockley Heath B94 6QT (01564 782075). Canalside, at bridge 25. A smart pub with a pleasant canalside garden and adventure playground, offering real ale and bar meals (carvery) *L and E daily.* Children very welcome. Moorings.

🍺 **The Boot Inn** Old Warwick Road, Lapworth B94 6JU (01564 782464; www.bootinnlapworth.co.uk). Near lock 14. Cosmopolitan country pub serving real ale. Fashionable bar meals *L and E.* Garden with gas heaters for cooler nights!

🍺 **The Navigation** Old Warwick Road, Lapworth B94 6NA (01564 783337). Canalside at Kingswood . By bridge 65 on the Grand Union. Real ale and real draught cider. Bar meals *L and E.* Children welcome. Outside seating. Moorings.

Edstone Aqueduct

WORCESTER & BIRMINGHAM CANAL

MAXIMUM DIMENSIONS

Length: 72' 0"
Beam: 7'
Headroom: 8'

MANAGER

0121 200 7400
enquiries.wmw@britishwaterways.co.uk

MILEAGE

KING'S NORTON JUNCTION to:
BIRMINGHAM Gas Street Basin: 5½ miles

No locks

The Bill for the Worcester & Birmingham Canal was passed in 1791 in spite of fierce opposition from the Staffordshire & Worcestershire Canal proprietors, who saw trade on their route to the Severn threatened. The supporters of the Bill claimed that the route from Birmingham and the Black Country towns would be much shorter, enabling traffic to avoid the then notorious shallows in the Severn below Stourport. The Birmingham Canal Company also opposed the Bill and succeeded in obtaining a clause preventing the new navigation from approaching within 7ft of their water. This resulted in the famous Worcester Bar separating the two canals in the centre of Birmingham, replaced by a stop lock in 1815.

Construction of the canal began at the Birmingham end following the line originally surveyed by John Snape and Josiah Clowes. Even at this early stage difficulties with water supply were encountered. The company was obliged by the Act authorising the canal to safeguard water supplies to the mills on the streams south of Birmingham. To do this, and to supply water for the summit level, ten reservoirs were planned or constructed. The high cost of these engineering works led to a change of policy: instead of building a broad canal, the company decided to build it with narrow locks, in order to save money in construction and water in operation.

The canal was completed in 1815. In the same year an agreement with the Birmingham Canal proprietors permitted the cutting of a stop lock through Worcester Bar. The canal had cost £610,000, exceeding its original estimate by many thousands of pounds. Industrial goods and coal were carried down to Worcester, often for onward shipping to Bristol, while grain, timber and agricultural produce were returned to the growing towns of the Midlands. However the opening of railways in the 1840s and 1850s reduced traffic considerably and had a profound effect on the fortunes of the canal.

By the early 1900s the commercial future of the canal was uncertain, although the works were in much better condition than on many other canals. Schemes to enlarge the navigation as part of a Bristol–Birmingham route came to nothing. Commercial carrying continued until about 1964, the traffic being mostly between the two Cadbury factories of Bournville and Blackpole, and to Frampton on the Gloucester & Sharpness Canal. After nationalisation, several proposals were made to abandon the canal, but the 1960s brought a dramatic increase in the number of pleasure boats using the waterway thus securing its future use. The whole of the canal is covered *in Book 2.*

King's Norton

To the north of King's Norton Junction, where the Stratford-on-Avon Canal (*see* page 144) joins the Worcester & Birmingham Canal, the canal passes through an industrial area, but thankfully seems to hold the factories at bay on one side, while a railway line, the main line from Worcester and the south west to Birmingham, draws alongside on its west flank. Canal and railway together drive through the middle of Cadbury's Bournville works, which is interesting rather than oppressive. Beyond it is Bournville station, followed by a cutting.

King's Norton
West Midlands. Tel, stores, garage, bank, station. The village still survives as a recognisable entity, for the suburbs of Birmingham have now extended all around it, and the small village green, the old grammar school buildings and the soaring spire of the church ensure that it will remain so. The church is set back a little from the green in an attractive churchyard, and is mainly of the 14th C, although two Norman windows can still be seen. The grammar school is even older – it was probably founded by King Edward III in 1344. An interesting puzzle is that the upper storey is apparently older than the ground floor... The school declined during the last century and was closed in 1875. Now restored, it is an ancient monument.

Wast Hills Tunnel To the south of King's Norton Junction, and once referred to as King's Norton Tunnel, this 2726yd bore is one of the longest in the country. It is usually difficult to see right through, and there are plenty of drips from the roof in even the driest weather. A steam-powered – and later a diesel-powered – tunnel tug service used to operate in the days of horse-drawn boats, as there is no towpath. The old iron brackets and insulators that still line the roof were installed to carry telegraph lines through the tunnel. Grandiose bridges (nos. 69 and 70) span the cuttings at either end.

Bournville Garden Factory Bournville, Birmingham B30 1UB. The creation of the Cadbury family, who moved their cocoa and chocolate manufacturing business south from the centre of Birmingham. The Bournville estate was begun in the late 1800s and is an interesting example of controlled suburban development. There were once old canal wharves here, which became disused when most of the ingredients travelled by rail – but the sidings closed in the late 1960s and now regrettably everything comes by road.

Cadbury World Linden Road, Bournville B30 2LU (Information line 0845 450 3599; www.cadburyworld. co.uk). It is by the factory and signposted from the canal, where there are moorings. An exhibition dedicated to the history and the love of chocolate. Audio-visual displays, a jungle to explore, and Victorian Birmingham. *Open Mon–Fri 10.00–15.00, Sat and Sun 09.30–16.30 (restricted in winter – please telephone).* Reservation for admission is advised. Telephone or visit the website for details. Charge.

Selly Manor and Minworth Greaves Corner of Sycamore Road and Maple Road, Bournville (0121 472 0199). Two half-timbered Birmingham houses of the 13th- and early 14th-C re-erected in the 1920s and 1930s in Bournville. They contain a collection of old furniture and domestic equipment. *Open all year Tue–Fri 10.00–17.00, also Apr–Sep, Sat and Sun 14.00–17.00; closed Nov–Mar, Sat–Mon.* Charge. The nearest point of access from the canal is at Bournville station: walk west to the Cadbury's entrance. There is a public right of way (Birdcage Walk) through the works: bear right at the fork, then turn right at the village green. The two houses are close by, on the left. Selly Oak and Bournville both have a PO. For more information contact the Bournville Village Trust, Estate Office, Oak Tree Lane, Bournville B30 1UB (0121 472 0199; www.bvt.org.uk).

Pubs and Restaurants

🍴 ✕ **The Navigation Inn** Wharf Road, King's Norton B30 3LS (0121 458 1652). About 100yds west of bridge 71. Guest real ales change regularly in this large rambling pub, which offers food *all day*. There is a garden. Karaoke *Fri and Sat*. Children welcome in the restaurant. Moorings.

WALKING & CYCLING
The towpath on this section is in excellent condition, and is much-used by both walkers and cyclists.

Selly Park

155

77A

Ten Acres

CADBURY'S WORKS

BOURNVILLE
Visitor Moorings

STIRCHLEY

Recn Gd

Wks

Breedon
75 Pershore Road Bridge

74 Railway Bridge
ord

Cotteridge

Stratford-on-Avon Canal

Lifford Lane 73
Bridge

Swing Bridge (left open) 2

144

Kings Norton Business Centre

| 5½m 0L |
| Gas St Basin |
| Diglis |
| 24½m 56L |

Junction Bridge 72

Pipe Bridge

1 (Guillotine Lock – open)

King's Norton Junction

FB
138 Playing Fields

| Kingswood Jnc |
| 12½m 18L |

King's Norton Park

KING'S NORTON

71 Parsons Hill Bridge

Bells Farm

Pipe Bridge

Walker's Heath

Moundsley Hall

King's

70 Primrose Hill Bridge

Walker's Heath Farm

HAWKESLEY

Lilycroft Farm

Pits (dis)

Crabmill Farm

West Heath

Golf Driving Range

Gay Hill

Crabtree Farm

Goodrest Farm

Meadow Hill Farm

Gay Hill Farm

Headley Heath Farm

Headley

Playing Fields High Hill

University Farm

Redhill Road

Redhill Farm

Seal's Green Farm

Lehing Farm

Dingle House

Wast Hills Tunnel
2726 yds

Red Hill

Wast Hills

Bell Green

WAST HILL

HOPWOOD DINGLE

See Book 2

Forhill

Yew Tree Farm

Big Forhill

Little Forhill

Birmingham

Soon the railway vanishes briefly behind the buildings of Selly Oak. Between bridge 80 and the next, skewed, railway bridge is the site of the junction with the Dudley Canal, but no trace remains here now of either the junction or the canal itself. North of here the canal and railway together shrug off industry and town, and head north on an embankment towards Birmingham in splendid isolation and attractive surroundings. Below on either side is the green spaciousness of residential Edgbaston, its botanical gardens and woods. A hospital is on the west side. The University of Birmingham is on the east side; among its many large buildings the most conspicuous is the Chamberlain Campanile Tower, which was erected in 1900. At one of the bridges near the University, two Roman forts used to stand; but most of the evidence of them was obliterated by the building of the canal and railway. Only a reconstructed part of the larger fort now exists. There is a useful Sainsbury's just south of bridge 80. Past the University's moorings, canal and railway enter a cutting, in which their enjoyable seclusion from the neighbourhood is complete; the charming old bridges are high, while the cutting is steep and always lined by overhanging foliage. It is a remarkable approach to Birmingham. The railway is the canal's almost constant companion, dipping away here and there to reappear a short distance further on; but trains are not too frequent, and in a way their occasional appearance heightens the remoteness that attaches to this length of canal. At one stage the two routes pass through short tunnels side by side: the canal's tunnel, Edgbaston, is the northernmost of the five on this canal and the only one with a towpath through it. It is a mere 105yds long. The Worcester & Birmingham Canal now completes its delightful approach to Birmingham. The railway disappears underneath in a tunnel to New Street station, while the canal makes a sharp left turn to the basin. The terminus of the Worcester & Birmingham Canal is the former stop lock at Gas Street Basin; this is known as Worcester Bar: originally there was a physical barrier here between the Worcester & Birmingham Canal and the much older Birmingham Canal. The latter refused to allow a junction, and for several years goods had to be transhipped at this point from one canal to the other. This absurd situation was remedied by an Act of Parliament in 1815, by which a stop lock was allowed to be inserted to connect the two canals. Nowadays the stop gates are kept open and one can pass straight through, on to the Birmingham Canal (see page 31). Don't leave your boat unattended in this area, although Gas Street Basin should be OK.

The Dudley Canal This canal used to join the Worcester & Birmingham Canal at Selly Oak, thus providing a southern bypass round Birmingham. The eastern end of the canal has been closed for many years, and will certainly remain so. The tremendously long (3795yd) Lappal Tunnel, now collapsed, emerged 2 miles from Selly Oak. This bore was more like a drainpipe than a navigable tunnel – it was only 7ft 9in wide, a few inches wider than the boats that used it, and headroom was limited to a scant 6ft. Boats were assisted through by a pumping engine flushing water along the tunnel, but it must still have been a night-marishly claustrophobic trip for the boatmen.

● **Edgbaston**
West Midlands. A desirable residential suburb of Birmingham, Edgbaston is bisected by the canal.
Botanical Gardens Westbourne Road, Edgbaston, Birmingham B15 3TR (0121 454 1860; www. birminghambotanicalgardens.org.uk) Founded over

100 years ago. Alpine Garden, lily pond and a collection of tropical birds. *Open daily.*
Perrott's Folly Waterworks Road, off Monument Road, Edgbaston. About ¾ mile west of bridge 86, not far from the Plough & Harrow Hotel. This seven-storey tower was built in 1758 by John Perrott and claims to be Birmingham's most eccentric building. One theory as to its origin is that Mr Perrott could, from its height, gaze upon his late wife's grave 10 miles away. One of the Two Towers of Gondor, featured in J.R.R. Tolkien's *Lord of the Rings*, is thought to have been based upon this building. Tolkien's last address in Birmingham was at 4 Highfield Road, opposite the Plough & Harrow. From 1884–1984 the folly was used as a weather station and was subsequently renovated. At the time of going to print Perrott's Folly was undergoing a major makeover. Visit www.perrottsfolly.co.uk for more details.
For more information on Birmingham, *see* page 41.

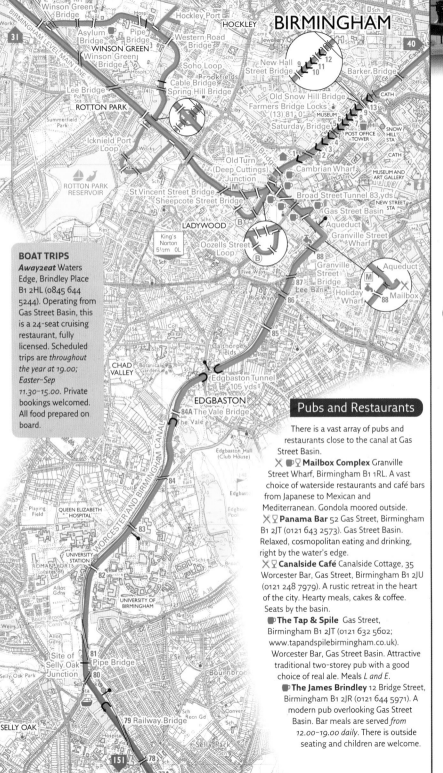

BOAT TRIPS

Away2eat Waters Edge, Brindley Place B1 2HL (0845 644 5244). Operating from Gas Street Basin, this is a 24-seat cruising restaurant, fully licensed. Scheduled trips are *throughout the year at 19.00; Easter–Sep 11.30–15.00*. Private bookings welcomed. All food prepared on board.

Pubs and Restaurants

There is a vast array of pubs and restaurants close to the canal at Gas Street Basin.

✗ 🍺🍷 **Mailbox Complex** Granville Street Wharf, Birmingham B1 1RL. A vast choice of waterside restaurants and café bars from Japanese to Mexican and Mediterranean. Gondola moored outside.

✗🍷 **Panama Bar** 52 Gas Street, Birmingham B1 2JT (0121 643 2573). Gas Street Basin. Relaxed, cosmopolitan eating and drinking, right by the water's edge.

✗🍷 **Canalside Café** Canalside Cottage, 35 Worcester Bar, Gas Street, Birmingham B1 2JU (0121 248 7979). A rustic retreat in the heart of the city. Hearty meals, cakes & coffee. Seats by the basin.

🍺 **The Tap & Spile** Gas Street, Birmingham B1 2JT (0121 632 5602; www.tapandspilebirmingham.co.uk). Worcester Bar, Gas Street Basin. Attractive traditional two-storey pub with a good choice of real ale. Meals *L and E*.

🍺 **The James Brindley** 12 Bridge Street, Birmingham B1 2JR (0121 644 5971). A modern pub overlooking Gas Street Basin. Bar meals are served *from 12.00–19.00 daily*. There is outside seating and children are welcome.

153

WILDLIFE

The *Speckled Wood* is a double-brooded butterfly, flying April–June and July–September. It favours clearings and is fond of sunbathing. The upperwings are dark brown with pale markings; the underwings are rufous brown. The caterpillars feed on grasses.

The *Large Skipper* favours grassy places of all kinds and flies during June and July. The upperwings are dark brown and orange-brown with pale markings. The underwings are buffish orange with paler spots. In common with most other skipper butterflies, at rest the Large Skipper often holds its wings at an angle and can look rather moth-like. The caterpillars feed on grasses.

The *Holly Blue* actually appears silvery in flight. The violet-blue upperwings are seldom seen well as it rests showing white, black-dotted underwings. There are two broods, flying April–May, laying eggs on holly; flying August–September and laying eggs on ivy.

The *Orange-Tip* is an attractive spring butterfly, seen flying between April and June. The male has an orange patch on the dark-tipped forewing, which is absent in the female. The hind underwing of both sexes is marbled green and white. The larvae feed mainly on the cuckoo flower.

The *Banded Demoiselle* is an attractive damselfly, often found resting among waterside vegetation. Males are seen in small, fluttering groups hovering over water; the flight of the female is rather feeble. The body of the male is blue with a metallic sheen; the smoky wings show a conspicuous blue 'thumbprint' mark. The female has a green body, with metallic sheen, and greenish brown wings. Flies May–August.

The *Moorhen* is a widespread and familiar wetland bird: often wary, in urban areas they can become rather tame. The adult has brownish wings but otherwise mainly dark grey-black plumage. It has a distinctive yellow-tipped red bill and a frontal shield on its head, with white feathers on the sides of the undertail and a white line along the flanks. Juvenile birds have pale brown plumage. The moorhen's legs and long toes are yellowish. It swims with a jerky movement, with tail flicking. In flight the moorhen shows dangling legs.

The *Mute Swan* is a large and distinctive water bird, the commonest swan in Britain. The adult has pure white plumage, black legs and an orange-red bill. The black blob at the base of the bill is smaller in the female than the male. Young cygnets are often seen accompanying the mother. While swimming, the bird usually holds its neck in an elegant curve.

The *Great Crested Grebe* is a slender water bird with a long, thin neck. From a distance the bird looks strikingly black and white, although upperparts are mainly grey-brown and underparts white. In summer both sexes acquire a prominent orange-reddish-brown ruff and show a crest to their dark cap. In winter they lose the ruff but retain the dark cap and a suggestion of a crest. Pairs perform elaborate ritual displays in spring and build nests among the emerging vegetation.

The *Devil's-bit Scabious* is an erect perennial of damp grassland, woodland rides and marshes. The short, thick rhizome has an abruptly cut-off end – bitten off by the devil! The basal leaves are spoon shaped, in a rosette; the narrow stem leaves in opposite pairs, the upper ones narrow. Blue-purple flowers (rarely pink or white) are borne in rounded heads, 15–25mm across, and appear June–October. This plant is the food plant of the, declining Marsh Fritillary butterfly. The word scabious derives from the former herbal use of this and related plants to cure scabies and other unpleasant skin complaints. The lookalike Field and Small Scabious have lilac flowers, more than 25mm across.

The *Marsh Fritillary* has beautifully marked wings. It flies May–June but is only active when it is sunny. Favouring damp heaths and moors, but also dry chalk grassland, the larvae feed on devil's-bit scabious and plantains.

Shardlow (see page 158)

TRENT & MERSEY CANAL

MAXIMUM DIMENSIONS

Derwent Mouth to Horninglow Basin, Burton upon Trent
Length: 72'
Beam: 14'
Headroom: 7'
Stenson lock is very tight for 14ft beam craft and Weston Lock is tight for boats of 72ft length.

Burton upon Trent to south end of Harecastle Tunnel
Length: 72'
Beam: 7'
Headroom: 6' 3"

Harecastle Tunnel
Length: 72'
Beam: 7'
Headroom: 5' 9"

North end of Harecastle Tunnel to Croxton Aqueduct
Length: 72'
Beam: 7'
Headroom: 7'

Croxton Aqueduct to Preston Brook Tunnel
Length: 72'
Beam: 8' 2"
Headroom: 6' 3"

MANAGER:

Derwent Mouth to bridge 27a Willington:
01636 704481
enquiries.emidlands@britishwaterways.co.uk

Willington bridge 27a to Great Haywood bridge 75:
01827 252000
enquiries.westmidlands@britishwaterways.co.uk
Great Haywood bridge 75 to Preston Brook:
01606 723800
enquiries.walesandbordercounties@britishwaterways.co.uk

MILEAGE

DERWENT MOUTH to:
Swarkestone Lock: 7 miles
Willington: 12¼ miles
Horninglow Wharf: 16½ miles
Barton Turn: 21¼ miles
Fradley, junction with Coventry Canal: 26¼ miles
Great Haywood, junction with Staffordshire & Worcestershire Canal: 39 miles
Stone: 48½ miles
Stoke Top Lock, junction with Caldon Canal: 58 miles
Harding's Wood, junction with Macclesfield Canal: 63¾ miles
King's Lock, Middlewich, junction with Middlewich Branch: 76¼ miles
Anderton Lift, for River Weaver: 86½ miles
PRESTON BROOK north end of tunnel and Bridgewater Canal: 93½ miles

Locks: 76

This early canal was originally conceived partly as a roundabout link between the ports of Liverpool and Hull, while passing through the busy area of the Potteries and mid-Cheshire, and terminating either in the River Weaver or in the Mersey. Its construction was promoted by Josiah Wedgwood (1730–95), the famous potter, aided by his friends Thomas Bentley and Erasmus Darwin. In 1766 the Trent & Mersey Canal Act was passed by Parliament, authorising the building of a navigation from the River Trent at Shardlow to Runcorn Gap, where it would join the proposed extension of the Bridgewater Canal from Manchester. The ageing James Brindley was appointed engineer for the canal. Construction began at once and in 1777 the Trent & Mersey Canal was opened. In the total 93 miles between Derwent Mouth and Preston Brook, the Trent & Mersey gained connection with no fewer than nine other canals or significant branches.

By the 1820s the slowly-sinking tunnel at Harecastle had become a serious bottle-neck, so Thomas Telford recommended building a second tunnel beside the old one. His recommendation was eventually accepted by the company and the new tunnel was completed in under three years, in 1827. Although the Trent & Mersey was taken over in 1845 by the new North Staffordshire Railway Company, the canal flourished until World War I. Look out for the handsome cast iron mileposts, which actually measure the mileage from Shardlow, not Derwent Mouth. There are 59 originals, from the Rougeley and Dixon foundry in Stone, and 34 replacements, bearing the mark of the Trent & Mersey Canal Society – T & MCS 1977.

Shardlow

The Trent & Mersey Canal begins at Derwent Mouth, some 2½ miles upstream of the point where the Soar Navigation

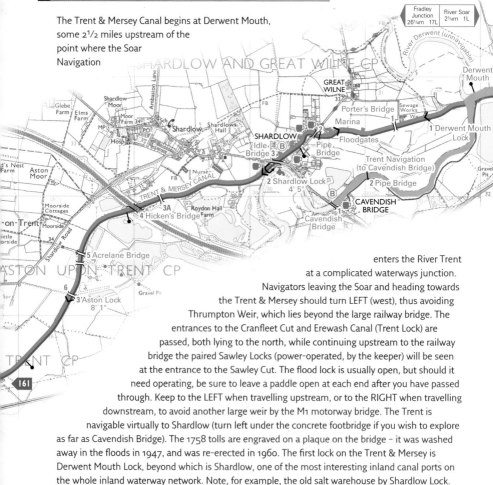

enters the River Trent at a complicated waterways junction. Navigators leaving the Soar and heading towards the Trent & Mersey should turn LEFT (west), thus avoiding Thrumpton Weir, which lies beyond the large railway bridge. The entrances to the Cranfleet Cut and Erewash Canal (Trent Lock) are passed, both lying to the north, while continuing upstream to the railway bridge the paired Sawley Locks (power-operated, by the keeper) will be seen at the entrance to the Sawley Cut. The flood lock is usually open, but should it need operating, be sure to leave a paddle open at each end after you have passed through. Keep to the LEFT when travelling upstream, or to the RIGHT when travelling downstream, to avoid another large weir by the M1 motorway bridge. The Trent is navigable virtually to Shardlow (turn left under the concrete footbridge if you wish to explore as far as Cavendish Bridge). The 1758 tolls are engraved on a plaque on the bridge – it was washed away in the floods in 1947, and was re-erected in 1960. The first lock on the Trent & Mersey is Derwent Mouth Lock, beyond which is Shardlow, one of the most interesting inland canal ports on the whole inland waterway network. Note, for example, the old salt warehouse by Shardlow Lock.

Boatyards

Ⓑ ✕ **Sawley Marina** Long Eaton, Nottingham NG10 3AE (01159 734278; www. bwml.co.uk).
⌂ ⌂ P D Pump out, gas, overnight and long-term mooring, winter storage, slipway, crane, boat and engine sales, engine repairs, telephone, chandlery, solid fuel, toilets, showers, restaurant, laundrette. groceries.
Ⓑ **Dobsons Boatyard** The Wharf, Shardlow DE72 2GH (01332 792271; sales@millermarine.com) ⌂ ⌂ ⚓ D Pump out, gas, overnight and long-term mooring, slipway, chandlery, boat building, boat and engine sales, engine repairs, wet dock, books and maps.

Ⓑ ✕ **Shardlow Marina** London Road, Shardlow DE72 2GL (01332 792832). On the River Trent.
⌂ ⌂ ⚓ D Pump out, gas, overnight and long-term mooring, winter storage, slipway, boat sales, chandlery, laundrette, toilets and showers. Caravan and camping site. Bar and restaurant on site.

BOAT TRIPS
Nb Pochard carries up to 70 people, with a bar and buffet. Based at Sawley Marina, NG10 3AE (01509 813311).

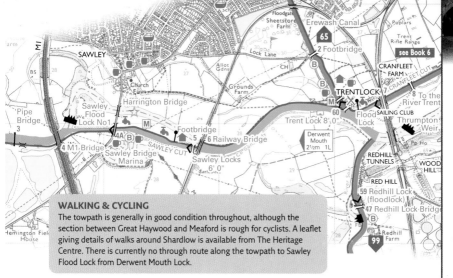

NAVIGATIONAL NOTES

1 Those leaving the canal and heading towards the River Trent should not pass Shardlow floodgates if the warning light shows red.
2 The Derwent is not navigable north of Derwent Mouth.

● **Sawley Cut**
In addition to a large marina and a well-patronised BW mooring site, the Derby Motor Boat Club has a base on the Sawley Cut. There are windlasses for sale at Sawley Lock, as well as the more conventional facilities, and BW showers. It is beautifully tended, with lots of flowers and some jokey sculptures. Have a look at the flood level markers – they are astonishing!

● **Shardlow**
Derbs. PO, tel, stores, garage. Few canal travellers will want to pass through Shardlow without stopping. Everywhere there are living examples of

large-scale canal architecture, as well as long-established necessities such as canal pubs. By the lock is the biggest and best of these buildings – the 18th-C Trent Mill, now the Clock Warehouse. Restored in 1979, it has a large central arch where boats once entered to unload.
Shardlow Heritage Centre London Road, Shardlow DE72 2GA (djacent to the Clock Warehouse (www.homepages.which.net/ ~shardlow.heritage/). Exhibitions of local canal history and replica of a narrowboat back cabin. Plus a calendar of canal-centred events. *Open Easter–Oct, Sat, Sun and B Hols 12.00–17.00.* Modest entry charge.

Pubs and Restaurants

🍽 **The Clock Warehouse** London Road, Shardlow DE72 2GA (01332 792844). Real ale, and food *L and E, all day.* Children welcome, and there is a garden. Moorings.

🍽 ✕ **The Old Marina Bar & Restaurant** Shardlow Marina, London Road, Shardlow DE72 2GA (01332 799797; www.theoldmarinabar. co.uk). Meals *L and E;* carvery *Sun 12.00–16.00;* specials during *week.* Outside seating. Children welcome. Live music *Fri and Sat.*

🍽 **The Navigation Inn** 143 London Road, Shardlow DE722HJ (01332 792918). By bridge 3. Haunted pub, serving real ale, and home-made food *L and E,* including *Sun* carvery. Garden with children's play area. Moorings. Live music *Fri.*

🍽 **The Malt Shovel** 49 The Wharf, Shardlow

DE72 2GH (01332 799763). By bridge 2. Friendly canalside pub, built in 1779 and serving real ale. Excellent food with home-made specials *L only (not Sun).* Children welcome. Outside seating.

🍽 **The New Inn** The Wharf, Shardlow DE72 2HG (01332 793330). Next to the Malt Shovel. Real ale, and bar meals *L and E.* Children welcome. Garden and outside seating.

✕ ♀ **The Thai Kitchen** 3 Wilne Lane, Shardlow DE72 2HA (01332 792331). Authentic Thai food *L and E* in a restaurant haunted by the 'lady in grey'. Children welcome.

🍽 **The Old Crown** Cavendish Bridge, Shardlow DE72 2HL (01332 792392). Friendly riverside pub. Real ale. Bar meals *L* , and *E Mon–Thur.* Children welcome. Garden with play area. B & B.

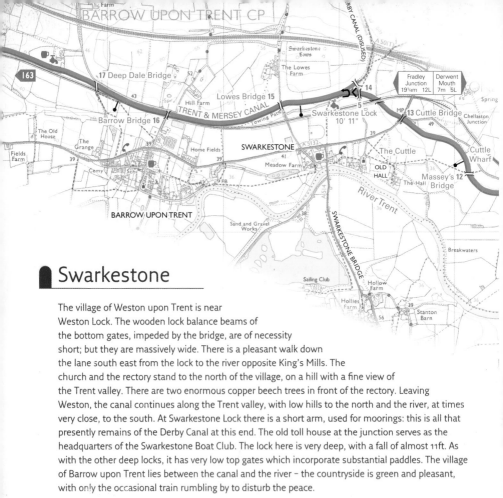

▌Swarkestone

The village of Weston upon Trent is near
Weston Lock. The wooden lock balance beams of
the bottom gates, impeded by the bridge, are of necessity
short; but they are massively wide. There is a pleasant walk down
the lane south east from the lock to the river opposite King's Mills. The
church and the rectory stand to the north of the village, on a hill with a fine view of
the Trent valley. There are two enormous copper beech trees in front of the rectory. Leaving
Weston, the canal continues along the Trent valley, with low hills to the north and the river, at times
very close, to the south. At Swarkestone Lock there is a short arm, used for moorings: this is all that
presently remains of the Derby Canal at this end. The old toll house at the junction serves as the
headquarters of the Swarkestone Boat Club. The lock here is very deep, with a fall of almost 11ft. As
with the other deep locks, it has very low top gates which incorporate substantial paddles. The village
of Barrow upon Trent lies between the canal and the river – the countryside is green and pleasant,
with only the occasional train rumbling by to disturb the peace.

● **Weston upon Trent**
Derbs. Tel, stores. A scattered village that is in fact not
very close to the Trent. The isolated church is
splendidly situated beside woods on top of a hill, its
sturdy tower crowned by a short 14th-C spire. Inside
are fine aisle windows of the same period. The lock
gardens make the approach from the canal
particularly attractive.
● **Swarkestone**
Derbs. Tel, stores. The main feature of Swarkestone is
the 18th-C five-arch stone bridge over the main
channel of the River Trent. An elevated causeway
then carries the road on stone arches all the way
across the Trent's flood plain to the village of Stanton
by Bridge. It was at Swarkestone that Bonnie Prince
Charlie, in the rising of 1745, gave up his attempt for
the throne of England and returned to his defeat at
Culloden. In a field nearby are the few remains of Sir
Richard Harpur's Tudor mansion, which was

demolished before 1750. The Summer House, a
handsome, lonely building, overlooks a square
enclosure called the Cuttle. Jacobean in origin, it is
thought that it may have been the scene of bull-
baiting, although it seems more likely it was just a
'bowle alley'. Restored by the Landmark Trust, it is
available for holiday lets – telephone (01628) 825925
for details. The Harpurs moved to Calke following the
demolition of their mansion after the Civil War. The
pub in the village, and monuments in the church,
which is tucked away in the back lanes, are a
reminder of the family.
● **Barrow upon Trent**
Derbs. Tel, stores. A small, quiet village set back from
the canal. A lane from the church leads down to the
River Trent. Opposite there is a 'pinfold', once an
enclosure for stray animals. The surviving lodge
house stands opposite a mellow terrace of old
workmen's cottages.

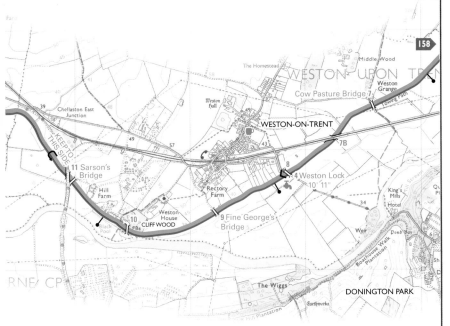

Pubs and Restaurants

🍺 **The Old Plough Inn** 1 Main Street, Weston-upon-Trent DE72 2BL (01332 700331). Attractive pub serving real ale. Food, with good choice for children, available *L and E*. Outside seating.

🍺 **The Crew & Harpur Arms** Woodshop Lane, Swarkestone DE73 1JA (01332 700641). By the river bridge. Real ale, and bar meals served *all day* in this handsome pub. Riverside seating and garden. Moorings.

🍺 **The Ragley Boat Stop** Deepdale Lane, off Sinfin Lane, Barrow-on-Trent DE73 1HH (01332 703919; www.king-henrys-taverns.co.uk). Large pub 300yds west of bridge 17, serving real ale. Food is available *L and E, and all day Sun*. Extensive vegetarian and children's menus. Children welcome. Outside seating in a 3-acre garden. Good moorings.

A HOP, A SKIP, AND A JUMP TO DERBY

The Derby Canal, which left the Trent & Mersey at Swarkestone and joined the Erewash at Sandiacre, has long been disused. One condition of its building, and a constant drain on its profits, was the free carriage of 5000 tons of coal to Derby each year, for the use of the poor.

But one of the most unusual loads was transported on 19 April 1826, when 'a fine lama, a kangaroo, a ram with four horns, and a female goat with two young kids, remarkably handsome animals' arrived in Derby by canal 'as a present from Lord Byron to a Gentleman whose residence is in the neighbourhood, all of which had been picked up in the course of the voyage of the *Blonde* to the Sandwich Islands in the autumn of 1824'.

Willington

Just by bridge 18 is Arleston House, an attractive old building with ground-floor walls of stone and the upper tiers of brick. This is followed by Stenson Lock, the last of the wide locks until Middlewich – it has a massive fall of 12ft 4in, and is overlooked by a useful coffee shop. Stenson is a small farming centre and a popular mooring spot with a large marina. After passing through a railway bridge, the canal changes course and heads off in a south easterly direction towards Burton upon Trent.

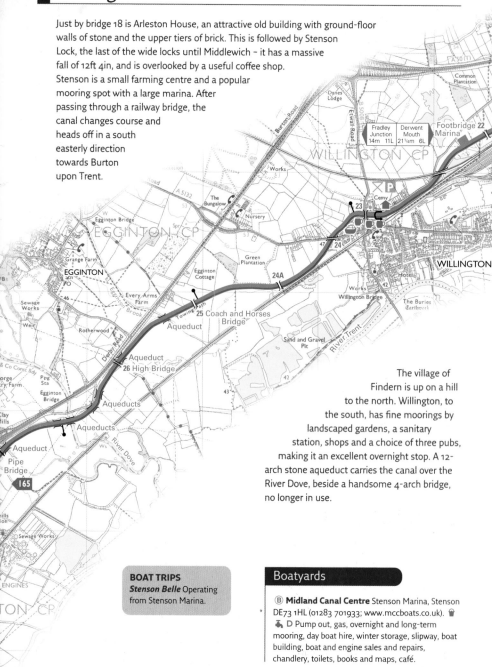

The village of Findern is up on a hill to the north. Willington, to the south, has fine moorings by landscaped gardens, a sanitary station, shops and a choice of three pubs, making it an excellent overnight stop. A 12-arch stone aqueduct carries the canal over the River Dove, beside a handsome 4-arch bridge, no longer in use.

BOAT TRIPS
Stenson Belle Operating from Stenson Marina.

Boatyards

Ⓑ **Midland Canal Centre** Stenson Marina, Stenson DE73 1HL (01283 701933; www.mccboats.co.uk). D Pump out, gas, overnight and long-term mooring, day boat hire, winter storage, slipway, boat building, boat and engine sales and repairs, chandlery, toilets, books and maps, café.

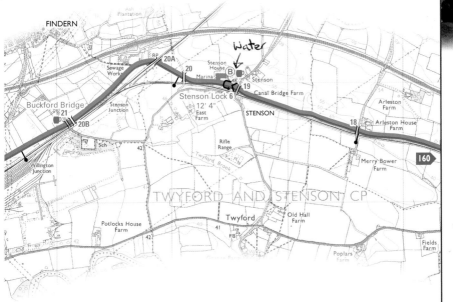

● **Repton**
Derbs. PO. 1½ miles south east of Willington (over the River Trent) is Repton, one of the oldest towns in England, which was once the capital of Mercia. The crypt below St Wystan's Church was built in the 10th C. One of the finest examples of Saxon architecture in the country, this crypt was completely forgotten until the end of the 18th C when a man fell into it while digging a grave. Repton public school dates from 1557, and there is much of historical interest in the school and the town.

● **Willington**
Derbs. PO, tel, stores, delicatessen. The railway bisects this busy little village on an embankment. There are three pubs, all close together.

● **Findern**
Derbs. PO, tel, stores. A small, quiet village where Jedekiah Strutt, the inventor of the ribbed stocking frame, served a 7-year apprenticeship with the local wheelwright. At one time the village green was no more than a waste patch used by cars as a short cut, and a parking place. When suggestions were made to turn it into a formal cross roads, the indignant Women's Institute galvanised the villagers into actually uprooting all traces of tarmac from the green and turfing the whole area properly.

● **Egginton**
Derbs. A quiet village lying off the A38. The church, set apart from the village, is pleasingly irregular from the outside, with a large chancel and a squat tower.

Pubs and Restaurants

⊕ **The Bubble Inn** Stenson DE73 1HL (01283 703113; www.thebubbleinn.com). Alongside Stenson Lock and Marina, this modern pub in a converted barn serves real ale and bar meals *L and E (not L & E Sun)*. Children welcome. Garden.

⊕ **The Wheel Inn** Main Street, Findern DE65 6AG (01283 703365; www.thefindernwheel.co.uk). Meals available *L and E, daily.* Garden, barbeque and children's play area. Quiz *Wed and Sun.*

⊕ **The Rising Sun** The Green, Willington DE65 6BP (01283 702116). Friendly village pub serving real ale. Reasonably priced bar food, including home-made pies, available *L and E.* Children welcome. Outside seating. Occasional live music.

⊕ **The Green Dragon** 11 The Green, Willington DE65 6BP (01283 702327). Popular and welcoming pub, with plenty of low beams. Real ale. Wide range of food available *L and E.* Garden. Children welcome away from the bar. Moorings.

⊕ **Nadee** Heath Lane, Findern DE65 6AR (01283 701333; www.nadeerestaurant.co.uk). Adjacent to canal at bridge 21. Bar and Indian restaurant. Landscaped garden, including a 5-a-side football pitch. Children welcome. *Open all day during season, E only during winter.*

Burton upon Trent

Logs, *coal* and *diesel* are available between bridges 28 and 29. *Fish & chips* can be obtained 100yds north of Horninglow Basin, which has some services and a butterfly garden. The canal then passes along one side of Burton upon Trent, without entering the town. Many of the old canalside buildings have been demolished, but the waterside has been nicely tidied up, making the passage very pleasant. The lovely aroma of brewing – malt and hops – often pervades the town, usually strongest to the west. Dallow Lock is the first of the narrow locks, an altogether easier job of work than the wider ones to the east. Shobnall Basin is now used by a boatyard, and visitor moorings nearby are available from which to explore the town. The A38 then joins the canal, depriving the navigator of any peace. On the hills to the north west is the well-wooded Sinai Park – the moated 15th-C house here, now a farm, used to be the summer home of the monks from Burton Abbey. There is a fine canalside pub at bridge 34, and a *shop* selling provisions, home-made cakes and crafts. It is *open Easter–Oct, daily 09.00–18.00.* The canal enters the new National Forest at bridge 30 – indeed an intricately carved seat reminds us of this – and will leave it just beyond Alrewas. The Bass Millennium Woodland, to the west of Branston Lock, is part of this major project.

● **Burton upon Trent**
Staffs. All services. Known widely for its brewing industry, which originated here in the 13th C, when the monks at Burton Abbey discovered that an excellent beer could be brewed from the town's waters, because of their high gypsum content. At one time there were 31 breweries producing 3 million barrels of ale annually: alas, now only a few remain. The advent of the railways had an enormous effect on the street geography of Burton, for gradually a great network of railways took shape, connecting with each other and with the main line. These branches were mostly constructed at street level, and until recent years it was common for road traffic to be held up by endless goods trains chugging all over the town. Only the last vestiges of this system now remain. The east side of the town is bounded by the River Trent, on the other side of which are pleasant hills. The main shopping centre lies to the east of the railway station. **Marston's Brewery Visitor Centre** Shobnall Road, Burton upon Trent DE14 2BW (01283 507391; www.marstonsbeercompany.co.uk). Tours of the brewery, including the unique and world-famous Burton Union system are available *Mon–Fri.* At the end of the tour you can enjoy a drink of real ale in the Visitor Centre. *Please telephone or visit website to check availability and to book.*
Brewhouse Arts Centre Union Street, Burton upon Trent DE14 1EB (01283 508100; www.little-theatre.co.uk). Live entertainment in a 230-seat theatre, plus a gallery and bistro bar.

Tourist Information Centre 183 High Street, Burton upon Trent DE14 1NG (01283 508111).
● **Shobnall Basin**
This is all that remains of the Bond End Canal, which gave the breweries the benefit of what was modern transport, before the coming of the railways.
● **Branston**
Staffs. PO, tel, stores, garage, butcher, Chinese takeaway, fish & chips. This is apparently the place where the famous pickle originated.

> **WALKING & CYCLING**
> Cycle Route 54 uses the towpath north of Burton upon Trent. It links Lichfield with Derby. Three walking trails around Burton upon Trent are available from the TIC. There are pleasant walks through Branston Water Park – telephone (01283) 508573 for more information.

Boatyards

Ⓑ **Jannel Cruisers** Shobnall Marina, Shobnall Road, Burton upon Trent DE14 2AU (01283 540006; www.jannel.co.uk). In Shobnall Basin. 🛆 🛆 🛆 D Pump out, gas, narrowboat hire, overnight mooring, long-term mooring, winter storage, slipway, dry dock, chandlery, books and maps, boat-fitting, boat sales, engine sales and repairs, toilets.

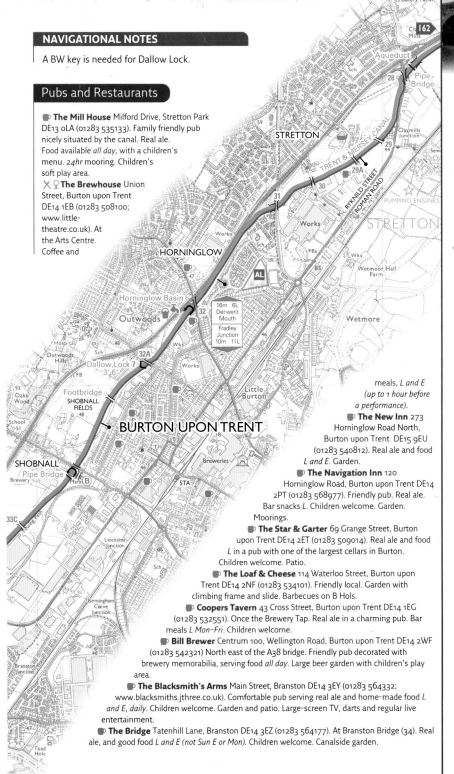

NAVIGATIONAL NOTES

A BW key is needed for Dallow Lock.

Pubs and Restaurants

The Mill House Milford Drive, Stretton Park DE13 0LA (01283 535133). Family friendly pub nicely situated by the canal. Real ale. Food available *all day*, with a children's menu. *24hr* mooring. Children's soft play area.

The Brewhouse Union Street, Burton upon Trent DE14 1EB (01283 508100; www.little-theatre.co.uk). At the Arts Centre. Coffee and meals, *L and E* (up to 1 hour before a performance).

The New Inn 273 Horninglow Road North, Burton upon Trent DE15 9EU (01283 540812). Real ale and food *L and E*. Garden.

The Navigation Inn 120 Horninglow Road, Burton upon Trent DE14 2PT (01283 568977). Friendly pub. Real ale. Bar snacks *L*. Children welcome. Garden. Moorings.

The Star & Garter 69 Grange Street, Burton upon Trent DE14 2ET (01283 509014). Real ale and food *L* in a pub with one of the largest cellars in Burton. Children welcome. Patio.

The Loaf & Cheese 114 Waterloo Street, Burton upon Trent DE14 2NF (01283 534101). Friendly local. Garden with climbing frame and slide. Barbecues on B Hols.

Coopers Tavern 43 Cross Street, Burton upon Trent DE14 1EG (01283 532551). Once the Brewery Tap. Real ale in a charming pub. Bar meals *L Mon–Fri*. Children welcome.

Bill Brewer Centrum 100, Wellington Road, Burton upon Trent DE14 2WF (01283 542321) North east of the A38 bridge. Friendly pub decorated with brewery memorabilia, serving food *all day*. Large beer garden with children's play area.

The Blacksmith's Arms Main Street, Branston DE14 3EY (01283 564332; www.blacksmiths.jthree.co.uk). Comfortable pub serving real ale and home-made food *L and E, daily*. Children welcome. Garden and patio. Large-screen TV, darts and regular live entertainment.

The Bridge Tatenhill Lane, Branston DE14 3EZ (01283 564177). At Branston Bridge (34). Real ale, and good food *L and E (not Sun E or Mon)*. Children welcome. Canalside garden.

165

Barton Turn

Beside Tatenhill Lock there is an attractive cottage; at the tail of the lock is yet another of the tiny narrow brick bridges that are such an engaging feature of this navigation. Note the very fine National Forest seat just north of the lock – there is another at Bagnall Lock, along with a 'living willow' sculpture. After passing flooded gravel pits and negotiating another tiny brick arch at bridge 36, the canal and the A38, the old Roman road, come very close together – thankfully the settlement of Barton Turn has been bypassed, leaving the main street (the old Roman road of Ryknild Street) wide and empty. It is with great relief that Wychnor Lock, with its diminutive crane and warehouse, is reached – here the A38 finally parts company with the canal, and some peace returns. To the west is the little 14th-C Wychnor church. Before Alrewas Lock the canal actually joins the River Trent – there is a large well-marked weir which should be given a wide berth. The canal then winds through the pretty village of Alrewas, passing the old church, several thatched cottages and a charming brick bridge.

● **Barton-under-Needwood**
Staffs. PO, tel, stores, bank, garage. Many years ago, when there were few roads and no canals in the Midlands, the only reasonable access to this village was by turning off the old Roman road, Ryknild Street: hence, probably, the name Barton Turn. The village is indeed worth turning off for, although unfortunately it is nearly a mile from the canal. A pleasant footpath from Barton Turn Lock leads quietly to the village, which is set on a slight hill. Its long main street has many attractive pubs. The church is battlemented and surrounded by a very tidy churchyard. Pleasantly uniform in style, it was built in the 16th C by John Taylor, Henry VIII's private secretary, on the site of his cottage birthplace. The former Royal Forest of Needwood is to the north of the village.

● **Wychnor**
Staffs. A tiny farming settlement around the church of St Leonards.

● **Alrewas**
Staffs. PO, tel, stores, garage, butcher, chemist, tearoom, fish & chips. Just far enough away from the A513, this is an attractive village whose rambling back lanes harbour some excellent timbered cottages. The canal's meandering passage through the village, passing well tended gardens and a bowling green, and the presence of the church and its pleasant churchyard creates a friendly and unruffled atmosphere. The River Trent touches the village, and once fed the old Cotton Mill (now converted into dwellings), and provides it with a fine background which is much appreciated by fishermen. The somewhat unusual name Alrewas, pronounced 'olrewus', is a corruption of the words Alder Wash – a reference to the many alder trees which once grew in the often-flooded Trent valley

and gave rise to the basket weaving for which the village was once famous.

Alrewas Church Mill End Lane, Alrewas DE13 7BT. A spacious building of mainly 13th-C and 14th-C construction, notable for the old leper window, which is now filled by modern stained glass.

Boatyards

Ⓑ **Barton Turns Marina** Barton Turn, Barton-under-Needwood DE13 8DZ (01283 711666; www.bartonmarina.co.uk). 🛈 🏕 🛠 D Pump out, gas, overnight and long-term mooring, winter storage, slipway, boat sales and repairs, engine repairs, chandlery, toilets, showers, books, maps and gifts, laundrette. Also pub, restaurant and shops, including a deli and bakery/butcher.

Ⓑ **Boat Doctor** (01332 771622). Emergency marine engineer with *24hr emergency breakdown call out.*

Ⓑ **Wychnor Moorings** Wychnor, Burton upon Trent DE13 8BY (07778 668388). 🛈 🏕 🛠 Pump out, gas, long-term mooring, coal.

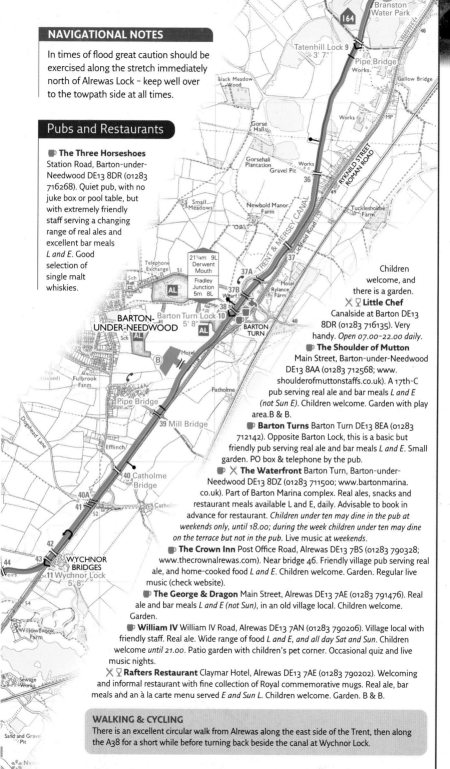

NAVIGATIONAL NOTES

In times of flood great caution should be exercised along the stretch immediately north of Alrewas Lock – keep well over to the towpath side at all times.

Pubs and Restaurants

The Three Horseshoes Station Road, Barton-under-Needwood DE13 8DR (01283 716268). Quiet pub, with no juke box or pool table, but with extremely friendly staff serving a changing range of real ales and excellent bar meals *L and E*. Good selection of single malt whiskies.

Children welcome, and there is a garden.

Little Chef Canalside at Barton DE13 8DR (01283 716135). Very handy. *Open 07.00–22.00 daily.*

The Shoulder of Mutton Main Street, Barton-under-Needwood DE13 8AA (01283 712568; www.shoulderofmuttonstaffs.co.uk). A 17th-C pub serving real ale and bar meals *L and E (not Sun E)*. Children welcome. Garden with play area. B & B.

Barton Turns Barton Turn DE13 8EA (01283 712142). Opposite Barton Lock, this is a basic but friendly pub serving real ale and bar meals *L and E*. Small garden. PO box & telephone by the pub.

The Waterfront Barton Turn, Barton-under-Needwood DE13 8DZ (01283 711500; www.bartonmarina.co.uk). Part of Barton Marina complex. Real ales, snacks and restaurant meals available L and E, daily. Advisable to book in advance for restaurant. *Children under ten may dine in the pub at weekends only, until 18.00; during the week children under ten may dine on the terrace but not in the pub. Live music at weekends.*

The Crown Inn Post Office Road, Alrewas DE13 7BS (01283 790328; www.thecrownalrewas.com). Near bridge 46. Friendly village pub serving real ale, and home-cooked food *L and E*. Children welcome. Garden. Regular live music (check website).

The George & Dragon Main Street, Alrewas DE13 7AE (01283 791476). Real ale and bar meals *L and E (not Sun)*, in an old village local. Children welcome. Garden.

William IV William IV Road, Alrewas DE13 7AN (01283 790206). Village local with friendly staff. Real ale. Wide range of food *L and E, and all day Sat and Sun*. Children welcome *until 21.00*. Patio garden with children's pet corner. Occasional quiz and live music nights.

Rafters Restaurant Claymar Hotel, Alrewas DE13 7AE (01283 790202). Welcoming and informal restaurant with fine collection of Royal commemorative mugs. Real ale, bar meals and an à la carte menu served *E and Sun L*. Children welcome. Garden. B & B.

WALKING & CYCLING

There is an excellent circular walk from Alrewas along the east side of the Trent, then along the A38 for a short while before turning back beside the canal at Wychnor Lock.

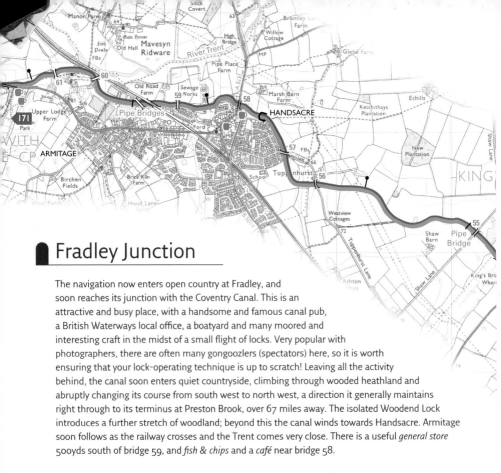

Fradley Junction

The navigation now enters open country at Fradley, and soon reaches its junction with the Coventry Canal. This is an attractive and busy place, with a handsome and famous canal pub, a British Waterways local office, a boatyard and many moored and interesting craft in the midst of a small flight of locks. Very popular with photographers, there are often many gongoozlers (spectators) here, so it is worth ensuring that your lock-operating technique is up to scratch! Leaving all the activity behind, the canal soon enters quiet countryside, climbing through wooded heathland and abruptly changing its course from south west to north west, a direction it generally maintains right through to its terminus at Preston Brook, over 67 miles away. The isolated Woodend Lock introduces a further stretch of woodland; beyond this the canal winds towards Handsacre. Armitage soon follows as the railway crosses and the Trent comes very close. There is a useful *general store* 500yds south of bridge 59, and *fish & chips* and a *café* near bridge 58.

NAVIGATIONAL NOTES

West of bridge 61 the canal is very narrow, due to the removal of Armitage Tunnel, and wide enough for one boat only. Check that the canal is clear before proceeding.

Boatyards

ⓑ **Swan Line Cruisers** Fradley Junction, Alrewras DE13 7DN (01283 790332). ⚓ D Pump out, gas, narrowboat hire, overnight mooring, long term mooring, boat building, boat sales and engine repairs, chandlery, books and maps, gifts, groceries.

ⓑ **King's Bromley Wharf Marina** Lichfield Road, Bromley Hayes WS13 8HT (01543 417209; www. kingsbromleymarina.co.uk). 🚿 🚽 ⚓ D Pump out, gas, overnight and long-term mooring, slipway, boat sales, chandlery, coal, toilets, showers, laundrette.

● **Fradley Junction**
Alrewas DE13 7DN. A long-established canal centre where the Coventry Canal joins the Trent & Mersey. Like all the best focal points on the waterways, it is concerned solely with the life of the canals, and has no relationship with local roads or even with the village of Fradley. The junction bristles with boats for, apart from it being an inevitable meeting place for canal craft, there is a boatyard, a British Waterways information centre and café (01283 790236, guided tours), BW moorings, a boat club, a popular pub and another café at the holiday park – all in the middle of a 5-lock flight.

Kings Bromley

Staffs. PO, tel, stores. A village 1½ miles north of bridge 54, along the A515. There are some pleasant houses and an old mill to be seen here, as well as what is reputed to have been Lady Godiva's early home. The Trent flows just beyond the church, which contains some old glass. A large cross in the southern part of the churchyard is known locally as Godiva's cross.

Armitage

Staffs. PO, tel, stores, garage. A main road village, whose church is interesting: it was rebuilt in the 19th C in a Saxon/Norman style, which makes it rather dark. The organ is 200 years old and it is enormous: it came from Lichfield Cathedral and practically deafens the organist at Armitage.

WALKING & CYCLING
You can complete a circular walk if you head off along the Coventry Canal to Fradley Bridge (90), walk through the village and on to Alrewas, returning along the Trent & Mersey. Fradley Pool Nature Reserve can be accessed from the towpath, and makes for a pleasant walk.

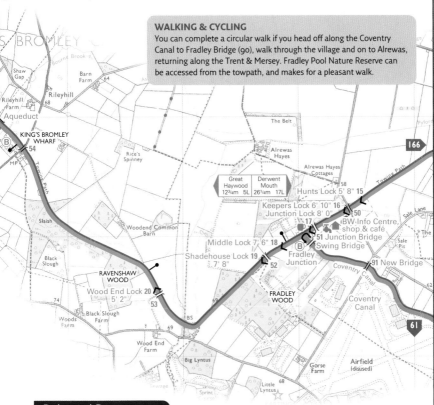

Pubs and Restaurants

🍺 **The Swan** Fradley Junction, Alewras DE13 7DN (01283 790330; www.theswanatfradley.co.uk). Known as 'The Mucky Duck'. Canalside, it is the focus of the junction and justly famous, this is reputedly one of the most photographed pubs in the country! It is in a 200-year-old listed building, with a fine public bar warmed by a coal fire, a comfortable lounge, and a vaulted cellar room. Real ale, and bar meals are served *L and E*, with a carvery *Sun L*. There is a flowered patio at the rear.

🍺 **The Crown** The Green, Handsacre WS15 4DT (01543 490239). At bridge 58. Welcoming 300-year-old pub serving real ale. Family room, and a garden. Good moorings. Occasional entertainment.

🍺 **Old Peculiar** The Green, Handsacre WS15 4DP (01543 491891). Traditional English pub. Real ale, and food available *L and E (not Mon or Tue L)*. Pretty garden. Children welcome.

🍺 **The Spode Cottage** Lower Lodge, Armitage WS15 4AT (01543 490353). Attractive pub serving real ale and meals *all day*. Children welcome. Outside seating, garden and children's play area. Live entertainment *first Sat of month*.

🍺 **The Plum Pudding Brasserie** Rugeley Road, Armitage WS15 4AZ (01543 490330; www.plumpudding.co.uk). Modern, award-winning restaurant serving real ale and meals *L and E*. Children welcome for meals only. Outside seating, including large, covered, canalside area used for eating and drinking. B & B.

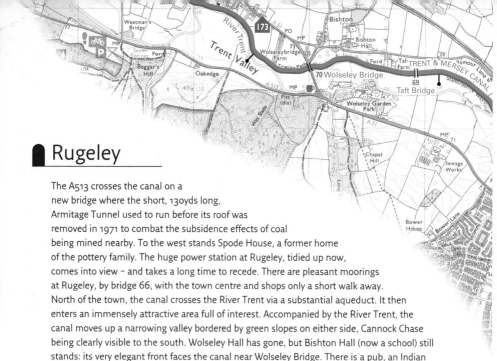

Rugeley

The A513 crosses the canal on a
new bridge where the short, 130yds long,
Armitage Tunnel used to run before its roof was
removed in 1971 to combat the subsidence effects of coal
being mined nearby. To the west stands Spode House, a former home
of the pottery family. The huge power station at Rugeley, tidied up now,
comes into view – and takes a long time to recede. There are pleasant moorings
at Rugeley, by bridge 66, with the town centre and shops only a short walk away.
North of the town, the canal crosses the River Trent via a substantial aqueduct. It then
enters an immensely attractive area full of interest. Accompanied by the River Trent, the
canal moves up a narrowing valley bordered by green slopes on either side, Cannock Chase
being clearly visible to the south. Wolseley Hall has gone, but Bishton Hall (now a school) still
stands: its very elegant front faces the canal near Wolseley Bridge. There is a pub, an Indian
restaurant and an antique, craft and garden centre just a short way to the south.

● **Spode House** WS15 1PU Spode House and
Hawkesyard Priory stand side by side. The priory
was founded in 1897 by Josiah Spode's grandson
and his niece Helen Gulson when they lived at
Spode House. The Priory is now known as
Hawkesyard Hall, and is a restaurant and spa.

● **Rugeley**
Staffs. PO, tel, stores, garage, banks, station, cinema.
A bustling and much re-developed town, with many
shops at the centre. There are two churches by
bridge 67; one is a 14th-C ruin, the other is the
parish church built in 1822 as a replacement.

● **Cannock Chase**
Covering an area of 26 square miles, and designated
as an Area of Outstanding Natural Beauty in 1949,
the Chase is all that remains of what was once a
Norman hunting ground known as the King's Forest
of Cannock. Large parts are recognised as Sites of
Special Scientific Interest, and exceptional flora and
fauna are abundant. This includes a herd of fallow
deer whose ancestors have grazed in this region for

centuries. An area of 4½ square miles forms a
Country Park, one of the largest in Britain. Near the
Sherlock Valley an area was chosen in 1964 as the
site of the Deutscher Soldatenfriedhof, and was built
by the German War Graves Commission. It contains
the graves of 2143 German servicemen from World
War I, and 2786 from World War II. It is an
intentionally sombre place. A small area is devoted
to the crews of German airships, shot down over the
UK in 1916 and 1917. There were two huge army
camps on the Chase during World War I, but today
little remains, apart from some anonymous and
overgrown concrete foundations.

Museum of Cannock Chase Valley Road,
Hednesford WS12 1TD (01543 877666;
www.cannockchasedc. gov.uk). This site was at one
time the Valley Colliery. Local history and interactive
galleries. *Open Jan-Mar, Mon-Fri 11.00- 16.00;
Apr-Oct, daily 11.00-17.00.* Free. Coffee shop, gift
shop, visitor information and walks.

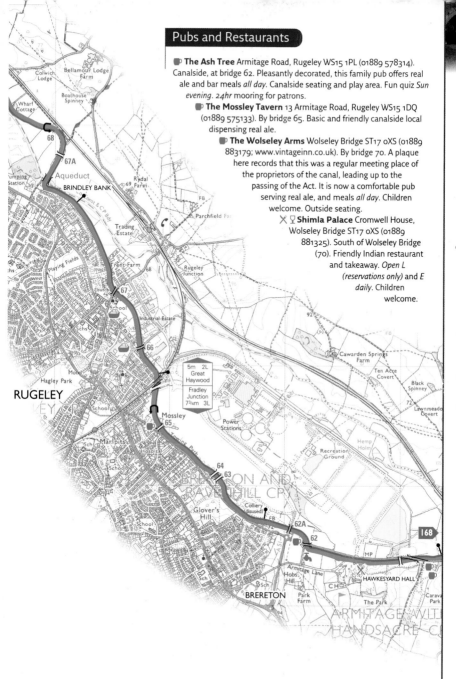

Pubs and Restaurants

🍺 **The Ash Tree** Armitage Road, Rugeley WS15 1PL (01889 578314). Canalside, at bridge 62. Pleasantly decorated, this family pub offers real ale and bar meals *all day*. Canalside seating and play area. Fun quiz *Sun evening*. *24hr* mooring for patrons.

🍺 **The Mossley Tavern** 13 Armitage Road, Rugeley WS15 1DQ (01889 575133). By bridge 65. Basic and friendly canalside local dispensing real ale.

🍺 **The Wolseley Arms** Wolseley Bridge ST17 0XS (01889 883179; www.vintageinn.co.uk). By bridge 70. A plaque here records that this was a regular meeting place of the proprietors of the canal, leading up to the passing of the Act. It is now a comfortable pub serving real ale, and meals *all day*. Children welcome. Outside seating.

✕ 🍷 **Shimla Palace** Cromwell House, Wolseley Bridge ST17 0XS (01889 881325). South of Wolseley Bridge (70). Friendly Indian restaurant and takeaway. *Open L (reservations only)* and *E daily*. Children welcome.

Great Haywood

The pleasant surroundings continue as the canal passes Colwich. As the perimeter of Shugborough Park is reached the impressive façade of the Hall can be seen across the parkland. Haywood Lock and a line of moored craft announce the presence of Great Haywood and the junction with the Staffordshire & Worcestershire Canal (*see* page 141), which joins the Trent & Mersey under a graceful and much photographed towpath bridge: just the other side there is a useful boatyard. Beyond the junction the Trent valley becomes much broader and more open. There is another boatyard by Hoo Mill Lock.

● **Little Haywood**
Staffs. PO box, stores. An elegant residential village, with a shop and two pubs.

● **Great Haywood**
Staffs. PO, tel, stores. Centre of the Great Haywood and Shugborough Conservation Area, the village is not particularly beautiful, but it is closely connected in many ways to Shugborough Park, to which it is physically linked by the very old Essex Bridge, where the crystal clear waters of the River Sow join the Trent on its way down from Stoke. Haywood Lock is beautifully situated between this packhorse bridge (which is an ancient monument) and the unusually decorative railway bridge that leads into Trent Lane. The lane consists of completely symmetrical and very handsome terraced cottages: they were built by the Ansons to house the people evicted from the former Shugborough village, the site of which is now occupied by the Arch of Hadrian within the park, built to celebrate Anson's circumnavigation of the globe in 1740–44. About 100yds south of Haywood Lock is an iron bridge over the canal. This bridge, which now leads nowhere, used to carry a private road from Shugborough Hall which crossed both the river and the canal on its way to the church just east of the railway. This was important to the Ansons, since the packhorse bridge just upstream is not wide enough for a horse and carriage, and so until the iron bridge was built the family had to *walk* the 300yds to church on Sunday mornings!
Shugborough Hall *NT.* Milford, near Stafford ST17 0XB (01889 881388; www.shugborough.org.uk). Walk west from Haywood Lock and through the park. The present house dates from 1693, but was substantially altered by James Stuart around 1760 and by Samuel Wyatt around the turn of the 18th C. It was at this time that the old village of Shugborough was bought up and demolished by the Anson family so that they should enjoy more privacy and space in their park. Family fortunes fluctuated greatly for the Ansons, the Earl of Lichfield's family; and crippling death duties in the 1960s brought about the transfer of the estate to the National Trust. The Trust has leased the property to Staffordshire County Council who now manage the whole estate. The house has been restored at great expense, and there are some magnificent rooms and many treasures inside.
Museum of Staffordshire Life This excellent establishment, Staffordshire's County Museum, is

housed in the old stables adjacent to Shugborough Hall. Open since 1966, it is superbly laid out and contains all sorts of exhibits concerned with old country life in Staffordshire. Amongst many things it contains an old-fashioned laundry, the old gun-room and the old estate brew-house, all completely equipped. Part of the stables contains harness, carts, coaches and motor cars. There is an industrial annexe up the road, containing a collection of preserved steam locomotives and some industrial machinery.
Shugborough Park There are some remarkable sights in the large park which encircles the Hall. Thomas Anson, who inherited the estate in 1720, enlisted in 1744 the help of his famous brother, Admiral George Anson, to beautify and improve the house and the park. In 1762 he commissioned James Stuart, a neo-Grecian architect, to embellish the park. 'Athenian' Stuart set to with a will, and the spectacular results of his work can be seen scattered round the grounds. The stone monuments that he built have deservedly extravagant names such as the Tower of the Winds, the Lanthorn of Demosthenes and so on.
The Park Farm Designed by Samuel Wyatt, it contains an agricultural museum, a working mill and a rare breeds centre. Traditional country skills such as bread-making, butter-churning and cheese-making are demonstrated.
Open Apr–Oct daily 11.00–17.00. Charge. Parties must book. Tea rooms, shop.

Boatyards

Ⓑ **Anglo Welsh** The Canal Wharf, Mill Lane, Great Haywood ST18 0RJ (01889 881711; www.anglowelsh.co.uk). 🛥 🛥 🔧 D Pump out, gas, narrowboat hire, day-hire craft, overnight and long-term mooring, boat sales, engine repairs, chandlery, toilets, books, maps and gifts.
Ⓑ **Engineering & Canal Services** Hoo Mill Boatyard, Hoo Mill Lane, Great Haywood ST18 0RG (01889 882611; mobile 07721 487561; engcanal@globalnet.co.uk) 🛥 🔧 (modest charge)D Pump out, gas, overnight and long-term mooring, winter storage, boat and engine sales and repairs, toilets, showers, laundrette.

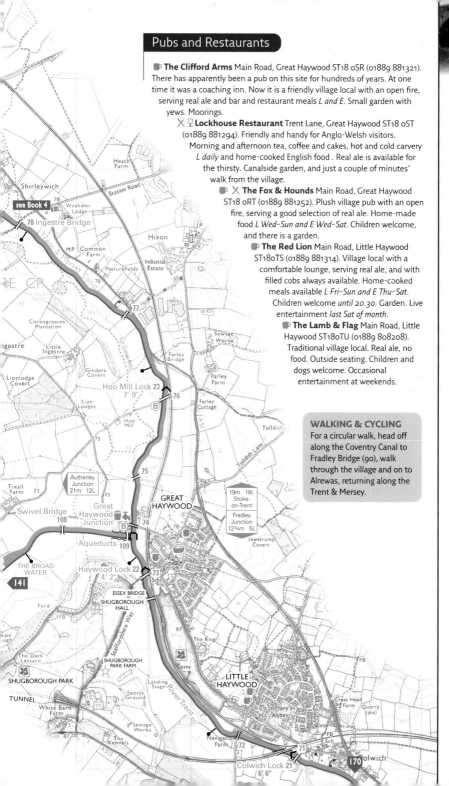

Pubs and Restaurants

🍺 **The Clifford Arms** Main Road, Great Haywood ST18 oSR (01889 881321). There has apparently been a pub on this site for hundreds of years. At one time it was a coaching inn. Now it is a friendly village local with an open fire, serving real ale and bar and restaurant meals *L and E*. Small garden with yews. Moorings.

✕ 🍷 **Lockhouse Restaurant** Trent Lane, Great Haywood ST18 oST (01889 881294). Friendly and handy for Anglo-Welsh visitors. Morning and afternoon tea, coffee and cakes, hot and cold carvery *L daily* and home-cooked English food . Real ale is available for the thirsty. Canalside garden, and just a couple of minutes' walk from the village.

🍺 ✕ **The Fox & Hounds** Main Road, Great Haywood ST18 oRT (01889 881252). Plush village pub with an open fire, serving a good selection of real ale. Home-made food *L Wed-Sun and E Wed-Sat*. Children welcome, and there is a garden.

🍺 **The Red Lion** Main Road, Little Haywood ST18oTS (01889 881314). Village local with a comfortable lounge, serving real ale, and with filled cobs always available. Home-cooked meals available *L Fri-Sun and E Thu-Sat*. Children welcome *until 20.30*. Garden. Live entertainment *last Sat of month*.

🍺 **The Lamb & Flag** Main Road, Little Haywood ST18oTU (01889 808208). Traditional village local. Real ale, no food. Outside seating. Children and dogs welcome. Occasional entertainment at weekends.

WALKING & CYCLING
For a circular walk, head off along the Coventry Canal to Fradley Bridge (90), walk through the village and on to Alrewas, returning along the Trent & Mersey.

INDEX

Abbey Park 88
Abbey Pumping Station 88
Ackers Trust Basin 118
Acton Trussell 138, 139
Albion Junction 34
Alder Wash 166
Aldersley 28
Aldersley Junction 28, 29, 36, 133
All Oaks Wood 128
All Saint's Church, Royal Leamington Spa 109
Alrewas 164, 166, 170
Alrewas Lock 166
Alvecote Priory 47, 58
Ambergate 68
American Adventure Theme Park 68
Amlington 59
Anglesey Basin and Chasewater 28
Anglesey Branch 28, 60
Anker, River 56
Anker Valley 54, 56
Ansty 130, 131
Ansty Hall 131
Arbury 47
Arbury Hall 52
Arlestone House 162
Armitage 168, 169
Armitage Tunnel 170
Ashby 18, 47
Ashby Canal 10-27, 52
Ashby Castle 26
Ashby Coalfields 18
Ashby de la Zouch 15, 24
Ashby de la Zouch Museum 29
Ashby Manor 29
Ashby Wolds 15
Ashted Flight 40
Ashted Tunnel 41
Assembly Rooms, Art Gallery & Museum 109
Aston Flight 40
Aston Junction 27, 39-41
Atherstone 39, 47, 54, 56, 57
Atherstone Locks 56
Autherley 133, 134
Autherley Junction 133-135
Avon, River 108, 126, 143
Avon Valley 77
Aylestone 71, 86, 87
Aylestone Hall 86
Aylestone Meadows 86
Aylestone Mill 84

Baddesley Clinton 113
Bagnall Lock 166
Banbury 123
Barby Hill 124
Barrow Mill Basin 94
Barrow upon Soar 71, 92
Barrow upon Trent 160, 161
Barton Turn 157, 166, 167
Barton-under-Needwood 166
Bascote 106
Bass Millennium Woodland 164
BCN Cottage 36
Bedworth 15, 16, 52
Bedworth Coalfield 47

Belgrave Lock 88
Bell Foundry Museum 94
Bentley, Thomas 157
Bilston Road Bridge 36
Birchill Junction 28
Birmingham & Fazeley Canal 30, 39-45, 47, 58, 60, 118
Birmingham & Liverpool Junction Canal 133
Birmingham & Warwick Junction Canal 39
Birmingham 28, 39-42, 72, 101, 104, 116-119, 123, 143, 144, 149, 150, 152, 153
Birmingham Airport 116
Birmingham Canal 39-41, 114, 133
Birmingham Canal Navigation (BCN) Main Line 28-38, 60, 118, 136
Birmingham Canal New Main Line 28, 27, 32
Birmingham Canal Old Main Line 28, 27, 32
Birmingham Gas Street 28, 149
Birstall 88, 91
Bishop Street Basin 48
Bishton Hall 170
Blaby 71, 85
Black Country 25, 133, 149
Black Country Museum 34-36
Black Works 136
Blackpole 149
Blegrave Hall and Gardens 88
Blisworth 123
Blythe, River 114
Boat Inn Cottage 128
Bodymoor Heath 42
Bodymoor Heath Bridge 39
Boot Bridge 52
Boot Wharf, Nuneaton 47
Bordelsey Basin 41
Bordesley Junction 40, 101, 114, 118
Bosworth Battlefield Centre 18, 20
Bosworth Water Trust 20
Bosworth Wharf Bridge 20
Bourne Brook Cut 44
Bournville 150
Bournville Garden Factory 150
Bradnall Junction 28, 34
Bradley Workshops 28
Brandwood Tunnel 144, 145
Branston 164
Branston Lock 164
Brasshouse Lane 32
Braunston 47, 71, 86, 101-104, 123-129
Braunston Church 129
Braunston Junction 47, 123
Braunston Puddle Banks 102
Braunston Tunnel 102, 103
Braunston Turn 101, 102, 123
Brentford 71, 101
Brewhouse Arts Centre 164
Bridgewater Canal 157
Brindley, James 28, 25, 27, 32, 36, 47, 123, 132, 133, 136, 140, 157

Brinklow 128, 129
Brinklow Arm 128
Bristol 133, 149
Broad Street Basin 36
Broad Street Bridge 30, 36
Brocks Hill Country Park & Environment Centre 85
Bromford Junction 28, 32
Broomey Croft 42
Brownhills 36
Budbrooke Junction 110
Burton 15
Burton Abbey 164
Burton Hastings 15-17
Burton Union 164
Burton upon Trent 162-165

Cadbury World 150
Cadeby Experience 20
Calcutt Locks 104
Calke Abbey 26
Cambrian Wharf 30, 40
Camp Hill Locks 118
Canal Art Trail 48
Canal House 48
Cannock Chase 140, 170
Cannock Road Bridge 36
Cape Locks 110
Carillon & War Museum 95
Carlton 20
Castle Gardens & Castle Motte 88, 90
Catherine de Barnes 116, 117
Catshill Junction 28
Causeway Green 32
Cavendish Bridge 158
Chamberlain Campanile Tower 152
Chapel Street 126
Charnwood Museum 95
Chase, The 170
Cheshire 157
Chester House 114
Chillington Wharf 36
Chilvers Coton 52
Clowes, Josiah 149
Coleshill 39
Colwich 172
Concordia Theatre 17
Congerstone 15, 20
Conkers 22, 24
Coors Visitor Centre 164
Cossall 66
Cossington 92
Cossington Lock 71, 92
Cotton Mill 166
Coven 134
Coven Heath 134
Coventry 39, 47-50, 101
Coventry Basin 47
Coventry Canal 15, 16, 39, 44, 47-61, 123, 130, 143, 157, 168
Coventry Cathedral 49
Crack's Hill 74
Cranfleet Cut 158
Crick 14, 71, 75
Crick Tunnel 72, 74
Cromford Canal 62, 68
Cross Green Bridge 134
Croxley 15
Culloden 160
Curdworth 42, 43

Curdworth Bridge 42
Curdworth Tunnel 39

Dadlington 15, 18, 19
Dallow Lock 164
Dane, River 64
Dartmouth Museum 50
Darwin, Erasmus 157
De Montfort Hall 90
Deep Cuttings Junction (Old Turn) 30
Deepfields 25, 36
Deepfields Junction 28
Deoraby 64
Derby Canal 62, 64, 160
Derbyshire 54, 62
Derwent Mouth 157, 158
Derwent, River 64
Devil's Elbow 96
Digbeth Branch 39, 41
Dixon 157
Dockholme Lock 64
Doebank Junction 28, 32
Donistorpe 24
Doomsday Book 29
Dove, River 162
Drayton 54
Drayton Bassett 44
Drayton Manor Family Theme Park 44
Dudley 34, 35
Dudley Canal 28, 34, 152
Dudley Port Junction 28, 34
Dudley Tunnel 25, 34, 35

Earlswood 145
Earlswood Reservoir 144, 145
East Midlands 62, 143
Eastwood 68
Eastwood Library 68
Eco House 90
Edgbaston 152
Edstone Aqueduct 145
Egginton 163
Elkington 75
Ellesmere Port 50
Elmdon Heath 117
Engine Branch 27
Engine Pool 145
Erewash 68
Erewash Canal 62-71, 158
Erewash Museum 66
Erewash, River 68
Erewash Valley 62
Ervin's Lock 84

Factory Junction 28, 34
Factory Locks 34
Farmer's Bridge 27, 39, 40
Farmer's Bridge Junction 39
Fazeley 25, 39, 42, 44, 45, 47, 101
Fazeley Junction 39, 42, 44, 47, 58, 59
Fazeley Mill 44
Ferrers Centre for Art/Craft 26
Filance Bridge 138
Findern 162, 163
Fisherwick 60
Fleckney 83
Fosse Locks 108
Fosse Way 129
Foxton 80, 82

Foxton Inclined Plane 78
Foxton Locks 78
Fradley 44, 47, 168
Fradley Junction 39, 47, 58,
    60, 157, 168, 169
Fradley Pool Nature Reserve
    169
Frampton 149
Frank Haynes Gallery 80

Gailey and Calf Heath
    Reservoirs 136
Gailey Reservoirs 136
Gailey Wharf 136, 137
Gainsborough 71
Gallows Inn 62
Gallows Inn Lock 66
Galton Bridge 32
Galton Tunnel 32
Galton Valley Canal Park 32
Gas Museum 86
Gas Street Basin 30, 152
Glascote 58
Glascote Bottom Lock 47
Glen Parva 86
Gloucester & Sharpness Canal
    149
Gloucester 133
Godiva, Lady 48, 50, 131, 169
Golden Mile 90
Gospall Park 22, 23
Gospall Wharf 15
Gospall Wharf Bridge 22
Gower Branch 28, 34
Grand Junction Canal 47, 71,
    101, 102, 104, 123, 129
Grand Union Canal 24, 41,
    71–119, 143, 144, 147, 148
Grand Union Canal, Leicester
    Section 71–91
Grand Union Canal, Main Line
    101–119
Grand Union Canal, River Soar
    71, 92–100
Great Central Way 86, 88
Great Haywood 140, 142, 172–3
Great Haywood Junction 133,
    157
Great Northern Basin 68
Great Train Robbery 24
Grendon 56, 57
Griff Colliery 50, 52
Grimshaw Hall 114
Guildhall 90
Gumley 83
Gumley Hall 83
Guru Nank Gurdwara & Sikh
    Museum 90

Hallam Fields Lock 62
Hampton-in-Arden 114
Handel 23
Handsacre 168
Hansons Bridge 42
Harborough Magna 129
Harborough Museum 80
Harborough Theatre 81
Harecastle 157
Hartshill 47, 54, 55
Hartshill Green 54
Hartshill Yard 46, 54
Hatherton Branch 136
Hatherton Junction 136
Hatton 111
Hatton Country World 111
Hatton Flight 110
Hatton Park 110

Hawkesbury 48
Hawkesbury Hall 48
Hawkesbury Junction 47, 48,
    50, 52, 123, 130, 131
Hawne Basin 34
Haymarket Theatre 90
Haywood Lock 172
Herbert Art Gallery & Art
    Museum 48
Heritage Centre 68
Higham on the Hill 19
Hillmorton 124
Hillmorton Bottom Lock 123
Hillmorton Locks 126
Hinckley 16, 17, 23
Hinckley & District Museum 17
Hinckley Wharf 15
Hockley Heath 143, 146, 148
Hockley Port 27
Holiday Wharf 152
Holy Trinity Church, Staunton
    Harold 26
Holy Trinity, Long Itchington
    106
Hoo Mill Lock 172
Hopwas 39, 47, 59
Hopwas Hill 58
Hopwas Village 58
Horninglow Basin 164
Horninglow Wharf 157
Horseley Fields Junction 28, 36
Horseley Ironworks 123
Huddlesford 60
Huddlesford Junction 47
Hull 157
Husbands Bosworth 78, 79,
    122
Husbands Bosworth Tunnel
    77, 78

Icknield Port Loop 27
Ilkeston 66, 67
Ivanhoe Baths 29

Jain Centre 90
James Gilbert Rugby Football
    Museum 126
Jephson Gardens 109
Jessop, William 15, 68, 71
Jewry Wall Museum 90
Johnson, Ben 54
Judkins Quarry 54

Kegworth 96, 97
Kegworth Deep Lock 96
Kegworth Museum 96
Kegworth Shallow Lock 98
Kettlebrook Wharf 58
Kilby Bridge 84, 85
Kilsby Tunnel 72
King's Bromley 169
King's Forest, Cannock 170
King's Mill 160
King's Norton 144, 146, 150,
    151
King's Norton Junction 143,
    144, 149, 150
King's Norton Stop Lock 144
King's Norton Tunnel 150
Kingsbury Water Park 42
Kingston on Soar 96
Kingswood 112, 113, 148
Kingswood Junction 101, 143,
    146, 147
Knowle 114, 115

Langley Mill 62, 66, 68–70

Lappal Tunnel 152
Lapworth 143, 144, 148
Lapworth Church 146
Lapworth Flight 146
Lapworth Link 147
Lapworth Locks 144, 146–148
Lawrence, D.H. 66, 68
Leam Valley 102
Leamington 108, 109
Leicester & Northampton
    Union Canal 78
Leicester 71, 82, 84–86,
    88–91, 101
Leicester Canal 71, 72
Leicester Cathedral 90
Leicester Navigations 62, 71,
    94, 96
Leicester Road Bridge 84
Leicester West Bridge 71
Leicestershire 18, 24, 71
Leighton Buzzard 24
Lenton 68
Lichfield 60
Lichfield Canal 60
Lichfield Cathedral 169
Little Haywood 172
Little Theatre 90
Liverpool 157
Lock Cottage 64
London 15, 24, 47, 48, 62,
    72, 101, 104, 123, 143
Long Eaton 64, 65, 98
Long Itchington 106
Longford 47
Longford Bridge 50
Longford Junction 48
Longwood Junction 28
Lord Leycester Hospital 111
Loughborough 62, 71, 94, 95
Loughborough Basin 71
Loughborough Canal 71
Loughborough Navigation
    71, 94, 96
Lower Shuckburgh 105

Mancetter 54
Manchester 157
Market Bosworth 20, 21, 23
Market Bosworth Wharf 15
Market Harborough 80, 81,
    101
Market Harborough Arm 71,
    78, 80
Market Harborough Canal
    Basin 81
Marston Jabbett 15
Marston Junction 15, 16, 47,
    52
Marston's Brewery Visitor
    Centre 164
Measham 15, 22, 24
Measham Museum 24
Melton Mowbray Navigation
    & Oakham Canal 92
Memorial Square, Coalville
    23
Merevale 57
Merevale Hall 56, 57
Mersey, River 133, 143, 157
Merseyside 133
Middlewich 162
Mile Straight 88
Milford 140, 142
Minworth 42
Minworth Locks 42
Minworth Top Lock 39
Moira 15, 22, 24–27

Moira Furnace 15, 22, 24
Moorgreen Reservoir 68
Mount Judd 54
Mountsorrel 92, 93
Mountsorrel Lock 94
Museum of Cannock Chase
    170
Museum of Staffordshire Life
    142, 172

Nantwich 133
Napton 123
Napton Hill 104
Napton Junction 47, 101, 104,
    105, 123
National Forest 22, 164, 166
National Space Centre 90
Netherton Tunnel Branch 28,
    34
New Street Station 152
Newarke Houses Museum 90
Newbold on Avon 127
Newbold Quarry Park 127
Newbold Tunnel 126, 127
Newbold, Thomas 15
Newtown Harcourt 84, 85
Normanton on Soar 96
North Kilworth 76
Northampton 80
Norton Canal Docks 28
Norton Junction 71–73, 101,
    102
Nottingham 68, 101
Nottingham Canal 62, 66, 68
Nottinghamshire/Derbyshire
    Coalfield 62, 71
Nuneaton 16, 50, 52–54, 131
Nuneaton Museum & Art
    Gallery 52
Nutbrook Canal 62, 66

Oakthorpe 24
Ocker Hill 32
Offchurch 108
Ogley Junction 28, 60
Old Roman Road 166
Old Turn Island 30
Oldbury Camp 54
Oldbury Locks Junction 28, 32
Oozell's Street Loop 27
Outram, Benjamin 15, 68
Oxford 24, 39, 47, 48, 101, 123
Oxford Canal 15, 47, 101, 102,
    104, 120–131, 143

Packwood House 112, 148
Park Farm, The 142
Pasture Lock 66
Peel's Wharf 58
Pelsall Junction 28
Pendeford Rockin' 134
Penk Valley 140
Penkridge 136, 138, 139
Penkridge Lock 139
Penk, River 138
Perrott's Folly 152
Perry Barr Top Lock 28
Phoenix Arts Centre 90
Pickfords Canal Carriers 84
Pillaton Old Hall 136, 139
Pillings Flood Lock 94
Polesworth 47, 56, 57
Pooley Hall 56
Potteries, The 133, 157
Preston Brook 157, 168
Pudding Green Junction 28, 32
Pump House, Smethwick 29

Radford Bridge 140
Radford Hall 109
Radford Semele 108, 109
Ratcliffe on Soar 98–100
Raw Dykes Ancient
  Monument 86
Red Deeps 52
Red Hill 98
Red Hill Lock 98
Repton 163
Rothen's Yard 56
Rothley 92
Rothley Brook 92
Rotton Park Reservoir 31, 32
Rowington 112
Royal Forest of Needwood
  166
Royal Hotel, Ashby de la
  Zouch 29
Royal Infirmary Museum 91
Royal Leamington Spa 108,
  109
Rugby 124, 126, 127
Rugby Wharf Arm 123, 126
Rugeley 170, 171
Runcorn Gap 157
Rushall Top Lock 28
Ryder's Green Bottom Lock
  28
Ryder's Green Junction 28
Ryder's Green Locks 25
Ryknild Street 166
Ryland Aqueduct 34

Saddington 83
Saddington Reservoir 82
Saddington Tunnel 82, 83
St Alphege Church, Solihull
  117
St Dionysius Parish Church,
  Market Harborough 81
St Helen's Church, Ashby de
  la Zouch 26
St James Church, Ansty 131
St John the Baptist, St
  Lawrence and St Anne
  Church, Knowle 114
St Lawrence's Church,
  Measham 24
St Martins Square & Loseby
  Lane 91
St Mary de Castro, Leicester 91
St Mary's Collegiate Church,
  Warwick 111
St Michael Cathedral Church,
  Coventry 49
St Nicholas Church, Leicester
  91
Salford 40
Salford Junction 28, 39, 40,
  101, 118
Saltersford Valley Picnic Area
  24
Saltisford Canal Centre 110
Sandiacre 64, 66
Sandiacre Lock 62
Sawley 98
Sawley Cut 100, 158, 159
Sawley Lock 98, 100, 158, 159
Scabious, Devil's-Bit 155
Scott, Sir Walter 29
Selly Manor and Minworth
  Greaves 150
Selly Oak 150, 152
Sence, River 20, 84, 86
Sephtons House 50, 131
Severn, River 39, 133, 149

Shackerstone 15, 23
Shakespeare, William 54
Shardlow 156–159
Shardlow Heritage Centre
  159
Shardlow Lock 158
Sheffield 66
Shenton Aqueduct 15, 20
Shenton Park 20
Shenton Village 20
Sherlock Valley 170
Shipley 66, 68
Shipley Lock 63, 68
Shire Hall Gallery, The 142
Shobnall Basin 164
Shrewley 111
Shrewley Tunnel 110–112
Shropshire Union 134
Shugborough Hall, Farm,
  Grounds, Museum & Park
  140, 142, 172
Shugborough Railway Tunnel
  140
Shutt Hill 138
Sileby 92
Sileby Lock 92
Simcock, Samuel 123
Sinai Park 164
Smeeton Westerby 82,83
Smethwick 25–33
Smethwick Junction 28, 27
Smethwick Locks 27
Smethwick Pool 27
Smockington Hollow 71
Snape, John 149
Snarestone 15, 22–24
Snarestone Tunnel 15
Sneyd Junction 28
Snibston Discovery Park 20,
  23
Soar, River 71, 86, 88, 92, 94,
  96, 98, 101, 158
Soar Valley 86
Soho Loop 27
Solihull 114, 116, 117
South Wigston 84, 85
Sow Aqueduct 132
Sow, River 140
Spa Lane 85
Spa Town 29
Spaghetti Junction 46
Spode House 170
Spon Lane Junction 28
Spon Lane Locks 28
Spon Street 48
Springfield Mill 66
Stafford 140, 142
Stafford Branch, The 142
Stafford Road (Gorsebrook)
  Bridge 36
Staffordshire &
  Worcestershire Canal 28,
  34, 36, 132–142, 149, 157,
  172
Stanford Hall 77
Stanton Gate 66
Stanton Ironworks 66
Stanton Lock 66
Star City 119
Staunton Harold 26
Staunton Hotel 26
Stenson 162
Stenson Lock 162
Stewart Aqueduct 32
Stockton 104, 106, 107
Stockton Locks 106
Stoke Golding 18, 19
Stoke Golding Wharf 15

Stoke-on-Trent 140, 143
Stone 157
Stonehurst Family Farm and
  Museum 92
Stoney Cloud 66
Stourbridge Canal 34
Stourport 133, 149
Stratford 143
Stratford Canal 143
Stratford-on-Avon Canal 112,
  143–148, 150
Stretton Arm 128
Stretton Baskerville 16
Stretton Stop 123, 128
Studio Theatre 90
Sulby Reservoirs 77
Sutton Cheney 18
Sutton Stop 50, 131
Swakestone Lock 157, 160,
  161

Tame, River 58
Tame Valley Canal 28, 32, 39
Tamworth 57–59
Tamworth Castle 59
Tangyes Engine 32
Tatenhill Lock 166
Teddesley Park 138, 139
Telford Aqueduct 27
Telford, Thomas 25, 27, 32,
  36, 157
Terry's Pool 145
Tettenhall & Autherley Canal
  133
Thames Embankment 106
Thames, River 39, 101, 123
Thrumpton Weir 64, 158
Thurmaston 91, 92
Tipton 34, 38
Tipton Junction 28, 34
Titford Canal 28, 32
Titford Pools 32
Tixall 140–142
Tixall Gatehouse 140
Tixall Lock 140
Tixall Wide 140
Trent & Mersey Canal 39, 44,
  47, 60, 101, 133, 140, 143,
  156–170
Trent Lane 172
Trent Lock 62, 64, 98, 158
Trent Navigation 64
Trent, River 15, 62, 68, 71,
  94, 98, 101, 133, 140, 158,
  160, 161, 164, 166, 168,
  170
Trent Valley 160, 172
Turner's Green 112
Tyburn 40, 42
Typhoo Basin 40, 41
Tyseley Locomotive Works
  and Visitor Centre 119

University of Birmingham 152

Valley Colliery 170

Walsall 25
Walsall Canal 28, 32
Walsall Junction 28
Warstock 145
Warwick & Birmingham
  Canal 110, 123, 143
Warwick & Napton Canal
  123, 143
Warwick 47, 101, 106, 108,
  110, 111

Warwick Bar 41
Warwick Castle 111
Warwick County Museum 111
Warwickshire 71
Warwickshire Coalfield 123
Watford 72
Watford Flight 78
Watford Gap 72
Watford Locks 72
Watling Street 16, 44, 136
Weaver, River 157
Wedgwood, Josiah 157
Wednesbury Collieries 28
Wednesbury Oak Loop 28
Wednesbury Old Canal 28,
  32
Welford 76, 77
Welford Arm 71, 77
Welton 72, 103
West Bridge 86, 88
Westminster 54
Weston Lock 160
Weston upon Trent 160
Wharf Cottage 136
Whatton House 96
White Horse 88
Whittington 44, 60
Whittington and Fradley
  Junction 60, 61
Whittington Bridge 60
Whittington Brook 39, 47
Whittington Firing Ranges
  58, 59
Whittington Junction 60
Whitworth 15
Wigston 84, 85
Wigston Framework Knitters
  Museum 85
Wigston Parva 85
Willington 157, 162, 163
Willoughby 124, 129
Wilmcote 143
Windmill End Junction 28, 34
Windmill Pool 145
Winson Green 27
Winwick 74, 75
Wistan Le Dale Model Village
  85
Wistow 83
Wistow Park 82, 83
Wollaton 68
Wolseley Bridge 170
Wolseley Hall 170
Wolverhampton 25, 32, 36,
  37, 134
Wolverhampton Locks 28
Woodend Lock 168
Worcester & Birmingham
  Canal 30, 133, 143,
  149–153
Worcester 150
Worcester Bar 30, 149, 152
Wreake, River 92
Wryley & Essington Canal 28,
  36, 47, 60
Wychnor 166
Wychnor Church 166
Wychnor Lock 166
Wygston's House Museum
  of Costume 91
Wyken Colliery Arm 130

Yardley Wood 145
Yelvertoft 74, 75

Zouch 96
Zouch Lock 71